Angela C. Wild is a political artist, lesbian feminist activist, and writer. An unapologetic radical feminist, her work is dedicated to promoting uncompromising lesbian visibility, building lesbian culture, defending women-only spaces, and dismantling patriarchal institutions such as compulsory heterosexuality, compulsory motherhood, sexual violence, and pornography.

She is a committed direct-action activist and has co-organised some of the most visible campaigns for lesbian rights in recent decades. A founding member of the grassroots lesbian group, Get the L Out UK, she authored Lesbians at Ground Zero: the first research on the "Cotton Ceiling" and founded Wild Womyn Workshop, a radical feminist shop for activists.

I WISH I WAS A
LESBIAN

WOMEN'S LIVES BEYOND HETEROSEXUALITY

EDITED BY ANGELA C. WILD

We respectfully acknowledge the wisdom of Aboriginal and Torres Strait Islander peoples and their custodianship of the lands and waterways. Country on which Spinifex offices are situated are Djiru, Bunurong and Wurundjeri, Wadawurrung, Gundungarra and Noongar.

First published by Spinifex Press, 2026

Spinifex Press Pty Ltd
PO Box 5270, North Geelong, VIC 3215, Australia
PO Box 105, Mission Beach, QLD 4852, Australia

women@spinifexpress.com.au
www.spinifexpress.com.au

Cover design by Deb Snibson
Front cover image by Angela C. Wild, *I Wish I Was a Lesbian*, 2025
paper collage and digital artwork
Typeset by Helen Christie, Blue Wren Books
Typeset in Minion
Printed and bound in Australia by Pegasus Media & Logistics

A catalogue record for this book is available from the National Library of Australia

ISBN: 9781922964304 (paperback)
ISBN: 9781922964311 (ebook)

I know I will be punished just as much for being an itty-bitty feminist as for going the whole way. And so I go the whole way.

—Mary Daly

There was a time when you were not a slave, remember that. You walked alone, full of laughter, you bathed bare-bellied. You say you have lost all recollection of it, remember. The wild roses flower in the woods. Your hand is torn on the bushes gathering the mulberries and strawberries you refresh yourself with. You run to catch the young hares you flay with stones from the rocks to cut them up and eat all hot and bleeding. You know how to avoid meeting a bear on the track. You know the winter fear when you hear the wolves gathering. But you can remain seated for hours in the treetops to await morning. You say there are no words to describe this time, you say it does not exist. But remember. Make an effort to remember. Or, failing that, invent.

—Monique Wittig, *Les Guérillères*

Acknowledgements

To Michelle Kerwin, with love – thank you for your faith in my wild ideas, for supporting this project from the very beginning and walking beside me through it all.

I am deeply grateful to Renate Klein and Susan Hawthorne for their enthusiasm and their careful guidance at every stage.

My thanks to Sheila Jeffreys for recognising the importance of this project and for connecting me with so many women who helped shape it.

Special thanks to Julie Bindel; being interviewed for her book *Lesbians: Where Are We Now?* helped me find my political lesbian voice again and gave me the confidence to begin this work.

Thank you, Frances Woods, for your friendship, cheerleading and for the hours of conversation that helped refine my analysis.

Thank you to Rachel Ara for all the creative conversations including those that helped perfect the cover artwork.

I am also grateful to S. for opening up international connections that enriched this work.

Thank you to all the amazing contributors to this book whose enthusiasm and excitement for the project helped me make it a reality.

I extend my deepest appreciation to the political lesbians whose work came before mine – your writing, courage, analysis, and vision continue to inspire, strengthen, and illuminate the path for all of us. Reading your work has literally changed my life.

Contents

Introduction

Angela C. Wild

Women, the wind is changing! Are you feeling it?

For a while, I wondered if it was just my imagination. Are we currently not witnessing one of the most important social shifts of our time? Does it not look like women are, quietly but unmistakably, stepping away from men?

For years I watched, mesmerised and hopeful, as South Korean women created and embraced new movements for change. It started in 2013. The country has been grappling with the 'molka' epidemic – a nationwide scandal involving men using spy-cams to secretly film women without their consent (McCurry and Kim, 2018). Public anger grew as the state failed to respond effectively, culminating in massive feminist protests in 2018 under the slogan 'My life is not your porn' (Taylor and Kim, 2018). Online spaces like Megalia and Womad became hubs of resistance, exposing misogyny and rejecting the suffocating expectation that women must marry, bear children, and serve men (Kuk, Park and Norma, 2018). In 2016, when the government released a "birth map" showing the number of women of childbearing age in each district, outrage erupted once again, with women declaring, "My womb is not national property" (Gao, 2024). Building on earlier movements like Escape the Corset and the Korean #MeToo, women publicly rejected femininity – some collectively shaving their heads and rebelling against beauty standards (Haas, 2018). Out of these waves of protest, many women came to the conclusion that true liberation meant complete separation from men. This is now known internationally as the 4B movement. Four simple, radical principles: no dating men, no sex with men, no marriage to men, and no children with men. For some, the movement later evolved into 6B4T, adding more radical principles such as boycotting misogynistic products, rejecting femininity and religion, and providing mutual support among unmarried women. In 2025, South Korea had the lowest birth rate in the world (Organisation for Economic Co-operation and Development, 2025).

The South Korean 4B movement made worldwide headlines, rattled the traditional press, and eventually spread abroad – to China, Europe, the US – with their core ideas going viral via social media platforms such as TikTok and Instagram. And here's the striking thing: ordinary women, online, through the unlikely medium of short videos, seemed to have achieved a spontaneous, collective consciousness – women sharing how fed up they are with men, recognising that dating men is not only deeply unsatisfactory but also plainly dangerous.

This is a generation of women facing the worst kind of incels (involuntary celibates): boys-turned-men raised in the manosphere, fed on red pill content,[1] a generation of young men idolising Andrew Tate, using violent porn, openly misogynistic, traditionalist and sexist to the point of embracing far-right ideology. You know something is wrong when even patriarch Jordan Peterson understands dating apps as training-grounds,

---

1 "Red pill content" is a metaphor from *The Matrix* film. It refers to online misogynist and far right content spread within the manosphere. It urges men to "awaken" to the "truth" that society is controlled by feminism and that men are oppressed as a result. It promotes the return of patriarchal traditionalist values such as rigid gender roles: male dominance/female submission. It is deeply anti-feminist. The "Red pill content" acts as a foundational ideology for many incels (involuntary celibate).

teaching men psychopath and predatory behaviour (Peterson, in Henderson, 2021).

Meanwhile, many men, incels or not, seem to believe choking a woman or imposing anal sex on her are normal ways to treat women sexually (Kotecha, 2025; Valentin, 2025; Ifop, 2025). They believe paying for dinner means paying for sexual access. They believe that if she agrees to sex, it is proof she is a 'whore'; if she accepts dinner but refuses sex, that makes her a 'gold-digger'. If she pays for her own meal, she's either a feminist (to be avoided like the plague), or she's 'friend-zoning' them. You see the type.

If you think this is bad enough, male violence often goes much deeper. And so does women's growing awareness of the risks of dealing with men: women and girls, killed because they politely rejected a man's advances make the headlines a bit too frequently for any of us to feel safe (CBS New York, 2024). The toxic mix of male sexual entitlement and rage is too often deadly.

On a very regular basis on social media, I see women detailing the horrors they have had to go through as a part of their hetero-sexual mandatory coupling history – the realisation of the inadequacy of men, whether husbands, boyfriends or dates: their inability to communicate; their failure to take responsibility for their own emotions; their unwillingness to share domestic tasks and childcare – ever heard of the married single mum syndrome? (Mayer, 2023). Women share their experiences of the practical and emotional parasitism of men. And then, of course, the abuse, including sexual abuse; violence, both in the form of coercive control and physical abuse; the rapes. A whole dimension of sexual violence was uncovered when Gisèle Pelicot decided to make her story of systematic abuse by her husband and the seventy men he recruited to rape her, a political statement about male violence (Harding, 2024). Because that's what it is.

Men online are also increasingly more comfortable being overtly misogynist (Lennon, 2025). Every cruel rape joke or sexualised personal attack facilitates women's growing awareness. Many women realise we are better off on our own – more grounded, more focused, safer, happier, healthier, and more successful. Women do not have to provide any form of labour – sexual, emotional, or domestic – for men who somehow wormed their way into our lives and claimed the title of husband.

The fact that married men and single childless women are the happiest demographics is now well-known (Oppenheim, 2019). These statistics highlight the obviously exploitative nature of heterosexuality for women. Many women cannot understand why on earth they would want to make their lives miserable when they can be happy and self-sufficient while being single. In the heterosexual game, women are the losers.

In the American context, women are losing abortion rights after the overturning of *Roe v. Wade* and face declining access to reproductive healthcare. Women have been confronted with criminal charges after a miscarriage (Aspinwall, 2024) and are now watching President Trump systematically dismantle anti-discrimination laws that once offered women a slightly fairer playing field in the workforce. Many women are waking up to these grim realities. They realise that their husbands voted for Trump, effectively voting against their rights (Whitesides, 2017). They see that in a collapsing economy, pregnancy presents an enormous risk: hospital bills, childcare costs, and the very real possibility of bankruptcy. In such a context, engaging sexually with men starts to look like a very dangerous gamble.

Women also leave heterosexuality after escaping abuse. Despite the familiar refrain society repeats, "there are some good ones out there" and the classic "#NotAllMen," they now know better. They've learned that man-keeping isn't worth the hassle, the energy, the time, or their health (Ferrara and Vergara, 2024). Many are leaving – and not coming back.

For the first time in history, women in the west have real access to education and economic independence. Men still own more property overall, but single women in the US are now out-buying single men (Brooks, 2023). Girls outperform boys from primary school through university in the UK (Carroll, 2023), and recent data shows that young women – in their 20s and early 30s – are, in some cases, earning slightly more than their male counterparts (British Business Excellence Awards, 2025). All this means very real possibility in terms of liberation.

The press, worried, is reporting on this 'new phenomenon'. Elon Musk is having public meltdowns over the dropping birth rates (Bouris, 2025). *Vogue* announced that 'the boyfriend' was now embarrassing (Joseph, 2025). The now-famous report predicting that by 2030, 45 per cent of women aged 25 to 40 will be single and childless (Morgan Stanley, 2019) is being waved around in alarm – as if it signals the collapse of society – and to guilt trip us about the 'a male loneliness epidemic' for the very men who so visibly hate us. Of course, feminists are to blame!

This isn't my imagination, there is a wind of change; it's women themselves blowing it. Women don't want men anymore. As a feminist, I rejoice at every one of these headlines.

Some Herstorical Context

But of course, it didn't all really begin in South Korea in 2013. That moment was part of a much longer political and feminist conversation, one that women have been having since the first wave of feminism. Feminists of the suffragette era had a broad and radical understanding of women's oppression, sexual power dynamics, and the role of male sexuality as a means of patriarchal control of women. They were very aware of the detrimental nature of male sexual behaviour on women. The British suffragettes' slogan that we know today – 'Votes for Women' – is not the full story. The slogan used by Christabel Pankhurst 'Votes for Women – Chastity for Men' (Pankhurst, 1913), was directly challenging men's sexual behaviour. First-wave feminists were campaigning to raise the age of consent (that men wanted to lower), working to abolish prostitution and trafficking, providing exit strategies for women trapped in prostitution, and campaigning to repeal the *Contagious Diseases Act* which imprisoned women. The discussions around the benefits of spinsterhood over marriage, the articulation of 'marriage as a trade' (Hamilton, 1909) and a survival necessity for most women, the campaign around divorce equality allowing women to divorce their husbands on the same grounds as men – all these indicate that women had grasped that heterosexuality was a con (Jeffreys, 1987; Jackson, 1994).

Second-wave feminists in the 1970s further highlighted the exploitative nature of heterosexual relationships and argued that the inequality between men and women in society was not conducive to women's liberation (Koedt, Levine and Rapone, eds. 1973).

But under patriarchy, every generation of feminists has to reinvent the wheel. The systematic erasure and demonisation of every generation of women who ever stood up for themselves explains why we either don't know, or don't take seriously, the work of our foremothers (Spender, 1983). For their critique of male sexual violence, Victorian women were branded 'prudish' and 'bigoted', second-wave feminists 'ugly' and 'man-haters'. The exact same slurs are hurled at feminists today.

So here we are again, a new generation of women with little understanding of our own herstory of liberation.

One could argue that the world has changed since the suffragettes. Hundreds of years of women's struggle have granted us the right to vote, to divorce on equal terms, to make and keep our own money. And yet fundamentally, men still rape and kill us. Some of the institutions may have changed, yet the violence remains the same. Some say it's getting worse.

In this context of increased violence and women's rising awareness, one of the phrases I see regularly on social media, whenever women discuss men is: "I wish I was a lesbian."

Heterosexuality is rebranded as hetero-pessimism (Seresin, 2019), and more recently, hetero-fatalism (Garnett, 2025). Heterosexuality is understood as unsatisfactory yet as something women are sadly unable to completely avoid because it is conceptualised as the natural fate of women. Many women no longer wish to be involved with men. But their choice, or perceived necessity, to opt out is often accompanied by a sense of loss: the belief that women must forgo romantic relationships, intimacy, and fulfilling sexual lives all together. There appears to be a way out. But not an alternative.

Interestingly, women recognise that as half of the population, they are nowhere near as oppressive or violent as men. Their most meaningful friendships are with women; they freely admit their best female friends know and understand them better than any husband or boyfriend ever will. Sometimes in the privacy of their own friendship group they admit having crushes on women. They wish they could love, sexually and romantically, other women. They also wish they could be free from their attraction to men.

More women have begun taking female lovers later in life, after decades in heterosexual relationships (Strock, 2025), but why is this still so rare? Why are so many women unable to do the same especially if they express the desire to do so?

To all the women who have ever written in despair, 'I wish I was a lesbian, but I can't be one', this book is for you.

The Personal Is Political

One of the most groundbreaking ideas to emerge from the second wave of feminism was that the personal is political (Hanisch, 1970). Through the group practice of consciousness-raising, women sharing their experiences started to realise that what they had so far understood as a personal, intimate and individual experience was in fact the shared experience of many women (Sarachild, 1978; Alderson, 2022). Consciousness-raising made it possible to draw patterns, understand men's strategy of oppression on a micro level and theorise. Women were able to coin concepts such as 'sexism', 'sexual harassment', 'marital rape' and other patriarchal forms of oppression that women had until then not understood as political – and had no name for. Women breaking the silence enabled the understanding that what happens repeatedly to women on a micro individual level has a political impact on a macro level. When a large number of women are harassed at work, this has an impact on women's ability to hold a job, let alone advance in their career; it impacts their self-confidence, their livelihood as well as their health, their financial safety and independence, and even their pension. The violent action of one man towards one woman, repeatedly inflicted by men as a class to a critical mass of women, has a global impact on all women everywhere.

Through the sharing and generalisation of women's experiences, and the knowledge gained from recognising what men do to us, women developed the concept of the sex class (Morgan, 1970). Men and women are distinct political classes. Men, as a class, oppress women as a class, through a range of interconnected structures of domination.

Crucially, 'patriarchy' is not a vague concept, an oppressive undefinable something floating over us with no detectable agent. Patriarchy is every man, even the 'good guys', even the ones we know. Patriarchy is a global oppressive political structure created and maintained by individual men every day. It is men who create and run oppressive organisations (like the state, the church, the police, the army). It is also men who choose at this very moment to dismantle anti-discriminatory laws; it is men who refuse to prosecute other men when they rape us; men who spike our drinks at the bar; men who watch passively while we are being sexually harassed in the street during our morning jog and laugh; men who restrict our freedom to access abortions; men who create porn; men who traffic women; men who place spy-cams in women's toilets; men who redefine the meaning of women to include themselves in it; men who rape their wives in their sleep; men who share revenge porn of their ex-girlfriend on the internet, men who create AI programs to produce endless pornified images of us at will, men who traffic women and girls on Little Saint James Island and elsewhere, men who chose to obey orders to not investigate suspected pedo-criminals when they are powerful, rich and famous.

But patriarchy is also men who do not engage in acts of violence but benefit from the violence carried out by other men. It is men who benefit if we have been traumatised from our previous abusive relationship so they don't have to do the job of subjugating us – someone else has already done it. It is men who benefit from wage inequality allowing them to earn more money than us just for being mediocre at their job. It is men who benefit from the system as it is, with its privileges for some. They don't have to be visibly contributing to patriarchy to be benefiting from it, but they never really effectively challenge the status quo. All of this is the patriarchy in action, carried out day after day, by random individual men near you and me.

It is essential to grasp that structures of oppression do not have to be front-facing organisations. Patriarchy does not only operate from official visible offices of power. It also happens all around us in our daily life; it also happens in the privacy of our own home every day.

The genius of Second Wave Feminism, following the understanding that the personal is political is to understand that everything, including our intimate and sexual life, is political. The fact that our number one killer is the man we chose to love and live with, calls into question the nature of love, romance, sex. So indeed, for feminists, everything needs to be put under feminist scrutiny; sexuality can and should be analysed with a feminist lens. This leads to the realisation that heterosexuality itself (not only marriage) is a structure of oppression that has to be analysed and dismantled. What happens at home and in the bedroom is political.

Yes, even sex. In fact, most especially sex.

Compulsory Heterosexuality

The idea that something is not logical about women loving men despite what men do to us, is one of the premises of Adrienne Rich's *Compulsory Heterosexuality and Lesbian Existence* (Rich, 1981). Why are women attracted to men despite the violence, the obvious lack of love, reciprocity or sexual pleasure? Or even safety? Why do women remain faithful to the class of people who oppress us? Why do women see themselves as innately heterosexual, committing themselves to a lifetime of unequal, exploitative relationships and bad sex? Why are most women willing to risk their lives in the name of romance? It defies all rational explanation.

Rich's analysis is critical because it defines heterosexuality beyond the biological imperative ensuring the survival of the species. From a feminist perspective, heterosexuality is a political institution that is imposed on women through social, cultural and economic means.

Rich asserts that in patriarchy, heterosexuality is organised, enforced and rendered unavoidable. Through a series of mechanisms of enforcements, women are expected, pressured and conditioned to desire, marry, and organise their whole lives around men. Rich lists examples such as women's enforced economic dependence on men, rape and sexual violence, pornography, denial of women's sexuality, social stigma against lesbians and the romanticisation of heterosexuality. These mechanisms not only restrict women's ability to achieve independence from men, but also make heterosexuality appear both inevitable and desirable. By binding women to men through heterosexuality, patriarchy secures women's labour, sexuality, and reproductive capacity thus ensuring the continuation of male dominance. In this framework, heterosexuality is not just a mere sexual orientation, not the natural and innate destiny of women, but a system created by patriarchy to maintain itself.

A Challenge to the Nature of Sexuality

Historically, the concept of an innate sexual orientation is fairly recent. It originates from the Victorian sexologists who theorised it. In the late nineteenth and early twentieth centuries, sexologists, led by Havelock Ellis, introduced the concept of 'sexual inversion' to categorise same-sex attraction as an innate condition. Ellis defined it as "sexual instinct turned by inborn constitutional abnormality toward persons of the same sex," framing it as a medical condition (Ellis, 1897). Sexologists were deeply invested in proving that homosexuality was a medical disorder, obsessively hunting for a so-called 'gay gene'. The aim of that quest was to 'cure' homosexuality. In their work, both Jeffreys (1987) and Jackson (1994) demonstrate that the concept of 'sexual orientation', as constructed by Victorian sexologists, served to reinforce patriarchal structures by pathologising same-sex attraction and promoting heterosexuality as the norm.

It is the patriarchal agenda of the sexologists that invented the idea that most people are born heterosexual, while a few others are not. This framing defines same-sex attraction as abnormal and deviant. Their search for a physiological basis for homosexuality remains unsuccessful to this day. In the absence of biological evidence, the concept of an innate sexual orientation can only be described as a belief system, not a biological fact. Yet, despite this lack of evidence, we live in a world that treats sexuality as an innate characteristic.

Personally, I am instinctively suspicious of any patriarchal thought system that declares something as 'natural', 'normal' or 'women's destiny' when there is no biological evidence to support these ideas; and men benefit from it. Surely this should constitute a major red flag for most feminists? If women aren't innately straight, then what? That's exactly the kind of question that demands feminist scrutiny!

Biological Essentialism and Biological Determinism

What we're talking about here are biological essentialism and biological determinism. Biological essentialism is the idea that biology defines the fixed, unchanging essence of a group. Biological determinism goes further, claiming that biology determines the behaviour and destiny of that group. Together, these ideas form the core of the ideology that has long supported and justified women's oppression by men, using differences between the sexes, real or imagined, biological or enforced, to sustain the belief that women are 'born that way', and therefore destined to be controlled and dominated by men.

While denying us of nutritious food and physical exercise, men have argued for centuries that women were born physically frail and had to be 'protected' by men. While denying us access to education, they have argued we were innately intellectually weak and therefore not fit to take part in professional activities or political life. While creating systems of exploitation restricting our capacity to be financially independent, stigmatising working women and sometimes forbidding us to make a living, they have argued we were innately dependent on them. While they have denied us the right to divorce, they have argued that marriage was the natural order of life, that men and women were naturally and innately drawn to a lifetime together, that men were the rightful heads of the household, and women the natural submissive helpers. All these and more have been used to justify men's power and control over us. Biological essentialism and determinism are how oppressors justify oppression. Biological essentialism and determinism are what feminism has been fighting against since its inception. The feminist struggle for liberation is partly about freeing ourselves from what men say we are, and by extension, what men say we are for: what use they can make of us. Feminism highlights that our sex doesn't justify our oppression, the limitations placed on our lives, how much we get paid or what activities we can and can't do.

Men have argued that women are naturally inferior in order to control us. Men have also argued that women are naturally heterosexual, while creating mechanisms and propaganda to prevent us from imagining any other possibility. While inventing theories to stop us from thinking of ourselves outside the heterosexual box, men have enforced heterosexual sex as unavoidable through a constant stream of sexual violence, rape and pornographic propaganda, demonising us if we resist the enforcement, and punishing us when we dissent. This is nothing but another layer of indoctrination ensuring that women don't leave men. Why are feminists not questioning the assertion that sexual orientation is an innate characteristic?

A Belief System

Lesbian feminists have been questioning the belief system that heterosexuality is inevitable. in the lesbian feminist framework, heterosexuality, homosexuality, and bisexuality are not equal, neutral and apolitical ways people relate sexually to each other – they are imbued with deep-rooted power dynamics that define how people of different sexes are expected and pressured to relate to each other in society according to their sex. Based on the idea that 'the personal is political', lesbian feminists suggest that heterosexuality is one of the ways in which patriarchy keeps women oppressed.

Through the individualisation of our oppression – the dividing of women by assigning each one to an oppressor through the institution of heterosexuality – patriarchy makes it difficult for women to connect and understand our experience as a collective, as a class, rather than as isolated and apolitical individuals. This, coupled with the naturalisation of our oppression through biological determinism, means that most women go through life unaware that they are spending their love, energy and support on their oppressor(s) within an institution that remains invisible to them.

Heterosexuality as an Institution

But surely, the critics say, heterosexuality is natural because it is needed for the survival of the species!

A degree of heterosexuality is indeed necessary for reproduction. But asserting that heterosexuality is an institution, as Susan Hawthorne did in 'In Defence of Separatism' in 1976, means that the way heterosexuality is organised, theorised and enforced is not natural despite what we are told.

It means there is nothing in the law of nature or the requirement for species survival that justifies the way heterosexuality exists, happens and is experienced by women. Nothing that requires that every woman should be coupled to a man for life. Nothing that dictates the 'right' amount of intercourse per week, or how long this intercourse should last. Nothing in nature justifies the production and consumption of pornography. There is zero biological imperative for the practice of anal sex, choking or other BDSM practices that men seem to impose on women and normalise everywhere they go.

The way heterosexuality is practised and lived and theorised in patriarchy is entirely political. None of it is required for the survival of our species. We could easily imagine countless alternatives to organising society, the division of labour, and sexual arrangements between men and women that don't involve any of these power dynamics and violence.

Pornography: Cultural Mechanism of Enforcing Heterosexuality through Sexual Violence

A lesbian feminist framework understands heterosexuality as a patriarchal institution imposed on women. Susan Hawthorne (2019)[2] highlights how such institutions control people, confining them to roles dictated by patriarchal power. This imposition takes place in a multitude of ways. Through cultural enforcements, financial pressure, but also a more physical enforcement: physical violence and threats (leading to the belief that women need men to protect us from other men), or sexual violence where heterosexuality is quite literally imposed on us, both in the endemic acts of rape, but also in the form of pornography.

A form of mass sexual terrorism and symbolic rape of all women and girls streaming non-stop on the internet, porn defines heterosexuality as the norm for women – whether we want it or not. The message is so pervasive, so hegemonic, so unavoidable, that most fail to recognise it as propaganda. To be constantly exposed to pornography, or to have pornified images made of oneself as we have seen recently with the Grok/X deepfake scandal, is to be subjected to political enforcement. Pornography is a propaganda

---

2   While *In Defence of Separatism* by Susan Hawthorne was finally published in 2019, it was written in 1976 as an Honours thesis in Philosophy.

strategy using both visual culture, the media and social media, as well as sexual violence as a means of indoctrination and a mechanism of social control of women.

What pornography says about the nature of heterosexuality for women is equally political (Dworkin, 1989). Recently, the album cover of Sabrina Carpenter has made the headlines. It represents the singer on all fours, her hair pulled by a nameless man. The title of the album is *Man's Best Friend*. While critics have argued this is a degrading image that sends a negative message to young girls, most liberal feminist commentators on social media defend Carpenter by saying she is free to express 'her' sexuality. Allegedly, Carpenter's sexuality is innately to be humiliated by men. 'That is what she likes, stop shaming her' is a common refrain. No one seems to question why women's sexuality would revolve around having one's hair pulled by a man. While I have no intention of shaming women, I think analysing and understanding politically the reasons for our behaviour – including sexual – what we comply with, what our desires and fantasies are – are of crucial feminist interest and importance (Wild, 2021). If some women like to be humiliated and have their hair pulled during sex – or worse – could it be because all of us have been exposed to pornography (or indirectly to men who regularly consume pornography) where women's sexual humiliation is normalised, and eroticised? Could it be that we live in a world where men want us to be submissive, and imposing that submission via sexual means is a powerful way to enforce it? Sometimes the simplest explanation is the obvious one.

The title of Carpenter's album reasserts women's sexual submission to men as natural, biological, inevitable and desirable. To release such an album in 2025, the year so many women seem to be leaving men behind, sounds suspiciously like a strategic patriarchal backlash. The term 'man's best friend' also refers to dogs; loyal companions on all fours beside their masters. Dogs had to be groomed and domesticated for thousands of years to become obedient, compliant, of service. The title is a disturbingly accurate description of men's domination strategies.

Lesbian feminists argue that women and girls are groomed from birth to be heterosexual – taught to believe that our attraction to men is innate and unchangeable, taught to believe that we are innately submissive sexually, taught that this is where we extract our sexual pleasure from. This is one of the central lessons of pornography. The biological essentialist element explored earlier, coupled with layers of propaganda and the imposition of hetero-sexuality make us internalise that this is what we were born to be, and that we should enjoy it.

What Is a Straight Woman?

Questioning the nature of heterosexuality, and finding it is not innate but socially constructed and politically enforced, leads us to the question: what is a straight woman? From this analysis emerges the idea that it is more accurate to speak of women *in heterosexuality* rather than *heterosexual women*. In this framework, heterosexual is not *who we are*, not an identity or an innate characteristic. Rather it is *where we are*: an institution, an oppression, an ideology. Not a destiny but a situation we have been forced into, a situation we can liberate ourselves from.

A 'straight woman' is a woman who has internalised that she is innately straight without a shred of evidence. Biologically, there is no such thing as a straight woman. She is the product of internalising patriarchal lies.

Heterosexuality Is Hierarchy

Far from being neutral or apolitical, heterosexuality is the medium through which a powerful social hierarchy between men and women is created and enforced.

Feminists since the second wave have highlighted the power dynamics at play in sex between men and women. Dworkin (1987), Jeffreys (1990), MacKinnon (1991), and Barry (1984), among others, have analysed how heterosexual sex is structured around domination and submission. With men cast as dominant and women as submissive, sex does not merely *reflect* hierarchy – it *creates* it. It does so in the sexual act of intercourse, where MacKinnon (1991) argues, gender is learnt.[3] It is during heterosexual sex that women internalise femininity: our imposed and internalised status as inferior, while men internalise masculinity: their internalised status as superior.

This power dynamic is packaged as innate and natural and theorised as such by the same men who were invested in naturalising a supposedly innate sexual orientation. It is sexology, the science of sex, which declared that women are born to be sexually submissive, while men are born to be sexually dominant. Women were said to be passive to receive men's sexual advances. Sometimes women were seen as uninterested in heterosexual sex, a condition that had to be cured. Men's role in sex is to be the conqueror, the hunter, trying to woo an unwilling female participant to submit to his will. You would be forgiven to confuse this 'science' for a rape apology.

Unsurprisingly, the sexologist propaganda has implications to this day. Most of the BDSM practices and theory are built on the principles laid out in those early texts.

Heterosexuality as the Cornerstone of Patriarchy

For lesbian feminism, all this makes heterosexuality *the core institution*, the cornerstone that holds all the other patriarchal institutions together. Without the individual oppression of each woman by men, in heterosexuality; without women thinking ourselves as innately straight; without the internalisation of our

---

3   Catharine MacKinnon uses the word gender to mean internalised sex roles.

so-called attraction, loyalty and submission to men, there couldn't be any patriarchy. If heterosexuality were natural, it wouldn't take propaganda or violence to enforce or uphold it.

Beyond Heterosexuality

Through challenging the myth of sexuality as 'natural', making lesbian existence visible, resisting patriarchal mechanisms of control and centre women in our lives, Adrienne Rich encourages women to decentre men and centre women. She calls this spectrum of woman-centred relationships that resist compulsory heterosexuality *the lesbian continuum*. She argues that free from the constraints of compulsory heterosexuality, loving women – including erotically and sexually – becomes a real possibility. She describes lesbian existence as both an act of resistance to patriarchy and a reclaiming of women's capacity for joy, intimacy, and power outside of men's control. She insists that taking a woman lover isn't just a 'private' act but has political meaning, because it refuses the institution of male access to women's bodies.

Many brilliant lesbian feminists have followed Rich's path. I truly encourage every woman to dive into this rich, fascinating, challenging and so often overlooked literature! From Lynn Alderson (2022), Julie Bindel (2014, 2025), Susan Cavin (1985), Cheryl Clarke (2015), Mary Daly (1987), Mary Ann Douglas (1990), Andrea Dworkin (1987), Marilyn Frye (1983, 1992), Carolyn Gage, Dee L. R. Graham (1994), Lynne Harne and Elaine Miller (1996), Susan Hawthorne (2019, 2025), Sarah Hoagland (1988), Sheila Jeffreys (1990, 1993, 2014, 2018), Jill Johnson (1973), Sonia Johnson (1991), Celia Kitzinger (1987), Celia Kitzinger and Sue Wilkinson (1993), Renate Klein (2025), Robin Ruth Linden (1983), Audre Lorde (2007), Catharine MacKinnon (1991), Ann E. Menashe (1999), Janice Raymond (1999/2000), Radicalesbians (1970), The Lesbian History Group (1996), Monique Witting

(1971, 1992) and more, lesbian feminists have developed these ideas further with subtle analyses and real depth of understanding, so that we can explore them, connect the personal and the political, and ultimately ask ourselves the crucial question that logically arises.

If lesbian feminist theory is true, if women aren't innately heterosexual, if we have all been groomed in heterosexuality, then what? If indeed you could choose – really choose – what would you choose? Would you choose to be a willing participant in a system that exploits you and your sisters?

This is an important question to ask women. Once we realise the nature of compulsory heterosexuality, the next logical step is to question whether we want to stay in it.

Political Lesbianism

At the heart of the question stands one concept: 'political lesbianism'. Scandalous, shocking, complex, multi-layered, often misunderstood – and just as often wilfully distorted and misinterpreted. The blurring, silencing, and demonisation surrounding this term form the core of much of today's fear, discord, and division among feminists. With such a reputation, why raise it at all?

Because the ferocity of the attacks on political lesbianism is directly proportional to how radical, strikingly effective, and brilliant the idea truly is.

What is political lesbianism? The answer largely depends on who you ask.

Critics often dismiss it as straight women abandoning men and adopting the label 'lesbian' out of spite or for activism, without genuine love, desire, or commitment to women. In this view, it is treated as inauthentic – an act of appropriation rather than 'real' lesbianism.

In truth, political lesbianism is far more profound than these misreadings suggest. Political lesbianism and lesbian feminism are often used interchangeably. A lesbian feminist is *not* simply a lesbian who happens to be a feminist, but a woman for whom lesbianism and feminism are inseparable. For a lesbian feminist, lesbianism emerges from, and is grounded in, her feminist politics. Political lesbianism is a strategy that stems directly from lesbian feminist thinking, the framework that connects everything: the personal, the political, the theoretical, the strategic, and the practical. Put simply, it is feminism in its most radical form. It is feminism carried through to its logical conclusion. For me, it has meant following my political thinking wherever it leads, without stopping short or censoring myself along the way, without shying away from exploring the meaning of my experiences. In pure radical fashion, political lesbianism tackles the problem at its root. It encourages women to stop fuelling the oppressor with our love, desire, attention, resources, in order to redistribute it all to ourselves, women and the feminist movement. It challenges the idea that sexuality is innate and immutable and declares that women and the fight for women's liberation would benefit, not only from leaving men, but from choosing women as lovers and life partners.

So, a political lesbian is a woman who has connected the personal and the political, understood the political nature of her heterosexual involvement, the grooming she has been subjected to, the oppression, limitations and violence inherent to her life while she centres men over herself – and she has decided to leave it behind.

But of course, this is only half of the story.

Every lesbian in the world has had to say no to men and to heterosexuality in its many forms a thousand times. A political lesbian is a woman who has made the conscious decision to decentre men but also to centre women in every aspect of her life, including romantically and sexually.

Is Political Lesbianism Fake Lesbianism?

I can hear the detractors and sceptics already: 'You can't manufacture sexual desire; this is not something that you choose on demand!'

Very true. No one leaves men and wakes up the next morning with a fully formed sexual desire for women and a lesbian consciousness. This is both simplistic and a misrepresentation of what it is like to become a lesbian.

In her essay in this book, author Hazel Holloway describes the process as a form of decolonisation. Once we remove the exploitative elements from our life that don't serve us and disconnect us from ourselves (heterosexuality and men), there is room for exploration and change. There is also room for mental space, consciousness, creativity, love available for ourselves and other women. I have seen women leave heterosexuality and witnessed our lives' focus shift. We also become more able to *see* women in all our richness, beauty and complexity. Seeing women as Marilyn Frye (1983) explains in 'To Be and Be Seen' is what lesbians and only lesbians can do. Only lesbians really see other women as full human beings. With that new vision comes the possibility to see women as potential romantic and sexual partners. I believe, as Julie Bindel does, that any woman, given the right circumstances, can experience that path. I also believe that in the absence of a lesbian gene or a lesbian brain, wanting to be a lesbian is what makes us one: that all-encompassing woman-centredness and that desire to share our time with women.

What About Sex?

The sexual element may come. If and when it does, it is a wonderful thing. To discover a way to relate sexually to someone who wasn't raised holding institutional and systematic political power over us is liberating and delightful. Having a sexual experience that is not based on our objectification to satisfy the male gaze, but on our own true desires, free from hierarchy, power dynamic and most importantly from coercion and violence, is a joyful and A-mazing experience. Lesbian feminism offers the possibility of a sexuality based on reciprocity and equality (Alderson, Holloway and Jeffreys, this volume). The experience of it changes everything.

But decolonisation from male-centred sexuality and the impact of a patriarchal porn-riddled culture on our body, sexual imaginary and intimacy takes time. Dismantling sexual traumas learnt in rape is hard work. Being a lesbian without a feminist consciousness is not a guarantee of experiencing an intimacy based on the eroticisation of equality either. After all, the lesbian S&M scene's raison d'être is to is replicate heterosexual-based dominance and submission dynamic. Nothing could be less feminist than that.

Detractors of lesbian feminism often claim that political lesbians are either faking their lesbianism, lack genuine sexual desire or attraction toward women, or are straight or asexual. We are, at times, expected to *prove* we are lesbians. I once read online that I wasn't a 'real lesbian' because I didn't publicly discuss the women I'm attracted to or the relationships I'm in. Some of us value privacy and refuse to overexpose our intimate lives – especially to political opponents, let alone to random men on the internet. Wild, I know, but not everyone performs for the social media machine. And what kind of 'proof' would even be required here – photographic evidence? Videos?

Recently, I heard of lesbians fleeing persecution in African countries who have been asked by British immigration authorities to *prove* their lesbianism. The fact that some of these women had children was taken as evidence that they were, in fact, straight – attempting to enter the country under false pretences. In some cases, documented by Susan Hawthorne, authorities even demanded photographs or videos of them engaging in sexual acts with women as 'proof' (2020). Not only does the performance of lesbianism for the camera fail to constitute evidence of lesbian identity – 'lesbian pornography' is performed by women for the male gaze and is never an expression of a genuine lesbian sexuality – but the very demand for pornographic images of women to verify their sexuality is itself an act of sexual violation. Women demanding proof of lesbianism rely on the same logic of male control over women's bodies that patriarchy enforces.

For those reasons, feminists committed to genuine women's liberation reject the imposition of any form of compulsory sexuality – whether heterosexual or homosexual – upon women. I do not believe anyone should be forced to have sex with a woman to be able to call herself a lesbian. Sexual desire is a spontaneous and intimate impulse. No one is sexual at all times and no one should be forced to have sex to prove anything. After all, as Sheila Jeffreys (this volume) observes, no one ever demands that women prove their heterosexuality; it is assumed by default. The expectation that women must 'provide receipts' to validate their lesbianism reproduces the patriarchal mechanisms of sexual control that feminism seeks to dismantle.

Liberal vs Radical: A Different Worldview

This focus on sexuality *as the sole marker of lesbianism* is also brandished by lesbians who see themselves as *born this way* and who are against political lesbianism. This is a profound ideological difference. Celia Kitzinger (1987) analysed how this narrow and liberal approach was developed by psychologists, some of whom have at times wilfully denied women's lesbianism if it was framed within a political context. In her study, Kitzinger identified the psychologists' sign of a 'well-adjusted' lesbian ('well-adjusted' to what?): one whose sexuality is merely a personal trait, unrelated to her decisions, worldview, behaviour, or beliefs. Such dissociation aims to depoliticise lesbianism and reduce it to a harmless personal characteristic. It is yet another patriarchal tool to defang feminism. *"Oh! Incidentally, I happen to be a lesbian! But don't worry, it's not my fault and I promise it won't spread!"*

It is – just about – okay for patriarchy to accept lesbians as long as we do not have any political understanding of our lesbianism. It is okay for patriarchy to accept feminists as long as we do not connect the dots and leave men to choose to liberate ourselves and love each other. But a woman who loves women and understands it in political terms? She is a real threat.

In contradiction to this liberal viewpoint, lesbian feminists understand lesbianism as a whole; a holistic way to view themselves and the world. *Political, personal, cultural, creative, strategic,* you name it. Sexuality is one part of who we are as lesbians, but so is the feminist ethos we share, the love and desire to be together, the collective work to dismantle patriarchy, the spaces we inhabit, the lesbian culture we create, the art we make, the events we build, the protests we organise, the songs we sing, the imagined world we want to live in …

Lesbian feminism is feared because it is a direct challenge to patriarchy, but not in the shape of a reactionary, defensive movement. We are a collective creative force working for a different world.

My Own Journey

While there are disagreements on this point, the term 'political lesbian' remains relevant for me. However decried, distorted and attacked, it remains useful because it not only frames sexuality as political, it clarifies that the shift to lesbianism was done thanks to feminism. It also describes that shift as a political act.

I would have been unable to call myself a lesbian without the direct input of Sheila Jeffreys. I heard her vivid description in 2012 of how women in the Women's Liberation Movement were becoming lesbians; and, she added, cheerfully "and so will you!" That sentence changed my life. I took it as an authorisation to take the step that felt right for me. And then and there, in that room, I made the decision that this was what I wanted. I looked around wondering how many women were touched by the same revelation! Six months later, I left the man, called myself a lesbian – and never looked back.

I am also indebted to other women, who at crucial times asked me what I thought I was doing, being married to a man, and pointed out the contradictions of working for women's liberation but sleeping with the enemy. One can get defensive at such a direct challenge! The logic of the question was unescapable though. I was grateful for the clarity it offered. I decided in favour of radical political honesty.

What I had forgotten – deleted from my memory – were the years spent not recognising my admiration, love and attraction to women; I had forgotten how intensely I loved my best friends. As Ananda Castaño in her chapter in this book explains, women and girls are conditioned to deny, ignore, or dismiss the possibility of seeing the women in our lives as potential romantic or sexual partners. No matter how intense our feelings toward women, they are expected to remain firmly in the realm of platonic friendship. Sexual and romantic desire is reserved for men. Forgotten, too, are the times my mother firmly guided a questioning teenager back onto the heterosexual path; how important it once felt not to disappoint her. Forgotten, the sexual experience I had with my best friend as a teenager – and the cruel punishment we both endured for it, punishment that ultimately separated us.

That experience forced me to reframe desire in my own head and redirect it towards men: "I can't feel like that. Only men are allowed to feel like that. I am not a man." Forgotten the years spent trying to fit in, forcing myself to have a boyfriend I felt nothing for. The despair I felt at 21, already married because that's what I thought I should do, and how my life felt so empty and miserable. How I told myself I couldn't be a lesbian because I was married to a man, the repetition of the 'born-this-way' narrative, 'a real lesbian would have found a way by now', keeping me in heterosexuality.

All these could be read as proof that I was a lesbian all along. But I think that on the contrary, they reveal the strength of compulsory heterosexuality and the false consciousness it instils. I had fully internalised the belief that I was a straight woman. That belief kept me locked in a system that was harming me. How do we name being 'in the closet' if we have no consciousness of being in it? For most of us who end up in heterosexuality, I believe the pressure and propaganda have worked perfectly. We are living proof of the coercion and – as we leave heterosexuality – proof that nothing in it was ever innate. Ann Menasche's study of lesbians who left and those who later returned to lesbian life supports this (this volume and 1999). About ten years prior to the pivotal talk by Sheila Jeffreys, I read *The Woman-Identified Woman* manifesto (Radicalesbians, 1970). I was in an abusive heterosexual marriage, and in no position to leave, so this text was my first introduction to the idea. I agreed with every single word of it, closed the book and went home to my husband.

I believe all women's experiences are different but compulsory heterosexuality is universal. It takes various shapes depending on our background, age, culture, country. But it is there implacable, unavoidable, relentless. I also believe that political ideas are like seeds. They need planting. And sometimes, when the terrain is fertile and the conditions appropriate, they grow. If we let them.

The power I felt when I left heterosexuality and called myself a lesbian was unmatched. Empowerment is often decried as a liberal concept used to support women embracing patriarchally imposed practices. But I believe that true empowerment lies in the act of walking away from what patriarchy had planned for us. It is the act of saying no and to self-define. True power comes from defiance. It comes from going against the rules imposed on us.

The inability many women experience to see women as potential sexual and romantic partners is the work of patriarchy: it is forbidden and punishable to be a lesbian in patriarchy. Many articles in this book describe the banishment from family women have had to endure for declaring they loved women (Kerwin, Spinster, this volume), how they were bullied as teenagers (May, this volume) or lost friends (Ehrlich). It is both the imposition of heterosexuality, and the erasure and punishment of lesbianism combined that constitute compulsory heterosexuality. For some of us, the path to lesbianism had to include a cerebral element, a careful dismantling of our past, a conscious decision – a political awakening.

The 'Born-This-Way' Ideology

The 'born-this-way' ideology – the idea that one can only be a lesbian because one is born a lesbian – is an active and contemporary component of compulsory heterosexuality. A backlash against the Second Wave Feminist revolution, it is profoundly patriarchal. While today it is often bandied about by lesbians who have internalised the belief that they need a doctor's certificate to call themselves lesbians, we must not forget that this belief system originates from patriarchal sexologists and serves to restrict women's ability to liberate ourselves from men and to weaken the women's movement (Sheila Jeffreys, this volume).

This narrative defines most women as born for men's use and inherently unable to free ourselves from the institution of heterosexuality. In fact, the 'born-this-way' snarrative denies the existence of heterosexuality as an institution of oppression entirely. Alima in this volume who made the journey from 'born-this-way' to 'political lesbian' explains she used to feel sorry for straight women's bad luck as she believed they couldn't escape their fate.

Just think about how much men and patriarchy benefit if most women believe they are innately straight and incapable of leaving them; if women keep pouring ourselves into heterosexual marriages instead of giving each other love, energy and attention; if we believe lesbianism is a rare defect of nature rather than a political choice available to any woman who wishes to take it. It becomes clear why political lesbianism is such a threat to patriarchy – and why it attracts so many opponents. The fear is that it spreads. Given men's parasitic oppression, this fear is justified. Women could all choose to leave men tomorrow and love and support each other. What would happen if the male population suddenly found themselves stripped of their free labour? When conservative men say that feminism aims to destroy civilisation *this* is what they mean. Feminism has the potential to destroy men's civilisation. Pat Robertson was right to be worried![4]

So, the critiques keep pouring in, often ill-conceived or based on projections rather than facts. I have addressed some already, here are a few more common ones:

Assertion 1: *Political lesbianism is just as bad as conversion therapy.*
Conversion therapy is usually understood as a conservative practice employed so that homosexual men and lesbians are 'cured' of their

---

4   "Feminism encourages women to leave their husbands, kill their children, practice witchcraft, destroy capitalism and become lesbians." Written by Pat Robertson in fund-raising letter to supporters of the Christian Coalition, 1992.

homosexuality. Such practices do exist: Julie Bindel recounts her own experience in this volume. However, patriarchy as a whole operates as a conversion therapy system for all women and girls – working both preventively and correctively to ensure women never become lesbians (corrective rape is one of those strategies, as discussed by Consuelo Rivera Fuentes and Lynda Birke, 2001 and by Susan Hawthorne, 2020). Formal conversion therapy is simply the last resort when all other mechanisms fail. In contrast, political lesbianism is *not* a global, systematic structure of oppression that pressures, forces, or coerces women to sleep with women, nor does it punish those who don't. That would contradict basic feminist principles. And let's be honest: which lesbian group has that kind of institutional power? Political lesbianism simply exposes the coercive nature of patriarchy and offers women a conscious way out, if they choose to take it.

Assertion 2: *Political lesbians are as bad as men who identify as women; they appropriate lesbianism in the same way men who identify as women appropriate womanhood.*

Men who call themselves lesbians ('translesbian') are predatory heterosexual males who use the framework of gender identity to act out a sexual fetish for lesbian sex, seeking access to lesbian bodies as a means of validating their self-declared identity (this has been called the cotton ceiling). In this sense, transgenderism, as used by men identifying as lesbians, represents one of the newest forms of *compulsory heterosexuality* (Wild, 2019). Political lesbians, by contrast, are women who choose to opt out of compulsory heterosexuality, directing their love and allegiance toward women. In the absence of any evidence for a 'gay gene', the only requirement to be a lesbian is to be a woman who loves women. Detransitioner, Charlie May, in this volume, draws important parallels between the 'born-this-way' ideology – which naturalises sexual orientation as innate – and gender ideology, which naturalises 'transness' as innate. Both stem from patriarchal thinking that seeks to depoliticise sexuality and gender, framing them as biological inevitabilities rather than as sites of political struggle and feminist consciousness, ultimately serving to control women.

Assertion 3: *Political lesbians are not real lesbians. They are pretend lesbians who are in fact straight or bisexual.*

This claim rests on the notion of an innate sexual orientation which I discussed earlier. As there is no concrete evidence to prove women are innately lesbians or not, the point is moot. Underlying this is the idea that a woman can never be a lesbian if she ever had relationships with men. The glorification of the 'gold-star lesbian' (a lesbian who has never experienced sex with men) reflects a denial of the pervasive force of compulsory heterosexuality in women's lives. While I find it amazing that in a world built on compulsory heterosexuality some women manage to escape it completely, this shouldn't create a hierarchy between women. Sadly, it is often accompanied by a deeply misogynistic trope which implies that sexual contact with men render women impure. I was once called 'soiled' by a woman who took offence at my own journey toward lesbianism.

Assertion 4: *Political lesbianism disrespects and goes against heterosexual women's 'true nature' to love men.*

This reflects another denial of the compulsory nature of heterosexuality. Being trapped in an oppressive system is never a woman's true nature. Political lesbianism simply highlights the nature of this oppression and the potential for liberation.

Assertion 5: *Political lesbians are shaming 'real lesbians' for their sexuality.*

Lesbian feminism opposes not only heterosexuality but also patriarchal sexual practices, including patriarchal versions of lesbianism. Practices such as sexual objectification, the eroticisation of hierarchy, butch/femme dynamics, top/bottom role-playing, any form of sadomasochism, lesbian pornography, and other acts that replicate heterosexual power dynamics have been powerfully critiqued by lesbian feminists (Hawthorne, 2025; Jeffreys, 1993; Linden, 1983; Radicalesbians, 1970).

Jeffreys (1990) and MacKinnon (1991) both describe and analyse the construction of female desire in a heterosexual context as "eroticising subordination." Women learn our sexual responses based on our experiences of subordination: conditioned responses which are the result of the enforcement of patriarchal sexual scripts. Similarly, lesbians – who are exposed to the same oppression – also develop their sexual responses in a patriarchal world that defines sexuality through objectification, eroticises violence, and valorises power dynamics. Lesbian sexuality and patriarchal versions of lesbianism are not the same: the first is a spontaneous and intimate woman-centred desire and attraction; the second is a pornified social construction, structured around power dynamics to serve patriarchal interests. Lesbian pornography and lesbian BDSM represent the only forms of lesbianism that patriarchy truly embraces – precisely because they reinforce patriarchal norms and weaken women's struggle.

We all live in a patriarchy and have been subjected to a lifetime of misogynistic propaganda. It would be surprising if women had not internalised some of these norms, including in our sexual practices. How could we be immune? But as feminists, it is our responsibility to recognise, challenge, and dismantle patriarchy within ourselves – including in our sexual desires and responses. As a lesbian feminist, I refuse to replicate the sexual dynamics I learned through heterosexuality. I consciously reject them. I do not want to love women in the way men claim to love us. It is crucial to differentiate between genuine desire and sexual objectification. Genuine desire is inspired by a woman as a whole: the way she "lights a room when she enters it" (Uygarkızı, this volume), the passionate way she speaks about the things she cares about, the exquisite curve of her neck, the power of her mind at work, the wrinkles around her eyes when she laughs, her determination in the face of challenges, the softness of her skin, her vulnerabilities and fears as well as her strength – everything that makes her a woman. Desire is also born from the bond you share: the mutual curiosity, amazement, and yearning for each other's bodies, how she so often makes you snort with laughter, the daily wordless acts of love, the ways you care and encourage each other, the reciprocity and trust between you, how you cry at the same film, how you can be both so similar and yet so very different. Sexual objectification, by contrast, reduces a woman to a disconnected collection of fetishised body parts for sexual use. The pursuit of pleasure for its own sake and at all costs is a pornographic construction of sexuality which solely benefits men and deeply harms women. It is an act of dissociation – from ourselves, and from other women often born of our experiences of sexual trauma. So are butch/femme and top/bottom role playing and, of course, BDSM. These are in total contrast to the real intimacy and connection an equalitarian lesbian relationship can offer.

I reject the notion that this critical, analytical process is akin to shaming lesbian sexuality. Rejecting the ways we may have internalised patriarchy is not shaming; it is undergoing a feminist process – sometimes difficult, but politically essential and personally deeply enriching.

Assertion 6: *Political lesbianism is individualistic.*
Political lesbianism is sometimes wrongly portrayed as an individualistic act and therefore not feminist. Feminism, we are told, must dismantle political structures of oppression. This criticism rests on the false premise that heterosexuality itself is *not* one of those political structures – a claim easily dismissed. Women

are primarily harmed, raped, and killed by the men we share our intimate lives with (Scott, 2026). Leaving the men who oppress us is not merely a personal choice; it is a survival imperative. As Sonia Johnson (2016, cited in Slamolo) reminds us, this is true both on the micro and macro levels. It is good and necessary for women, individually and collectively, to leave our oppressors and to gather, organise, and work with the members of our own class.

The journey toward political lesbianism always begins through the process of consciousness-raising: whether in person, through reading lesbian feminist texts, online discussions, or in collective speak-outs. It is through women sharing our stories – about the nature of our oppression by men, and how heterosexuality creates and sustains that oppression – that we begin to free ourselves from our individual oppressors. Hearing that some women have become lesbians gives others permission to take the same journey, should they wish to do so. If the personal is political when discovering that what happens to us in the hands of individual men in the privacy of our own home, then the personal is also political when we dismantle and leave our imposed allegiance to those men and their system. It goes both ways. And when a critical mass of women undergoes this political awakening, the result is a collective transformation. A movement.

After all, as Sonia Johnson said, "the only genuine Revolution possible, the only Revolution that … really changes anything, is an internal Revolution" (Sonia Johnson 2016, in Slamolo). Patriarchy is enforced and internalised in each of us individually – one by one, one rape at a time. Liberation must also occur on the individual level. We have both the power and the responsibility to initiate this change in our own lives. We each have the capacity to embody change, to act in accordance with our ideals, to live our politics. We must work through our experiences until we understand them and move on from them; until we uproot the patriarchal lies within us; until we stop believing and enacting them in our lives. There is no contradiction between individual and collective transformation here. Politically, this is the only sustainable way to create change: by being, embracing and embodying that change ourselves.

Compulsory Heterosexuality vs Every Woman

It is often misunderstood that the concept of compulsory heterosexuality refers to a specifically *lesbian* oppression – as popularised recently, for instance, in the *Lesbian Masterdoc* (Luz, 2018). The *Masterdoc* supports the idea that compulsory heterosexuality affects every woman, defining it as social pressure and "the assumption that straight is the default." However, it sadly muddles the issue by framing lesbianism as something women either *are* or *are not* – the "you might be a lesbian if …" approach.[5] It ultimately fails to challenge the nature and construction of sexuality itself under patriarchy. This kind of framing uses the concept of compulsory heterosexuality to promote a biologically determinist idea: that some women are simply born lesbians, while others are not. This is a grave misinterpretation that directly contradicts Adrienne Rich's essay and her motivation for writing it. By definition, compulsory heterosexuality affects *all* women. Lesbians are the visible tip of the iceberg, those who have escaped and survived it.

When some women come out as lesbians after years of heterosexuality, the usual explanation offered is that heterosexuality was never fulfilling for them *because they were lesbians all along.* Their lesbianism is then used to explain their inability to find satisfaction with men – an argument rooted in individualism

---

5   The *Lesbian Masterdoc* also promotes the idea that men can be lesbians if they identify as 'transwomen' or 'translesbians'. This perspective ignores trans ideology as a manifestation of compulsory heterosexuality, and how the so-called 'cotton ceiling' – the notion that lesbians should not exclude males from their dating pools if they identify as women – acts as a form of conversion therapy specifically targeting lesbians.

and biological determinism, rather than in a feminist analysis of heterosexuality as a political institution.

The premise of this book is this: heterosexuality doesn't work for women – full stop.

It's not you. It's them.

The fact that you find heterosexuality unfulfilling, exploitative or painful doesn't mean you were *born* a lesbian – it's much simpler than that. Heterosexuality is a system designed by men, for men. It can never work for us.

Next Step on My Feminist Journey

After becoming a lesbian, it became important to me to share the lesbian feminist knowledge I was discovering. My understanding of feminism had always been radical – centred on women's liberation – as opposed to a reformist feminism working for equal opportunity. One obvious step toward liberation is to remove ourselves, as much as possible, from physical danger.

Depending on the country, men commit between 95 to 99 per cent of sexual crimes (ONS, 2025; Peytavin, n.d.; United States Sentencing Commission, 2018). Men commit between 75 and 95 per cent of violent crimes, especially the most serious ones like homicide (ONS, 2017; Federal Bureau of Investigation, 2020). In the UK, men kill a woman on average every three days (Centre for Women's Justice, 2020). In Mexico, ten women and girls are killed every day by intimate partners or other family members (United Nations Office, Geneva, 2024). In the US, 34 per cent of murdered women are killed by intimate partners; 76 per cent by someone they know (Smith, 2022). In the UK, women killed by a current or former partner average 62 per cent of all femicides (Femicide Census, 2025).

The data on marital rape are often unconclusive: A UK study from 1998 found that approximately one in seven British wives had been raped by their husbands without use or threat of violence; and one in 17 had been violently raped by their husbands (Painter and Farrington, 1998). Rape can be difficult for women to define or acknowledge, especially when it occurs outside the patriarchally sanctioned scenario of 'stranger rape in a dark alley'. A recent French survey by the French polling and market research firm IFOP for *Elle* magazine, conducted in July 2025 on 3,015 people (including 1,710 women), found that 57 per cent of women reported having had marital sex when they did not want to, and ten per cent said they often had sex with their partner against their will. Yet only a small fraction explicitly labelled these experiences as rape, even when they met the legal definition (IFOP – Institut français d'opinion publique, 2025)

These figures demonstrate that heterosexuality is one of the most dangerous institutions for women, because it grants men 24/7 access to women on an intimate level. It is also the setting where gaslighting – blurring the line between sex and rape – leaves many women unable to recognise the rape they endure, sometimes sharing entire lifetimes with their rapists. Free from heterosexuality in 2013, I started talking about all this, candidly and spontaneously, without any expectation of the backlash that was about to come.

The Backlash: Heterosexual Defensiveness

Opponents to the idea that women can opt-out of heterosexuality and become lesbians can be found among heterosexual women and lesbians alike. The main premise for this opposition in both those groups of women is an internalised patriarchal vision of sexuality. It is very challenging to think critically and politically about aspects of our lives we have been indoctrinated to understand as our own since birth. Even more so when we are living in this oppression daily. Consequently, being confronted by the idea that it may not be the case is challenging. Hey, I get it! I was there, remember? I understand that anger towards the messenger is a natural way to deal with what we are saying.

Challenging heterosexuality in us is painful because of the intimate nature of the task and the uncovering of the trauma involved. As Catharine MacKinnon says, "Sexuality is to feminism what work is to Marxism: that which is most one's own, yet most taken away" (1991). It requires examining one's lifetime of sexual experiences with the lens of lesbian feminism, one that understands that sexual violence is systematically applied in order to make us compliant. It is not a journey to be taken lightly. But it's life-changing and definitely worth it. The contributors to this anthology agree.

The anger some heterosexual women feel towards political lesbians is misplaced. A healthy alternative would be to direct it towards men, and that is much harder to do. We are not your enemy.

The Backlash: Lesbian Defensiveness

The second demographic opposing political lesbianism is lesbians who have internalised the 'born-this-way' narrative. Their opposition stems from the belief that they felt they never had a choice. Many also claim that if they had had a choice, they would have chosen to be heterosexual. The level of internalised anti-lesbianism that this reveals is heartbreaking. It also infers that given the same circumstances, every woman would make the same choice, which is not the case.

I have no doubt that the circumstances and context of our journeys into lesbianism – including our age, religious background, the culture we live in, our friendship groups, whether we are feminist or not, our political affiliation, our family support or lack of it and many other factors – make a huge difference in how we experience and interpret that journey. Being a young lesbian has been traumatic for several women in this book, while women who came out later in life, have found it relatively easier than being in heterosexuality. For all lesbians in this book, the path to lesbianism was a wonderful experience that changed their lives for the better. None of this denies the experiences of others. What we may lack is women truly listening to and respecting the diversity of our experiences.

There is a concern that if women can *choose* to be lesbians, then they could – and worse, should – choose to be heterosexual. Critics often claim that because political lesbians argue that women can choose lesbianism, we therefore believe lesbians can or should choose to be straight. In reality, political lesbianism exposes that this expectation *already exists* under compulsory heterosexuality, which successfully pushes most women into heterosexual life. Naming this mechanism is not an endorsement of it – it is the basis of our resistance to it. Some people believe that challenging the 'born-this-way' notion of lesbianism runs the risk of losing the little protections we have under the law. Julie Bindel (this volume) and Lynn Alderson (1988) describe how claiming 'our sexuality is not a choice' was a strategic decision from the gay liberation movement to secure such legal protections. But this strategy comes at the expense of any lesbian feminist analysis by completely depoliticising lesbianism.

Opponents to political lesbianism use all of this rhetoric, and often lack basic respects for our experiences. While political disagreement is an important and necessary part of any feminist process, the opposition to political lesbianism has often taken the form of personal attacks. My own experience includes years of silencing, deplatforming, demonisation, attempts to make me lose my livelihood, harassment, character assassination, defamation, insults, and pile-ons. I have even been sent pornography online.

I have no doubt these attacks will continue and possibly intensify after the publication of this book.

Because of such threats, several potential contributors declined the opportunity to write a contribution for this book. This is why I have accepted submissions under pseudonyms. But I believe strongly that no one should have to face this level of violence for speaking the truth of our experiences and advancing political analyses.

The political consequences of normalising biological essentialism in sexuality – especially when dissent is suppressed through bullying and intimidation – are disastrous. We now find ourselves within a feminist movement that overwhelmingly silences an entire strand of feminist thought, dismissing it as 'controversial'. The institution of heterosexuality, the cornerstone of patriarchy, has become a taboo subject among feminists. This silencing not only obscures critical feminist analysis, it also undermines lesbian feminist activism and erases lesbian visibility as a whole.

This book aims to re-open this crucial discussion once more. I commend the women who chose to publish their thoughts in this anthology for their courage to put pen to paper and confront the ideology – and the bullies – trying to silence us. I thank them for their crucial work for the future of our collective liberation.

Why this book?

So why this book, despite the attacks? Because nobody does feminism for likes. Feminism is not about adjusting to patriarchal beliefs; it is not about staying silent or tailoring our politics to avoid offence. It isn't about caving in to bullies. Feminism is not people-pleasing.

Years of being silenced – and watching the most radical branch of feminism become an unspeakable taboo – drove me into depression. I realised it was better to face attacks for "going the whole way," as Mary Daly says, than to remain silent and get attacked anyway.

The pressing statement "I wish I was a lesbian … but I can't" called for a radically honest answer. This book is a collective response. Many contributors share the view that sexuality is politically constructed and enforced; many of these women have themselves left heterosexuality to live happy lesbian lives. In the context of a feminist movement that overwhelmingly silences political lesbianism, these women often lack the platform to discuss their decisions. My aim in this book is to address this lack by giving silenced political lesbians contributors the opportunity to write about their lives, their trajectories to lesbianism and how they conceptualise sexuality in a patriarchal world. Women from a variety of geographical backgrounds, ethnic groups and ages have responded in a wide range of ways – through theory, analysis, hybrid political-personal accounts of their experiences, prose, art, and poetry – reflecting the richness of lesbian feminist culture.

Ethos

Political lesbianism is sometimes criticised on the grounds that it tells women what to do. The famous pamphlet *Love Your Enemy?* asserts that all feminists *should* become lesbians (Leeds Revolutionary Feminists, 1981). While the text is brilliant, powerful and groundbreaking in many ways, I have always felt uneasy with this prescriptive approach.

Do I believe that women and feminism would benefit from all women leaving men and embracing lesbianism? Yes. Do I think a prescriptive method is the way forward? No. I agree with Stanley and Wise (1993) who emphasise that women's decisions and actions must be understood within the material and social conditions that shape their lives – not judged from an external feminist or theoretical standpoint. What may appear as compliance, contradiction or failure from the outside, can, within women's lived realities, be acts of survival, resistance, or simply the only viable option. Having been in such situations myself, I usually refrain from imposing such pressures on women.

This book is built on a different ethos. Its aim is not to tell women what to do, nor to blame or berate them for not taking the 'right decision' or for 'not being radical enough'. Instead, by presenting the stories of women who have made such changes and providing the feminist theoretical framework so often silenced, this book offers a sisterly suggestion: that, for those who feel so inclined, challenging heterosexual grooming and reshaping one's life is possible.

The book aims to present this conversation respectfully and peacefully. While it is impossible to predict or control the way anyone will respond to our words, I hope this collection offers women a serene and positive way to think about these questions.

Conclusion

This book exists because feminism is about telling the truth based on our own experiences so that others can interrogate their own life and begin taking tangible steps towards women's liberation. Challenging the biological-essentialist myths that women are biologically destined to pair up with men, while they sacrifice everything – joy, pleasure, career, hobbies, financial autonomy, friendships, and health – on the altar of male-centredness, is a tangible step toward women's liberation. So is supporting uncompromising female autonomy in our lives and our sexuality, and encouraging self-love and love for our sisters in a world that forbids it. Any of these actions is reason enough to speak up. Combined, they provide a powerful, explosive challenge to men's rule.

When women decide we have had enough of being drained of our energy, killed, raped, sold, commodified, impregnated, robbed of our labour, love, and emotional and practical support – the patriarchy loses its fuel. Its power is denied; its slaves withdraw. Control of access – saying no to men, creating women-only spaces, or adopting separatist strategies – is a fundamental form of power that women can reclaim. Not as yet another strategy to make men behave better, but to free ourselves. As Marilyn Frye (1983) writes: "The slave who decides to exclude the master from her hut is declaring herself not a slave."

The Herstory of women resisting heterosexuality – Beguines, Chinese marriage resisters, Suffragettes, second-wave separatists and political lesbians – has been systematically erased (Swan, 2016; Raymond, 1999; Gage, 2013; Jeffreys, 1987; Fougère, 2012). That's because women's collective refusal of men has always threatened patriarchy's survival. Women's collective resistance to heterosexuality, and their love for one another, has been a universal and consistent feature of women's struggle. What if the reason that becoming a lesbian feels like a homecoming for so many of us is not because we were lesbians 'all along', but because women loving women is a logical, universal, ancestral way of being, as well as a path of resistance – a truth patriarchy has tried to erase since its inception?

When we as individual women leave an abusive man, we take ourself seriously – our freedom, our survival, our dreams and aspirations, our creativity, everything that man has tried to crush in us. We choose to prioritise ourselves and focus on ourselves, sometimes for the first time in our life. Political lesbianism invites women everywhere to collectively take ourselves seriously, put ourselves first, and leave men and their oppressive regime. Stop engaging in it, giving it attention, stop begging for crumbs – liberal reforms authorised by men that keep us dependent and focused on softening a system built on our subordination. Only genuine women-centredness enables us to think beyond the male system:

beyond the laws designed to control us and the culture that demands we centre men.

The political lesbian revolution offers the only real path to change: building without patriarchy, creating the world we need, bypassing male power entirely. It is up to us – collectively – to decide that women, and women only, are the future of women. Women-centredness allows us to think outside the male system, beyond its laws and culture. Political lesbianism gives us a political space of our own, one where we find clarity, connection, creative solutions, and the sisterhood men have always disrupted. It allows us to give one another the love and support we have historically given to men, and to unleash the force and energy released when women centre women.

In 2026, patriarchy is destabilised by women's growing refusal of men, marriage and motherhood. In response, we see a concerted backlash. With its re-domestication of women, reinforcement of traditional gender roles, anti-feminist agendas, and attempts to roll back women's economic, public and cultural presence, Project 25 functions as a political strategy to push women back into reproductive and domestic service (Allen, 2024; National Women's Law Center, 2024). Compulsory heterosexuality makes a big comeback. In this climate, deep political resistance is required. We urgently need a feminism that recognises compulsory heterosexuality as a structuring force – and actively refuses it.

Monique Wittig (1971) urges us to remember the time when we were not slaves and, if we cannot remember, to invent it. By reinventing every day what it means not to be slaves in a male-dominated world, political lesbianism embodies that resistance. The political lesbian is a living, embodied memory of women's freedom and untamed possibilities – and an open door for every woman drawn to her own liberation.

So, you said you wish you were a lesbian?

Now you can.

References

Alderson, Lynn and Harriet Wistrich. (1988). 'Clause 29: Radical Feminist Perspectives', *Trouble and Strife*, No. 13.

Alderson, Lynn. (2022). 'In the Company of Women: Political Lesbianism and the War on Women'. In *The Radical Notion*, Issue Seven Spring/Summer 2022

Alderson, Lynn. (2022). 'How to Launch a Consciousness-Raising Group in Your Local Area'. FiLiA. <https://www.filia.org.uk/latest-news/2022/1/7/how-to-launch-a-consciousness-raising-group-in-your-local-area>.

Allen, Gemma. (4 December 2024). 'How Trump 2.0 and Project 2025 May Affect Women's Careers, According to the "Mamattorney"', *Forbes*. <https://www.forbes.com/sites/gemmaallen/2024/12/04/how-trump-20-and-project-2025-may-affect-womens-careers-according-to-the-mamattorney/>.

Aspinwall, Cary. (31 October 2024). 'Some States Are Turning Miscarriages and Stillbirths into Criminal Cases Against Women'. *The Marshall Project*. <https://www.themarshallproject.org/2024/10/31/stillbirth-oklahoma-arkansas-women-investigated>.

Barry, Kathleen. (1984). *Female Sexual Slavery*. Revised edition. New York: New York University Press.

Bindel, Julie. (2014). *Straight Expectations. What does it mean to be gay today?* London: Guardian Books

Bindel, Julie. (2025). *Lesbians. Where Are We Now?* London: Forum.

Bouris, Catherine. (29 March 2025). 'Elon Musk Says Shrinking Birth Rates Keep Him up at Night'. *Yahoo News*. <https://www.yahoo.com/news/elon-musk-says-shrinking-birth-010246947.html>.

Brooks, Khristopher J. (2 February 2023). 'Single Women Are Racing Ahead of Men in Homeownership. Here's Why', *CBS News*. <https://www.cbsnews.com/news/home-buying-single-women-outpacing-men-in-home-ownership/>.

British Business Excellence Awards. (4 March 2025). 'New Research Shows UK's Gender Pay Gap Reverses As Young Women Now Out Earn Men'. *British Business Excellence Awards*. <https://britishbusinessexcellenceawards.co.uk/from-the-awards/new-research-shows-uks-gender-pay-gap-reverses-as-young-women-now-out-earn-men#:~:text=Young%20women%20aged%2016%20to,jobs%20for%20non%2Duniversity%20graduates>.

Carroll, Matthew. (2023). *Sex Gaps in Education in England*. Cambridge: Cambridge University Press & Assessment. <https://www.cambridgeassessment.org.uk/Images/698454-sex-gaps-in-education-in-england.pdf>.

Cavin, Susan. (1985). *Lesbian Origins*. San Francisco: ISM Press.

CBS New York. (28 March 2024). 'Rejection Killings: Dangers Women Face when Telling Men "No"' [video]. *CBS News*. <https://www.cbsnews.com/newyork/video/rejection-killings-dangers-women-face-when-telling-men-no/>.

Centre for Women's Justice. (2020). *UK Femicides 2009–2018: Femicide Census Report*. <https://www.centreforwomensjustice.org.uk/news/2020/11/25/uk-femicides-2009-2018-femicide-census-report>.

Clarke, Cheryl. (2015). *Lesbianism: An Act of Resistance*. In Moraga, Cherrie and Gloria Anzaldúa (eds). *This Bridge Called My Back*. Albany: SUNY Press.

Daly, Mary. (1987). *Gyn/Ecology: The Metaethics of Radical Feminism*. London: The Women's Press.

Daly, Mary. (1992). *Outercourse: The Be-Dazzling Voyage*. San Francisco: HarperSanFrancisco, Melbourne: Spinifex Press.

Douglas, Carol Anne. (1990). *Love and Politics. Radical Feminist and Lesbian Theories*. San Francisco: ISM Press.

Dworkin, Andrea. (1987). *Intercourse*. New York: Free Press.

Dworkin, Andrea. (1989). *Pornography. Men Possessing Women*. London: Pluto Press.

Ferrara, Angelica P. and Dylan P. Vergara. (2024). 'Theorizing Mankeeping: The Male Friendship Recession and Women's Associated Labor As a Structural Component of Gender Inequality'. *Psychology of Men & Masculinities*, Vol. 25, No. 4, pp. 391–401.

Fougère, Myriam. (Director and writer). (2012). *Lesbiana* [Film]. Canada/USA: National Film Board of Canada.

Femicide Census. (2025). *Femicide Census Publishes Its Annual Report.*: <https://www.femicidecensus.org/femicide-census-publishes-its-annual-report/>.

Frye, Marilyn. (1983). *The Politics of Reality: Essays in Feminist Theory*. First edition. Trumansburg, NY: The Crossing Press.

Frye, Marilyn. (1992). *Willful Virgin. Essays in Feminism 1976–1992*. Freedom: The Crossing Press.

Gage, Carolyn. (8 July 2013). 'Sworn Sisters and Marriage Resisters'. *Carolyn Gage Blog*. <https://carolyngage.weebly.com/blog/sworn-sisters-and-marriage-resisters>.

Gao, Ming. (11 November 2024). '"A woman is not a baby making machine": a brief history of South Korea's 4B movement – and why it's making waves in America', *The Conversation*. <https://theconversation.com/a-woman-is-not-a-baby-making-machine-a-brief-history-of-south-koreas-4b-movement-and-why-its-making-waves-in-america-243355>.

Garnett, Jean. (21 July 2025). 'The Trouble with Wanting Men'. *The New York Times Magazine*. <https://www.nytimes.com/2025/07/21/magazine/men-heterofatalism-dating-relationships.html>.

Graham, Dee L. R. (1994). *Loving To Survive. Sexual Terror, Men's Violence and Women's Lives*. New York: New York University Press.

Haas, Benjamin. (26 October 2018). 'Escape the Corset: South Korean Women Rebel Against Strict Beauty Standards'. *The Guardian*. <https://www.

theguardian.com/world/2018/oct/26/escape-the-corset-south-korean-women-rebel-against-strict-beauty-standards>.

Hamilton, Cicely. (1909). *Marriage as a Trade*. New York: Moffat, Yard & Company. <https://digital.library.upenn.edu/women/hamilton/marriage/marriage.html>.

Hanisch, Carol. (1970). 'The Personal Is Political'. In *Notes from the Second Year: Women's Liberation* [online]. New York: Radical Feminism. <https://www.carolhanisch.org/CHwritings/PIP.html>.

Harding, Andrew. (18 December 2024). 'Gisèle Pelicot: How an Ordinary Woman Shook Attitudes to Rape in France'. *BBC News*. <https://www.bbc.co.uk/news/articles/cd75v8eqz44o>.

Harne, Lynne and Elaine Miller. (eds). (1996/2021). *All the Rage: Reasserting Radical Lesbian Feminism*. London: The Women's Press; Mission Beach: Spinifex Press.

Havelock Ellis, Henry. (1897). *Studies in the Psychology of Sex, Volume 2: Sexual Inversion*. Philadelphia: F.A. Davis Company.

Hawthorne, Susan. (2019). *In Defence of Separatism*. Melbourne: Spinifex Press.

Hawthorne, Susan. (2020). *Vortex: The Crisis of Patriarchy*. Mission Beach: Spinifex Press.

Hawthorne, Susan. (2025). *Lesbian: Politics, Culture, Existence*. Mission Beach: Spinifex Press.

Hoagland, Sarah Lucia. (1988). *Lesbian Ethics: Towards New Values*. Palo Alto: Institute of Lesbian Studies.

Henderson, Rob. (4 April 2021). 'Does Modern Dating Drive Men to Psychopathy?' [video] YouTube. <https://www.youtube.com/watch?v=IrVMj0ecV74&t=177s>.

Institut français d'opinion publique (IFOP). (2025). Marital rape in France in 2025. <https://www.ifop.com/en/article/marital-rape-in-france-in-2025>.

Jackson, Margaret. (1994). *The Real Fact of Life: Feminism and The Politics of Sexuality c 1850–1940*. London: Taylor & Francis.

Jeffreys, Sheila. (1987). *The Spinster and Her Enemies: Feminism and Sexuality 1880–1930*. Melbourne: Spinifex Press.

Jeffreys, Sheila. (1990/2011). *Anticlimax: Feminist Perspective on the Sexual Revolution*. London: The Women's Press; Melbourne: Spinifex Press.

Jeffreys, Sheila. (1993). *The Lesbian Heresy*. Melbourne: Spinifex Press.

Jeffreys, Sheila. (2014). *Gender Hurts A Feminist Analysis of the Politics of Transgenderism*. Oxon: Routledge.

Jeffreys, Sheila. (2018). *The Lesbian Revolution*. Oxon: Routledge.

Johnston, Jill. (1974). *Lesbian Nation: The Feminist Solution*. New York: Touchstone.

Johnson, Sonia. (1991). *Going Out of Our Minds: Metaphysics of Liberation.* Freedom: Crossing Press.

Joseph, Chante. (2025). 'Is Having a Boyfriend Embarrassing Now?'. *British Vogue.* <https://www.vogue.co.uk/article/is-having-a-boyfriend-embarrassing-now>.

Kitzinger, Celia. (1987). *The Social Construction of Lesbianism.* London: SAGE Publications Ltd.

Koedt, Anne, Ellen Levine and Anita Rapone (eds). (1973). *Radical Feminism.* New York: Times Books.

Kotecha, Sima. (13 March 2025). 'Why Gen Z Needs Rom Coms'. *BBC News.* <https://www.bbc.co.uk/news/articles/c62zwy0nex0o>.

Kuk, Jihye, Hyejung Park and Caroline Norma. (7 November 2018). 'Radical Feminism Paves the Way for a Resurgent South Korean Women's Movement'. *Feminist Current.* <https://www.feministcurrent.com/2018/11/07/radical-feminism-paves-way-resurgent-south-korean-womens-movement/>.

Lennon, Connor. (7 March 2025). 'Online "Manosphere" Is Moving Misogyny to the Mainstream'. *UN News.* <https://news.un.org/en/story/2025/03/1160876>.

Leeds Revolutionary Feminists. (1981). *Love Your Enemy? Debate Between Heterosexual Feminism and Political Lesbianism.* London: Onlywomen Press Ltd.

Lesbian History Group. (1996). *Not a Passing Phase.* London: The Women's Press

Linden, Robin Ruth. (ed.). (1983). *Against Sadomasochism: A Radical Feminist Analysis.* New York: Frog in the Well.

Lorde, Audre. (2007). *Sister Outsider: Essays and Speeches.* Berkeley: Crossing Press.

Luz, Angeli. (2018). *Am I a Lesbian? Masterdoc* [PDF]. Available at: <https://ia802308.us.archive.org/24/items/am-i-a-lesbian-masterdoc/Am%20I%20a%20Lesbian_%20Masterdoc.pdf>.

MacKinnon, Catharine A. (1991). *Toward a Feminist Theory of the State.* Cambridge, MA: Harvard University Press.

Mayer, Beth Ann. (2023). 'What Is a "Married Single Mom"?', *Parents.com,* 4 May. <https://www.parents.com/what-is-a-married-single-mom-7488576>.

McCurry, Justin and Nemo Kim. (3 July 2018). '"A Part of Daily Life": South Korea Confronts its Voyeurism Epidemic', *The Guardian.* <https://www.theguardian.com/world/2018/jul/03/a-part-of-daily-life-south-korea-confronts-its-voyeurism-epidemic-sexual-harassment>.

Menasche, Ann E. (1999). *Leaving the Life: Lesbians, Ex-lesbians and the Heterosexual Imperative.* First edition. London: Onlywomen Press.

Morgan, Robin. (ed.). (1970). *Sisterhood Is Powerful: An Anthology of Writings from the Women's Liberation Movement.* New York: Random House.

Morgan Stanley. (2019). *Rise of the SHEconomy*. Morgan Stanley. <https://www.morganstanley.com/ideas/womens-impact-on-the-economy>.

National Women's Law Center (NWLC). (2024). *Project 2025: What It Means for Women, Families, and Gender Justice*. Washington, DC. <https://nwlc.org/wp-content/uploads/2024/09/Project 2025 Full Report.pdf>.

Organisation for Economic Co-operation and Development (OECD). (2025). *Korea's Unborn Future, Understanding Low-Fertility Trends*. <https://www.oecd.org/en/publications/korea-s-unborn-future_005ce8f7-en/full-report.html#preface-d1e20-2726fe8f33>.

Oppenheim, Maya. (4 April 2019). 'Unmarried, Childless Women Are Happiest People of All, Says Expert'. *The Independent*. <https://www.independent.co.uk/news/uk/home-news/women-happy-children-spouse-partner-relationship-unmarried-a8931816.html>.

Office for National Statistics (ONS). (2017). *Overview of Violent Crime and Sexual Offences: Year Ending March 2016*. <https://www.ons.gov.uk/peoplepopulationandcommunity/crimeandjustice/compendium/focuson violentcrimeandsexualoffences/yearendingmarch2016/overviewofviolent crimeandsexualoffences>.

Office for National Statistics (ONS). (2025). *Sexual Offences in England and Wales Overview: Year Ending March 2025*. <https://www.ons.gov.uk/peoplepopulationandcommunity/crimeandjustice/articles/sexualoffences prevalenceandtrendsenglandandwales/latest>.

Painter, Kate and David P. Farrington. (1998). *Marital Violence in Great Britain and Its Relationship to Marital and Non-Marital Rape*. NCJ Report 178714, Office of Justice Programs. <https://www.ojp.gov/ncjrs/virtual-library/abstracts/marital-violence-great-britain-and-its-relationship-marital-and-non>.

Pankhurst, Christabel. (1913). *The Great Scourge and How to End It*. London: E. Pankhurst.

Peytavin, Lucile. (n.d.). *Gender and Statistics*. Lucile Peytavin Consulting. Available at: <https://www.lucilepeytavin.com/en/copie-de-gender-statistics>.

Radicalesbians. (1970). *The Woman-Identified Woman*. United States: Know, Inc. Reprinted in *Women's Liberation Movement Print Culture*, Duke University Libraries. <https://idn.duke.edu/ark:/87924/r3gx1t>.

Raymond, Janice G. (1999/2000). *A Passion for Friends: Toward a Philosophy of Female Affection*. Boston, MA: Beacon Press; Melbourne: Spinifex Press.

Rich, Adrienne. (1981). *Compulsory Heterosexuality and Lesbian Existence*. London: Onlywomen Press.

Rivera-Fuentes, Consuelo and Lynda Birke. (2001). 'Talking With/In Pain: Reflections on bodies under torture'. *Women's Studies International Forum*. Vol. 24, No. 6, pp. 653–668.

Sarachild, Kathie. (1978). 'Consciousness-Raising: A Radical Weapon'. In *Notes from the Second Year: Women's Liberation* [online]. New York: Radical Feminism. <https://www.rapereliefshelter.bc.ca/wp-content/uploads/2021/03/Feminist-Revolution-Consciousness-Raising-A-Radical-Weapon-Kathie-Sarachild.pdf>.

Scott, Marion. (2025). 'The most dangerous place in Scotland to be a woman… Her own home'. The Sunday Post. <https://www.sundaypost.com/fp/violence-against-women-for-many-home-is-more-dangerous-than-the-street/>.

Seresin, Asa. (9 October 2019). 'On Heteropessimism'. *The New Inquiry*. <https://thenewinquiry.com/on-heteropessimism/>.

Slamolo. (2016). *Going Farther Out of Our Minds Part 1* [YouTube video]. <https://www.youtube.com/watch?v=VGDfCQmKuPA>.

Slamolo. (2016). *Going Farther Out of Our Minds Part 2* [YouTube video]. <https://www.youtube.com/watch?v=CyLYZ5bKXuc>.

Smith, Erica L. (2022). *Female Murder Victims and Victim Offender Relationship, 2021*. Just the Stats Report, Bureau of Justice Statistics, U.S. Department of Justice. NCJ 305613. <https://bjs.ojp.gov/female-murder-victims-and-victim-offender-relationship-2021>.

Spender, Dale. (1983). *Women of Ideas and What Men Have Done to Them*. London: Ark.

Stanley, Liz and Sue Wise. (1993). *Breaking Out Again*. Second edition. London: Routledge.

Strock, Carren. (2025). 'The Awakening Women May Experience Later in Life: When Women Love – Really Love – Other Women'. *AARP Ethel*. <https://www.aarpethel.com/relationships/the-awakening-that-sometimes-happens-late-in-life>.

Swan, Laura. (2016). *The Wisdom of the Beguines: The Forgotten Story of a Medieval Women's Movement*. New York: BlueBridge.

Taylor, A. and Min Joo Kim. (3 July 2018). 'My Life Is Not Your Porn: South Korea's War Against Spy Cameras and Sexual Harassment'. *The Independent*. <https://www.independent.co.uk/news/world/asia/south-korea-spy-cams-metoo-sexual-harassment-ahn-hee-jung-a8470771.html>.

United Nations Office Geneva. (2024). 'Mexico: Boom in Organised Crime Making Femicide Invisible, Local Activist Says'. UN Geneva. <https://www.ungeneva.org/en/news-media/news/2024/12/101036/mexico-boom-organised-crime-making-femicide-invisible-local-activist>.

United States Sentencing Commission. (2018). *Final Fiscal Year 2018 Quarterly Data Report on Federal Sentencing*. Washington DC: USSC. <https://

www.ussc.gov/sites/default/files/pdf/research-and-publications/federal-sentencing-statistics/quarterly-sentencing-updates/USSC-2018_Quarterly_Report_Final.pdf>.

Valentin, Annabelle. (13 March 2025). 'Sodomie: Une Première Fois Non Désirée Pour Plus D'une Femme Sur Deux' [Sodomy: A First Unwanted Experience for More Than One Woman In Two]. *Elle.* <https://www.elle.fr/Love-Sexe/Sexualite/Sodomie-une-premiere-fois-non-desiree-pour-plus-d-une-femme-sur-deux-4413958>.

Whitesides, John. (7 February 2017). 'Wife Leaves Husband of 22 Years Because He Voted for Donald Trump', *The Independent.* <https://www.independent.co.uk/news/world/americas/donald-trump-wife-leaves-husband-22-vote-republican-democrat-a7567356.html>.

Wild, Angela C. (2019). *Lesbians at Ground Zero: How Trans Ideology Is Conquering the Lesbian Body.* Lampeter, Wales: Get The L Out. <https://www.gettheloutuk.com/attachments/LesbiansAtGroundZeroFindings.pdf>.

Wild, Angela C. (2021). Understanding Heterosexuality: "Eroticising subordination" and colonisation—A lesbian feminist perspective. In Elizabeth Miller (ed.), *Spinning and Weaving: Radical feminism for the 21st century,* Mason: Tidal Time Publishing

Wilkinson, Sue and Celia Kitzinger. (1993). *Heterosexuality. A Feminism and Psychology Reader.* London: Sage Publication.

Wittig, Monique. (1971). *Les Guérillères,* translated by David. Le Vay. London: Peter Owen.

Wittig, Monique. (1992). *The Straight Mind.* Boston: Beacon Press.

Late-blooming 'Privilege'

Hazel Holloway

I am using a pseudonym to protect my identity from those who would disrespect me simply for speaking my truth. As a quiet, reserved woman who avoids conflict, this opportunity to speak anonymously is invaluable.

I was entirely heterosexual until age 40. By 'entirely heterosexual' I don't just mean in terms of my experiences, but my feelings as well. I had only ever experienced attraction to males; never to females. I fancied lots of boys/men in my youth. It feels quite embarrassing to recall it now and writing this is difficult because it is so far removed from who I am today. But sharing my experience is important so that other women can know that change is possible (including drastic change) and that they need not be trapped in heterosexuality for life. That you can quit men without forgoing love, sex and intimacy.

I was a typical boy-mad teen with pictures of male rock stars on my bedroom wall. I read *Jackie* magazine and romance novels. My friends and I were preoccupied with which boys we fancied at school. By college, I was obsessed with getting a boyfriend and jealous of anyone who had a boyfriend, especially if he was 'fit' and was in a band. I had my first 'real' boyfriend at 18 and was quickly hooked on PIV which, while not particularly satisfying, made me 'bond' with this utterly unsuitable, immature dude. I had three other boyfriends over the next decade, and the sex felt like a drug at times, even though it was a battle to train boyfriends in how the female body worked. And to not be such entitled misogynists – though I had little success there!

Although I dodged the violent men, my relationship experiences were disappointing, to say the least. I found that while I felt drawn to men, I struggled to relate to them. I felt objectified, disrespected and neglected. My self-worth and confidence took a big hit, and with hindsight, I can see that this wore me down and primed me, as it does so many women, to settle for a mediocre man by the time I got to my late 20s. I stayed with this man in a monogamous relationship for over 15 years and reproduced with him. I was pleased to have found one that wasn't a porn user and had at least *some* sympathy with feminism. How low the bar was!

I had always been a feminist and had endured the normal societal gaslighting that equality had been won, and feminism was no longer needed. Yet, I saw a male-centric world all around me, and so my feminist curiosity persisted. The so-called relationships that I had with men only strengthened my beliefs. Men so clearly had the power in heterosexuality and they revelled in it. I came to see how the institution of heterosexuality is, in fact, one of the fundamental bases of their power and egotism. It is at the heart of gender itself.

I began reading feminist books in my late teens, starting with *The Female Eunuch* and this progressed on to radical feminist texts throughout my 20s and 30s. I encountered many mind-expanding theories that have contributed to me becoming the feminist I am today, and I owe a huge debt of gratitude to women such as Sheila Jeffreys, Marilyn Frye and Adrienne Rich. These theories included political lesbianism and compulsory heterosexuality. The fact that a 'wave' of women in previous decades had quit men and loved women instead was a revelation. It sounded wonderful!

Just imagine being able to have equal relationships without the male/female power dynamic! But I never encountered any real-life connection to this lifestyle. Plus, of course, I believed that I was doomed to be always heterosexual. After all, surely I would have experienced attraction to women by now if I had it in me. I was one of those people who used to say: "I wish I was a lesbian, but I just don't fancy women."

The early years of motherhood were grim and incredibly hard work. I lost myself completely and my resentment grew tenfold. I began a long period of celibacy. Around this time, social media became a thing, and this was a lifeline. I joined feminist groups online, ones that were actually radical. Women shared invitations to radical feminist events, and I planned a handful of weekends away in women-only spaces. And wow, these spaces were revelatory! I had read about the power of women-only spaces and activism, but I had to experience the phenomenon for myself to truly understand. My consciousness went up a gear!

At a feminist discussion weekend in a wonderful, women-centric location, I spoke at length with an older radical feminist who is sadly now deceased. She was a lifelong lesbian but had experienced first-hand the mass exiting of heterosexuality by women of her own age in the 1970s. We exchanged a great deal about our respective life journeys and on the final day of the event, she took me to one side and said, "I strongly recommend that you become a lesbian" and that I should think of myself not as heterosexual, but as "pre-lesbian." My exposure to radical feminist theory meant that I was ready to hear this without feeling defensive. I decided to be open to the possibility!

Over the next few years, I attended numerous radical feminist conferences, social weekends and camping trips. I met lots of women who had exited heterosexuality and learned so much from hearing their stories. I also met many lifelong lesbians who asserted that any woman could be a lesbian and who would break into song (Alix Dobkin's *Every Woman Can Be a Lesbian*) once the drinking and merriment got underway. I met many women who had been impacted by the same radical feminist books that I had read and had also come to question compulsory heterosexuality (comp het for short) and seek to overcome it. These events, the shared times and deep conversations, were life changing. Women would inevitably flirt with one another, and when a lesbian started to flirt with me, I found myself flirting back and was hit with the realisation that I was most definitely attracted to her and that this included sexually.

After this, I started to have woman crushes all over the place! I assumed that I must be bisexual but I soon found any residual attraction to men quickly faded. And I now see it as rooted primarily in a need for male approval and validation. I think many women can relate to this. The attraction I was now feeling to women, and to radical feminists specifically, felt very different. I think that seeing our orientation as 'sexual' is a male, patriarchal idea, based on men sexually objectifying feelings about women. But for women in general, our attraction leans more heavily towards the relational as well. It is more about a romantic attraction with a sexual element. Indeed, many lesbians speak of how lesbianism is about so much more than sex, yet we are stuck with the inadequate masculinist definition of it being a 'sexual' orientation.

Fast forward to the present, and the UK radical feminist movement that we had a decade ago has waned somewhat. The 'gender critical' (i.e. transgender ideology critical) movement is now seen by many to be the face of radical feminism, despite being single-issue and often alarmingly opposed to lesbian feminism. But happily, I have retained life-long friendships and connections from RadFems, most significantly my girlfriend whom I met via the movement. Ours is a healthy, reciprocal relationship. The support that we gain from one another, and from feminism more generally, supports us in our activism and working in the women's sector.

I do not fancy men now. The thought of kissing one, let alone touching his penis, gives me the ick! My orientation has changed, and this is the truth, regardless of how anyone else feels about it. I am now a menopausal 'elder' with a lot of life experience. I look out upon a world where compulsory heterosexuality is real and powerful. It directs as many women as possible into heterosexuality, which is the primary place that the patriarchy wants us to be. The mass compliance of ordinary males with the wishes of the male elite are founded on the promise of women's sexual and domestic availability. I would like all women trapped in heterosexuality to have an experience such as mine; to realise that you *can* exit, but that this need not mean an end to intimacy in your life. This realisation puts you in a much more powerful position in terms of your life destiny and significantly diminishes the hold that men have over you. It shifts your life perspective in so many ways. I used to believe that men age like wine while women age like milk and was apprehensive about getting older. But I now think older women (lesbian feminists especially) are fabulous! They sparkle with wisdom and character, the lines on their faces showing experience and status which are very attractive qualities. Such shifts in perspective are truly liberating. Our worldview is so heavily impacted by patriarchy, but it can change with consciousness raising and the right environment. We owe it to future generations of women to create this environment.

Those who support the 'born-this-way' ideology insist that women like me are in fact bisexual, but that we somehow hadn't realised this until middle age. But if the definition of lesbian is a woman who is exclusively attracted to women, then many ex-het women *do* fit into this category. I sympathise with the fact that some lifelong lesbians have struggled with their sexuality in a deeply homophobic world. That they do not feel that they had any 'choice' and that theirs is a fundamentally different experience from mine. And they are correct in this – 'coming out' in my 40s was easy and I am very grateful for this. To exit heterosexuality and discover my love for women, in middle-age, has been a huge privilege. It has improved my life immensely. It is not my intention to disrespect lesbians, and I would not argue with those who feel that their sexuality is innate. The right to a self-defined sexuality was one of the seven demands of the Women's Liberation Movement after all. But the experience of political lesbians/lesbian feminists is also worthy of respect. I would not have taken this journey were it not for the encouragement of many lifelong lesbians in the radical feminist movement. There is huge disagreement regarding this issue amongst lesbians, and the idea that 'real' lesbians reject the theory of political lesbianism is a myth. In fact, many lifelong lesbians call *themselves* political lesbians.

But heterosexual women are in a very different position. I refute the notion that encouraging a heterosexual woman to consider how her sexuality might be socially constructed and could change is the same as gay conversion therapy. I see this as a false conflation, because the history and context are so radically different. I do not understand why a feminist would want to lock women into heterosexuality when we know that many can exit. Insisting that everyone has an innate and unchanging sexuality prevents women from leaving. It is a fundamentally anti-feminist stance. It is also untrue. It reminds me of the transgender movement's insistence that we all have an innate gender identity. We don't! Our sex is fixed, but to whom we are attracted is all about our subjective feelings, which can change over the life course. My girlfriend has always been a lesbian but does not know if this is innate or not for her. She wonders whether her childhood observation that heterosexuality is not good for women had an impact. And when seeing a lesbian kiss on TV she recalls thinking, "Oh, you can do that! That makes a lot more sense."

The word 'choice' is often used in the sexuality debates, and I think this can lead to misunderstanding because it is open to such different interpretations. When ex-het women say that they have 'chosen' lesbianism, some people interpret this as saying that it was a simple choice that any woman can make at any time. But I would describe the 'choice' as more like a commitment to cult de-programming; a choice to be open to new possibilities, inspired by those who went before and demonstrated that change is possible. But change is heavily dependent upon the correct circumstances and support being in place. Many women may never encounter these circumstances. But many more *would* do if the goal of feminism were to facilitate this.

I have heard ex-het women criticised for treating lesbianism like it is a second choice; that we are only with women because men were disappointing. I think that this ignores the nuance of our experiences under patriarchy. If we are brainwashed into heterosexuality then we *do not know* about the alternatives because they have been hidden from us. Becky Birtha's poem 'How I Became a Lesbian' encapsulates this, when she speaks of women feeding "thick, pulpy slices" of mango "into each other, mouths open in astonishment" and realising that this love of mangos might have come earlier "only you never knew they existed until you were halfway through your life." The final line describes "the startling comprehension of the possibilities of life in a world that included this incredible, sweet reality" and for me, this encapsulates the joy of late-blooming lesbianism.

People sometimes say, "But what about women who are just straight and/or are happy with men?" and I always find this to be an odd question to ask. What about them? Lesbian feminists are not compelling women to do anything that they don't want to do. It's an invitation, not a diktat. What we *do* know is that a lot of women wish they could exit heterosexuality, and many *can* in the right circumstances. I would love to see a mainstream feminist movement that prioritises this. Happy heterosexual women can support and encourage this. If every town had a strong feminist community that women could escape to, this would seriously raise the bar for how men would need to treat women in heterosexual relationships.

I have come to see my relationship choices as central to my feminism and as such, I am a lesbian feminist. Giving my love to a woman rather than a man is a core part of my activism and I would urge more women to do the same. Not only is this better for us as individuals, but it benefits all women regardless of whether they participate or not. Women's creative energy (our 'gynergy') is powerful and is extracted from us via heterosexual norms to fuel the patriarchy. Redirecting it to women instead is a powerful and positive choice, whether we relate to women monogamously, via ethical non-monogamy or platonically.

Compulsory Heterosexuality

Radfem Kollektiv Berlin

Compulsory heterosexuality lays the foundation for patriarchal institutions, such as the nuclear family, prostitution and marriage: it aims to control women, our bodies, and our sexual practices for the benefit of men. It is the dominant social and cultural force that limits women's sexuality by creating the illusion that it is in our nature to be drawn to, or be sexually available for, men. With the words of Adrienne Rich in her insightful essay 'Compulsory Heterosexuality and Lesbian Existence' (1980), this dogma contains all constraints and sanctions that enforce or ensure 'the coupling of women with men' and obstruct and penalize 'women's coupling or allying in independent groups with other women'. Alternatives, like lesbianism, are concealed, ensuring that the majority of women worldwide direct their emotional and sexual energies away from other women and instead towards men.

Women are convinced or socialized to believe that marriage and sex with men are inevitable parts of our lives, even if we do not want it, even if it causes us great pain. As radical feminists, we assume that if all women were free, and heterosexuality was not forced or demanded by penalty, women's coupling with men would not occur in the way we observe under patriarchal rule.

When the standard family is nuclear, heterosexuality is normalized: the heterosexual couple is positioned at the core, which serves as the central unit of society. As radical feminists, we recognize this as male supremacist propaganda. Within the patriarchal framework, the possibility of an egalitarian heterosexual relationship flourishing is unlikely.

In patriarchy, heterosexuality is a relational model based on dominance and submission that functions as the blueprint for all social interactions. Lesbian and gay relationships – although lacking the sex-based power differential – are of course molded by these same social forces. In recent discourse, we observe that the word 'queer' attempts to challenge heteronormativity, but instead it simply obscures female sexual boundaries by discouraging women from using the term 'lesbian' and thus from embracing lesbianism.

Traces of women's real, tangible resistance to this doctrine of compulsory heterosexuality can be found worldwide and across history. Therefore, we assume that women do not have an internal or innate drive for life-long monogamous emotional and sexual relations with men. Quite to the contrary, heterosexual coupling is not natural to women, and women resist compulsory heterosexuality because it hinders our creativity, joy, freedom and eroticism. We encourage and celebrate the mental, emotional, physical, erotic and sexual connections shared among and between women worldwide.

As feminists, the male invention of compulsory heterosexuality and man's urge to repress, restrain and redirect women's emotional and sexual energies must make us furious. Women are constantly told that we need men (our oppressors) in every facet of our lives, and that any deep bond shared between women is an unnatural expression of man-hating. Compulsory heterosexuality reinforces women's dependence on men in every social, legal, and religious context. Thus, women are prevented from experiencing the pleasures and challenges of independent self-actualization – as well as the joys and demands of sisterhood and woman-love!

This text is an extract from the RadFem Kollectiv Berlin Manifesta. <https://radfemkollektivberlin.net/manifest/>.

References

Rich, Adrienne. (1980). 'Compulsory Heterosexuality and Lesbian Existence'. In *Signs*, Vol. 5, No. 4, Women: Sex and Sexuality, pp. 631–660.

Flame, Kelly Frost 2025

Flame

Kelly Frost

In my favourite local junk market, I found a collection of girls' annuals from the 1950s. These included a mix of short stories, comic strips, puzzles and beautiful black and white illustrations. They linked with popular girls' magazines of the time such as *School Friend* and *Girls' Crystal*.

What hit me immediately was the stark contrast between these and the teen magazines of today. I was appalled to learn, through Radfem chats, that these modern publications feature articles about anal sex and how to 'choke' 'safely' with men and boys. They euphemistically call it 'choking' because they can't sell the idea of strangulation to us (who knew?) but that is what it is.

And then there are the endless adverts for make-up, pornified fashion, cosmetic injections and hair removal. Depressing.

Girl magazines of the '50s contained no such horrors! What a pleasure it was for me to read stories about girls playing tennis and hockey. These games were always played with joy and good spirit. The girls don't really mind who wins; it's all about being active, getting better at a sport and spending time with friends.

I read stories about rescuing puppies from a cliff edge or about their best friend who got into trouble in a boat. They ride horses, ski and have chats in their dorm rooms about their hopes and dreams. Yes, they are often set in posh boarding schools but I forgive them for this class bias because they do everything else so well! There is no talk of boys or how to be attractive to them. They are a breath of fresh air!

I started removing the illustrations and cutting paper to create hearts between and around two friends.

In these hearts are cut-outs from the piles of wrapping paper and birthday cards I've kept over my nearly 50 years of having birthdays.

This piece is called *Flame* and it's from the series celebrating love between girls and women and the power and pleasure of female connection.

I've lived and loved the past 25 years without men in my life and I wish these annuals had been around for me in my childhood. Perhaps then I wouldn't have been forced into a youth of compulsory heterosexuality and worry about the male gaze.

But my life now, thanks to radical feminism, is full of sisterhood and support, laughs and occasionally romance. I got there in the end!

On Dating Men (And Reasons Not To)

Yağmur Uygarkızı

If you're a feminist (do feminism, read feminism, breathe feminism) and you're not (yet) a lesbian, it is likely that you've had or are currently having the tremendous pleasure of dating men – that mandatory rite of passage in womanhood under compulsory heterosexuality.

As I look back to my pathetic attempts to square my feminist politics with my heterosexuality, I wonder, why was I dating men despite everything I knew thanks to feminism?

It took me several years to incorporate feminist theorist Sheila Jeffreys' teachings on heterosexuality, mainly through *Anticlimax* (1990) and her autobiography *Trigger Warning* (2020; see also Leeds Revolutionary Group, 1981). I had to stop being dissociated to conclude this piece and exited heterosexuality on the fast track. The myth of *The One* or *Prince Charming* held me back for too long, and the contemporary release of his *Exclusive Unlimited Feminist Edition* made everything worse. This is my own 'What was I thinking?' moment, how I translated political lesbianism in my own words, so please don't take it personally. You, my dear reader, you take it politically.

Y B A Feminist 2 B A Wife?

There's a tale that goes a little bit like this. One exceptional man alone could absolve all others for their mediocrity, if not cruelty: 'Prince Charming'. He'll come and save me one day – from my lurid home, depressing life, poverty, lack of love.

Things get worse when that exceptional Good Guy Greg is vested with feminist superpowers. Initiatives to include men into feminist conversations abound. I'm thinking of the French feminist movement, wherein any man capable of putting three consecutive non-sexist sentences together is put on a pedestal.

The aggressive campaign for heterosexuality, having exhausted the film and beauty industry, went for the last unchartered territory, the largest niche but most fruitful segment of the market: feminism. Feminism has become an insidious way for men to make themselves relevant in women's lives. My Prince shall come and save me one day – from my lurid home, depressing life, poverty, lack of love … and *male violence*. We were once told we each needed our individual copy of a man at home to fix the cable; now we're told we need one to fix men. 'Ah! Men? Violent?! Hahaha what do you mean? My husband's more feminist than me, he changed the bedsheets in 2023!'

They kill us, rape us, beat us and then we offer them feminism to fuck us better?

Houston, we have a problem.

Radical feminist, Ti-Grace Atkinson, magisterially debunked the myth of 'love' as a respite from violence in heterosexual relationships. In one address to female college students in 1969, she challenges those in the audience who want to get married: "What does going to college have to do with getting married?" (Atkinson, 1974, p. 28). After all, as she puts it, studying psychology in no way equips you to be a better wife than learning how to clean and cook.

So here is my question: What does feminism have to do with dating men?

Just like higher education seemed to be a promise of better male treatment of women, all sorts of women are flocking to all sorts of feminisms in the hope of escaping male violence. In the political economy of dating men, feminism is the new hot currency.

But you don't need feminism to spend your days with a mediocre man. Why open your eyes to their violence if you're going to shut them up the moment he wants to mount you? (Why did I do it?)

"Don't you realise it's against your interests?" (Atkinson, 1974)

Just look at the argument of feminism as a token for better sex with men. Thousands of years of burning, mass raping, mutilating … all gone with one, big … FUCK. You heard it ladies! You just need to get laid and soon you'll feel better about the whole thing. Hm, weird … I feel like I've heard that one before. Lesbian writer Jill Johnston certainly saw the irony way before me in 1973 in *Lesbian Nation*: "The angry feminists after all, all they needed was a good fuck" (p. 26).

Because isn't this precisely the definition of compulsory heterosexuality? The mandatory fucking of women to keep us subordinate to men as lesbian thinker Marylin Frye put it:

> It is very important to the maintenance of male-supremacy that men fuck women, a lot. So it is required; it is compulsory. Doing it is both doing one's duty and an expression of solidarity. (1983 cited in Graham, 1994).

If anything, the argument then only reinforces the case against heterosexuality. Heterosexuality is so compulsory that even with a feminist mindset, you're supposed to just do it.

Squaring feminism with heterosexuality is the most pernicious form of male sexual stronghold of women. Suppose you find your *Prince Charming Exclusive Unlimited Feminist Edition*, you are now stuck with the schmurf for life because you know how much more violent all the others are. You're trapped. You know (I knew) women depend on men for economic survival, do you realise (did I realise) you now depend on one for *moral* survival?

Again, this does nothing to challenge the heterosexual model. Clinging on to *Prince Charming Exclusive Unlimited Feminist Edition* is the typical female reaction to male kindness. But what is kindness in that context? What is decency under patriarchal captivity, Psychologist Dee Graham, *In Loving to Survive* (1993), compares heterosexuality for women to a collective Stockholm Syndrome, in which captives bond with their captors hoping they'll be spared cruelty. Victims trapped with perpetrators, as in the infamous Swedish robbery case, blow out of proportion any act of kindness from the aggressor, including the mere cessation of violence, wrongly interpreting it as a sign of the perpetrator's benevolence. In any other context, a human being wearing clean socks would have gone completely unnoticed, but under a regime of massive destruction of women by men, any man engaging in such behaviour is erroneously perceived as good, 'sexy' even ('feminist', I hear?).

Salvation from the problem cannot come from the problem. I get it, a vaccine requires injection of the venom, but full immersion? Come on! Wasn't the first jab enough?

Ultimately, the quest for feminist solace in heterosexuality denotes a clear misunderstanding of the problem. If you think that men can be allies in women's liberation, you haven't understood where the danger's coming from. You haven't done the math. Or read *Amazon Odyssey* (1974). Or both. Because "[if] women are being oppressed, there's only one group left over to be doing the oppressing: men" (p. 74).

The Other Woman

Mr Right has a wife. Since they're both so progressive, she's kept her surname: Mrs Myhusbandisbetterthanyours.

If we follow through with the argument that patriarchy will end thanks to Good Feminist Guys in good heterosexual relationships, and if we bear in mind that their supply in the political economy of heterosexuality is scarce, how do we deal with distribution? Who gets whom? Good feminist boyfriends do not challenge a core feature of heterosexuality which is female rivalry for men. Given this blatant contradiction one cannot help but wonder whether the safeguard of the long-beaked echidna in Papua New Guinea was out of stock at the supermarket of charitable causes the day defendants of heterosexuality visited. Just listen to how it sounds. Turn the music on, *Milkshake* by Kelis (2003) – remix:

> My feminist man's so much better than yours,
> damn right, he's better than yours,
> damn right, he's better than yours,
> I could share him,
> But I'm better than you!

How do you maintain feminist solidarity then? How do you square such condescension with feminist politics, Madam? Would you bother coming down from your Sperm Castle and grace us with your presence from time to time?

It's the unbearable sense of superiority that bothered me when dating men. Even if I got correct treatment from one man, what did it say about my attitude towards other women and ultimately my own blindness towards my 'romance'? Should I have just pitied other women my whole life? Would I just put the kettle on for my sobbing friends while I was going full Alhamdulillah for having the best man a woman could possibly ask for?

In *In Defence of Separatism* (2019) political theorist Susan Hawthorne warns against the frailty of the status gained by women in heterosexual relationships. She reminds her reader that you're still a woman in a man's world. You might get a preferential treatment over other women because of your *social* status, but you'll still get a worse treatment than your male partner because of your *sexual* status.

I couldn't stand that.

Ti-Grace Atkinson obviously didn't miss the class aspect. She reacts to one of the countless stories of women abandoned by their husbands after decades of good and loyal service: "While I was moved by this woman's situation," Ti-Grace Atkinson says, "still the question nags me – how could she have believed she was not one of 'them'?" (Atkinson, 1974, p. 129).

Well, Mrs Myhusbandisbetterthanyours, what makes you think you're so special?

What made *me* think *I* was so special?

Girl you're cute, but you ain't Beyoncé. And you know what? Even Beyoncé was treated badly. Do you think us common mortals stand a chance?

I'm glad my self-confidence wasn't shattered by heterosexual encounters, but I told myself: if you think you're so special, you might want to have a look at what happened to women lionised across the globe and supposedly those getting the best treatment. I've looked at global icons and their human-shaped cumbersome accessories aka boyfriends. Madonna: cheated on; Miley Cyrus, she made a song about it; Natalie Portman; Halle Berry; Siena Miller … You name it (see Laconte, 2021). That women with such exceptional lifestyles had such ordinary experiences should alert you to the quality of your own.

From there I rated celebrities on the Jay-Z Scale of Ugly Boyfriends from 0 to Jay-Z. This non-linear system of measurement makes inequalities in heterosexual couples blatant. You don't need statistics and arguments, just open your eyes. Here's how it works: Julia Roberts and her first husband Lyle Lovett? That's a *Jay-Z-10*

– only because Julia Roberts's marriage to Mr Lovett was much shorter than that of Beyoncé and Mr Z. But how much does the Sophia Loren/Carlo Ponti couple fare on the Jay-Z Scale of Ugly Boyfriends from 0 to Jay-Z? *Carlo Ponti.* I'm telling you it's not linear. You can play around it. Here's some ideas:

- Jack Antonoff and Margaret Qualey,
- Roger Vadim and Brigitte Bardot or Jane Fonda,
- Andrew Upton and Cate Blanchett,
- Vincent Cassel and Monica Bellucci or Tina Kunakey …

Beauty is not the eye of the beholder but in front of the ugly man.

Celebrity culture, by dissecting women's lives publicly, can help us read our own. Celebrities also provide the perfect *ceteris paribus* examples. I can't think of a better proof of compulsory heterosexuality than these women who by having the economic means of escaping heterosexuality still put up with those ugly schmurfs.

No, but in all seriousness, please look at what some of these pop icons endured.

Rihanna and Chris Brown. The man disfigured her in 2009. Had I not heard Oprah Winfrey on a loop on TV stating, "If a man hit you once, he will hit you again," I wouldn't be writing this today (Kennedy, 2009).

Beyoncé was only 18 when that creepy Mr Z, aged 30, started lurking around her. She didn't just have to put up with him cheating on her, she also had to lift up that big sack of flesh of a man after allegations of him raping a 13-year-old girl with fellow rapper P-Diddy emerged (Melas, 2024).

Enough showbiz, what about one truly exceptional globally famous woman, Gisèle Pelicot? Spectacular by all accounts. By holding a public trial against her former husband who pimped her for free during decades, she showed the entire world what a happy heterosexual couple is about: deceits and rapes (Pélicot in Chrisafis, 2024).

You want your Feminist Prince Charming but look who fights the dragons. Are you not afraid to wake up 40 years later next to the same now-crumpled face and realise your whole life was a lie? A woman who's happy in a heterosexual relationship is just a woman who hasn't noticed what's going on.

"I Became a Lesbian Because I Didn't Want to Clean a Man's Toilets"[1]

If you were presented with a basket of shiny beautiful apples and told that only of them was not poisonous, would you take the risk?

The heterosexual bet is about gambling your whole life on the infinitesimal chance of ending with the right guy. You just have to look at the global rates of femicide to see that I'm not exaggerating. Russian roulette's a joke next to the *hetbet*.

The apple metaphor is now well-known in feminist circles, but how many noticed that right next to that basket stands one full of exquisite mangosteens? Ok, for the sake of the story, let's say that two are rotten. Wouldn't you rather revel in their honey?

My point is not that I think you *should* be a lesbian. Magniloquent terms like integrity, solidarity or even sacrificial terms like 'for the cause' are all good, but that's not what you need to hear me out.

My point is that, eventually, you *will* become lesbian (Jeffreys cited in Wild, this volume). Past a certain point of feminist awareness, you will not want to have anything to do with men, let alone date them.

What is it that you seek in a man?

---

1   Heard at a feminist conference organised by Bec Wonders (around 2021).

Mutual trust? Companionship? Understanding? If you went to the butcher for a vegan meal, people would call you crazy! Why isn't there the same common sense when it comes to heterosexuality?

What do you want to do with a man?

Talk to him? Might as well talk to a tree – at least it grows!

Have S.E.X? That Sensual Exclusion of XX they turn it to be? You'll be bored out of your tits!!

Have kids?

Buy a house?

Watch him prey on teenage girls?

Observe him as he skilfully tries to juggle his male habits of nights-with-the-lads and his feminist politics with the elegance of a donkey intent on algebra?

Lightyears, neurons, protons,
No unit to measure the density of women's pleasure,
Nothing to account for the layers of experience.
Archaeology excavates the earth, feminism unravels the pain.

I am every woman and so is every woman.

Now tell me: where does a man fit in this picture?

How can a man understand the depth of my experiences?

How can a man handle the gynergy? Hell-bent on destruction as he is, he'll suffocate over the beam of life you exude.

How could he catch the luminous streaks of your expressions?

Does he know of all the secrets he will never learn? How would he welcome them if he knew?

Can he hear the rumblings of your wild thoughts from the movement of your eyes?

Does a man have a heart and is there space in that heart for your love?

How can a man make sense of the imperceptible tightness of a woman's lips and turn it into a smile?

The way we walk, the way we talk, lighten a room when we enter it. What does a man understand about that?

Tell me now, do you still want to listen to him whine about that corporate job he couldn't get?

You can keep looking if you want, at the end of the day, we all know that the perfect man is a woman.

References

Atkinson, Ti-Grace. (1974). *Amazon Odyssey*. New York: Links Books.

Chrysafis, Angelique. (2024, September 5) Woman tells trial of husband who invited men to rape her: 'I was sacrificed on altar of vice'. *The Guardian*. <https://www.theguardian.com/world/article/2024/sep/05/french-woman-world-fell-apart-alleged-rapes-men-invited-by-husband-gisele-pelicot#:~:text=The%20accused%20men%20recruited%20by,ideal%20couple%2C"%20she%20said>.

Frye, Marylin. (1983). The Politics of Reality: Essays in Feminist Theory. Trumansburg, NY: The Crossing Press, In Graham, Dee L. R. with Edna I. Rawlings and Roberta K. Rigsby.(1994). *Loving to survive: Sexual terror, men's violence, and women's lives.* New York University Press.

Graham, Dee L. R. with Edna I. Rawlings and Roberta K. Rigsby. 1994). *Loving To Survive: Sexual Terror, Men's Violence, and Women's Lives.* New York University Press.

Hawthorne, Susan. (2019). [1976]. *In Defence of Separatism*. Mission Beach: Spinifex Press.

Jeffreys, Sheila. (1990). *Anticlimax: A Feminist Perspective on the Sexual Revolution.* London: The Women's Press; (2011) Melbourne: Spinifex Press.

Jeffreys, Sheila (2020). *Trigger Warning: My Lesbian Feminist Life.* Mission Beach: Spinifex Press.

Wild, Angela C. 2026. 'Introduction'. In Wild, Angela C. (ed). I *Wish I Was a Lesbian: Women's Lives Beyond Heterosexuality.* Mission Beach: Spinifex Press

Johnston, Jill. (1973). *Lesbian Nation: The Feminist Solution.* New York: Simon & Schuster.

Kelis. (2003). 'Milkshake' [Song]. On Tasty. Star Trak Entertainment/Arista Records. Released August 25, 2003.

Kennedy, Helen. (2009). 'Oprah Winfrey has a warning for Rihanna: 'Chris Brown will hit you again.'' *New York Daily News*. <https://www.nydailynews.com/2009/03/08/oprah-winfrey-has-a-warning-for-rihanna-chris-brown-will-hit-you-again/>.

LaConte, Stephen. (2021). 'Celebrities who've been cheated on'. *BuzzFeed.* <https://www.buzzfeed.com/stephenlaconte/celebrities-whove-been-cheated-on>.

Leeds Revolutionary Feminist Group. (1981). Political Lesbianism: The Case Against Heterosexuality. In *Love Your Enemy.* London: Onlywomen Press.

Melas, Chloe. (2024). 'JayZ accused in civil lawsuit of raping a 13yearold girl in 2000'. *NBC News.* <https://www.nbcnews.com/news/us-news/jay-z-accused-civil-lawsuit-raping-13-year-old-girl<-2000-sean-diddy-co-rcna183376>.

Choosing to Love Women:
A Korean 4B Story

Hyejung Kim

I entered university in Busan, South Korea in 1998, and became involved in leftist student activism. During this time, I experienced sexual violence within the activist community. I didn't even realize it was sexual violence until I read an article by a feminist scholar a year later, which explained why such acts are structural forms of violence against women. This revelation led me to become a feminist. I felt like I had been deceived by the world and was now discovering a new one. Although Busan is South Korea's second-largest city, feminist movements weren't very active on university campuses back then. I found a few female students interested in feminism, and together we studied it, sharing personal experiences and reflections – essentially forming a consciousness-raising group.

Unlike in Busan, I learned that feminist groups were forming at major universities in Seoul, where events and discussions were happening. Thirsty for feminism, I started attending feminist events in Seoul, such as the Women's Film Festival. Seeing free-spirited women there shocked me. Feminist ideas were being expressed and shared through various forms of art and cultural activities like art, music, and publishing, with vibrant discussions on topics like sexual violence and sexuality. One thing that struck me was that many of the feminists I met there were lesbians.

In fact, heterosexual feminists would jokingly say that they were the *minority* in those spaces.

Inspired by the vibrant feminist movement I had witnessed in Seoul, I wanted to create something similar in Busan. Along with three other feminists, I launched a feminist web magazine at Busan National University in 2000. Our first feature article criticized the military culture among male students. In South Korea, most male university students take a break from their studies to complete 18 months of mandatory military service. After returning, many would exhibit a stronger sense of male entitlement, engaging in behaviors such as sexual harassment and enforcing military-like discipline on younger students. This article quickly spread online, and soon, our website was flooded with angry male commentators from all over the country, causing it to crash. The comment sections were filled with threats and sexual insults. These men were outraged that women who hadn't served in the military dared to criticize them. Some of our members, whose personal information was exposed, were so frightened by the threats that they avoided attending classes.

This incident made me realize how difficult it was to communicate with men about women's issues. The leftist men I worked with were largely ignorant or indifferent to the daily sexism women faced. I began to see that men and women, due to their different social standings, had fundamentally different experiences, making it nearly impossible for men to truly understand women's perspectives. At the time, I was contemplating romantic relationships, and I found myself questioning whether I could be with someone who couldn't share my worldview shaped by my experiences as a woman. I thought that if I were to enter an intimate relationship, I would want a partner who could share this perspective. If someone could not understand or share this critical aspect of my life, could our relationship be truly deep and equal? Even now, I find that a very rational concern.

Around this time, I watched a film called *If These Walls Could Talk 2*, featuring Ellen Degeneres and Sharon Stone as a lesbian couple in one of the episodes. It depicted a story of a white middle-class lesbian couple in the US trying to have a child. Two women building a domestic life together seemed so appealing. Until then, I had never met a real-life lesbian. South Korea had no openly out lesbian celebrities or public figures and even today, there are none. After watching the movie, I started imagining what it might be like to live as a lesbian. But when I asked some feminist friends, "Could I live as a lesbian too?" their response was, "You'd have to try having sex with a woman first." Even my close feminist friends seemed to associate lesbianism primarily with sexual attraction since none of us had ever met a real-life lesbian.

I began searching for places in Busan where I could meet lesbians. Through the internet, I found a lesbian rights group that met monthly at a lesbian bar. I attended one of these meetings. The group was more of a social gathering than an activist one, as no one in the group had publicly come out. However, they still wanted to strengthen their group as a human rights organization. I actively participated in the group and helped transform it into a 'women of sexual minority' rights organization. Eventually, I began a long-term relationship with a woman I met through the group. As I experienced intimacy with another woman and met others living that way, I realized there was no longer any reason to consider men as potential partners.

In the early 2000s, there were a few gay rights organizations in South Korea, mostly based in Seoul. Gay men and lesbians had separate organizations, but their political agendas were largely aligned. Both groups focused on the common oppression they faced as gay people. However, the lesbian groups were more sensitive to issues of sexual violence and worked to raise awareness of it within the lesbian community, something gay male organizations didn't prioritize. At that time, queer politics was making its way into South Korean progressive academia and student movements from the West. Films supporting 'transgender' rights were also being introduced at the Seoul Women's Film Festival, reinforcing the notion that, like gender identity, one's sexual identity is innate and does not change despite social influences. For example, a man who identifies as a woman has a sense of gender identity as a female, so much so that he believes he has to surgically modify his body to align it with his unchangeable identity. The argument for an innate and unchangeable sexual orientation similarly offers no scientific evidence and is a mere belief system. However, radical feminist perspectives on political lesbianism were hard to find. I had heard about the term but did not know its meaning and implications in depth. The only book on homosexuality that I found was *Homosexuality and Psychology* by a male psychologist, in which he argued that homosexual tendencies are innate and that individuals experience discrimination and exclusion in a heterosexual-centered society.

As I was engaged in lesbian rights activism, I often gave lectures on gay rights at women's organizations or leftist groups, referencing materials that framed homosexuality as an innate trait. Despite the fact that I had chosen to become a lesbian from a feminist perspective, I adopted the dominant queer theory, which downplayed or erased experiences like mine. I told myself that I was an exception, believing that most lesbians had always been attracted to women and that those who became lesbians later in life were merely 'rediscovering' their true selves, which had been repressed by a heteronormative society. This narrative claimed that gay men and lesbians faced discrimination for something they hadn't chosen, and therefore, this oppression was unjust. According to this logic, homosexuality, in its attraction to the same sex instead of the opposite sex, is simply a sexual preference that differs from heterosexuality. Therefore, during these lectures I gave, I often emphasized the discriminations and problems I faced in society as a lesbian rather than positive aspects of being a lesbian.

As I continued to live as a lesbian and engage in anti-prostitution feminist activism, I began questioning the queer movement's tendency to frame prostitution as 'sex work' rather than sexual exploitation. In 2017, I discovered Sheila Jeffreys' books, which had not yet been translated into Korean. I borrowed them from my partner's university library, and reading them was an eye-opening experience. As well as radical feminist criticism against 'sex work' ideology, I learned about political lesbianism. Around the same time, a new wave of radical feminist movements began to emerge in South Korea. These movements rapidly spread through existing women-only spaces on the internet, where women shared their personal experiences of being women and raised their political consciousness. Topics like beauty practice, femininity, heterosexual relationships, and marriage were shared and debated from a feminist perspective, leading to the emergence of movements such as the 4B movement (rejecting dating, having sex with, marrying, and having children with men) and Escape the Corset movement, which rejected femininity and beauty practice as social oppression. I worked with other women involved in these movements and translated Jeffreys' books into Korean. I also wrote my master's thesis on the Escape the Corset movement in Women's Studies.

Even in the radical feminist movement in South Korea, lesbianism was initially understood only in terms of sexual orientation, and the idea that homosexuality was innate was generally accepted among feminists. Lesbians were often seen as *lucky* women who were born with this inclination. However, through the mass mobilization of women-only protests and feminist groups, many women were inspired by seeing other women who had cast off femininity with their own eyes. Women who witnessed others freeing themselves from imposed femininity and transforming their lives found the courage to take off their own *corsets*. They began to see other women as powerful agents of change. Through these experiences, many women came to choose to love women. Most radical feminists I met in this new movement were often already lesbians, wanted to become lesbians, or had at least excluded men from their romantic and sexual lives.

I realized that women choosing to become lesbians through political awakening – shifting their views on femininity, masculinity, and heterosexuality – was not only possible but also more common than I had thought. In a male-dominated society, women seldom have chances to see other women as human beings or share woman-centered perspectives. When women have spaces to interact with each other without male interference, they can start to see other women as full human beings. When feminist ideas are shared in these spaces, women can begin to understand their own experiences from a feminist perspective, and as a result, they often find themselves feeling affection toward other women.

I now see that the idea of sexuality as something innate is a major setback for the women's liberation movement. Heterosexuality as an institution is one of the main pillars that uphold male domination. The belief that women who have lived as heterosexuals cannot become lesbians or that women who choose to become lesbians are somehow 'fake' strips away a powerful tool for women's liberation. It reinforces the idea that heterosexual women are born with a heterosexual identity and thus cannot escape it. In the early 2000s, as a young feminist who had come to understand that men and women experienced the world differently, I began to feel a desire to turn my affection toward women. What I needed to become a lesbian was the time spent with other women sharing personal experiences as a woman, the mere images of fictional lesbians in American films, and witnessing actual lesbians in women-only spaces. Over 15 years later, during the radical feminist wave that swept through South Korea, I came to realize that my experience wasn't unique. I believe that if more spaces where women can gather, share, and dream of a life free from male domination emerge, more women will choose to become lesbians. I am grateful for the opportunities that opened my eyes and gave me the courage to live as a lesbian, and I thank those who have shared their experiences of choosing lesbianism. I hope that my story reaches other women and inspires them to dream of new possibilities.

I Wasn't Born This Way and I Am Proud of It

Julie Bindel[1]

I am regularly accused of being a 'fake lesbian', a 'heterosexual pretending to be a lesbian', told I must be bisexual rather than exclusively same sex attracted, and that I am colonising lesbian culture and identity.

All of this comes my way because I don't believe in the gay gene. What I do believe is that any woman, in the right circumstances, meeting the right person, and being in the right frame of mind could choose to embark on a sexual relationship with another woman, whether or not she has previously only had relationships with men. You may say that this would make her bisexual, but what about all those women who have never looked back, and from that moment on are exclusively attracted to and have relationships with other women? A so-called late-blooming lesbian isn't necessarily a woman who is older (by whatever measure) – it can simply mean a woman who has a heterosexual history.

In the past, when I have said I would describe myself as a 'political lesbian' (and partly because I was a little bit flippant in my description of what a political lesbian is), it has been assumed I was saying that straight women could talk themselves – or even be forced – into being sexually attracted to other women.

---

1   A version of this article was published in the *Queer Majority*, 15 June 2025.

What I actually meant was that I am very political about my lesbianism. I also refuse to accept that unless a woman is born with this imagined and rather elusive gene, she could never make a positive choice to be in a relationship with another woman; I know so many women who had no previous inkling that this could ever happen but who then met a woman, fell head over heels in love (or lust) with her, and for whom the rest is history.

Lesbians, whether consciously or not, inherently represent a major disruption to patriarchy; we have always been the movers and shakers within the women's liberation movement. Why then, are the majority either complacent about, or even hostile to, feminism?

And how come, rather than celebrate the fact that loads of women are now coming out later in life, having left heterosexuality behind, do so many remain wedded to the idea of a 'gay gene' and the notion that unless you were 'born that way' you should either resign yourself to remaining straight forever – or declare yourself bisexual?

I understand that some people are happy to settle for tolerance and acceptance and have no interest whatsoever in liberation movements. Lesbians and gay men are still punished for their same-sex attraction and encounters, even though things are very different now than they were back in 1977, when I came out in a traditional working-class community in a town in the northeast of England.

At that time, many (if not most) gay men were out – and therefore inevitably facing discrimination or even abuse, and what they pleaded for was to be seen as just the same as everyone else. "We were born this way," they shrugged, "We can't help it." By contrast, proud lesbians were on the streets, chanting, "Two, four, six, eight, is your wife really straight?" At the height of the women's liberation movement, huge swathes of women who had been in heterosexual relationships left their marriages to live lesbian lives. The movement had provided women with opportunities to see each other differently than they had before, and although some women would never feel the vaguest hint of sexual or romantic attraction towards another female, plenty of those who had never previously considered it an option grabbed the opportunity with both hands when it arose.

There's a great scene in the 2014 film *Pride* (a comedy drama film based on a true story involving lesbian and gay activists who raised money to help families affected by the British miners' strike in 1984) in which lesbians are singing (to the tune of *Solidarity Forever*): "Every woman is a lesbian at heart/Every woman is a lesbian at heart/Every woman is a lesbian at heart ..." Reggie, a gay male character, looks aghast: "You can't possibly say that every woman is a lesbian." The women beg to differ, even suggesting that Reggie's mum might be a bit Sapphic.

This was clever scripting, because the arguments about whether or not there is any genetic basis for same-sex attraction are often between lesbians and gay men. Or rather, between lesbian feminists and the more conservative type of gay man.

I am proud of being a lesbian, and certainly wouldn't want it any other way. When I first came out, I was regularly asked, "If there was a drug that would make you straight, would you take it?" The underlying assumption was that it was being a lesbian that was the problem, rather than anti-gay prejudice. Once my consciousness had been raised, I'd answer by suggesting we look at 'curing' the bigots.

I love being a lesbian and consider it way preferable to heterosexuality. I do not seek to be merely 'tolerated' by heterosexuals. There is no kink in my gene that resulted in my sexual orientation, and nor is my brain coloured with stripes of the rainbow flag.

This is what I meant when, in the past, I have described myself as a political lesbian. I no longer do because of the wilful and genuine misunderstanding about what it means, or rather, what I mean by it.

Lesbians were frontline warriors within the Lesbian and Gay Liberation Movement, campaigning for change by staging outrageous protests such as abseiling down the House of Lords during the debate about Section 28 (which banned the promotion of homosexuality by local authorities and the portrayal of it as a "pretended family relationship") or chaining themselves to the chair of a news anchor during a live broadcast at the BBC. The action I was involved in was an invasion of the Ideal Home Exhibition in London. We occupied the show home and unfurled banners reading 'Lesbians are everywhere' and 'Lesbian mothers make the best mothers'.

Seeking permission to replicate the behaviour and lifestyle of the mainstream heterosexual population didn't really change anything (despite the fact that this normality was indeed what many lesbians and gay men sought). It just meant that life became a bit of a lottery: there were those who accepted you as one of them, and those that didn't. This is why some of us rejected the notion that we were the same as straight people and kept on campaigning. Lesbians like me didn't campaign for equal marriage – as feminists, we wanted to abolish it as a patriarchal institution that could never be reformed.

In a bid to garner more sympathy from those who recognised that same-sex attracted people were oppressed, gay men (and some lesbians) would put forward the 'proof' that we were born with an inherent sexual orientation. Even putting aside the problematic nature of ascribing sexual attraction to a foetus or newborn baby, this so-called 'proof' has never materialised. The nature versus nurture question has engaged scientists, religious fundamentalists, parents and lesbians and gay men for well over a hundred years. Beyond the Nazi experimental stage, this was in many ways a valiant attempt to discredit the idea of homosexuality as a mental disorder – but there is still no evidence showing that same-sex attraction is innate.

Conversion therapy of the kind practiced by Christian fundamentalists and others who (for whatever reason) consider same-sex attraction dangerous or morally wrong, is not what it appears to be. I should know, because in 2013, I went undercover for an intensive week of lesbian conversion therapy at a Christian centre. I discovered that these people do not for one minute think they can change sexual attraction by simply telling you that you had an unhappy childhood, or that the kink in your nature was caused by early experiences of sexual abuse – they just want you to stop being a lesbian. They don't really care what the origin of this behaviour is. My therapist was very blasé when I asked her, in my adopted persona, if she thought I would ever meet a nice man and be able to settle down with him after all these decades of sinful behaviour with women. She simply shrugged, and her eyes glazed over. Her job would have been considered done only if I became a lifelong celibate and denounced lesbianism to my friends and the wider public.

The 'born this way' argument has never helped those who do have innate characteristics – such as black people, or women. Uttering the words, "Don't pick on me, I can't help it" has never protected anyone from abuse and discrimination.

Feminists (the actual as opposed to the fun kind) understand that lesbians have an advantage, in that we get to avoid the grossly unequal, patriarchal relationships that are upheld by every institution and normalised within society. Gay men are on the back foot, because they have missed out on being the head of household. This is rather a crude generalisation, but it is nevertheless true for many women. We recognise the liberatory elements of avoiding compulsory heterosexuality and being with women.

Political lesbianism has nothing to do with straight women claiming to be lesbians to make a point. Since the backlash against feminism and the distorting of lesbian politics by queer theorists, many women seem to think that being political about being a lesbian is 'fake lesbianism' done for the sake of punishing men.

Lesbianism is a political act in its own right – it doesn't mean pretended desire, and neither does it mean straight women appropriating a lesbian culture or identity. Political lesbianism is not about pretending *not* to be attracted to men as an act of feminist sacrifice. It is about giving women the option of asking themselves whether they have been railroaded into heterosexuality.

Claiming that lesbians are 'born this way' can be a barrier to women coming out in later life, having been previously heterosexual. It ignores the fact that social conditioning can result in women ignoring or suppressing their desire for other women and seeing it as a 'passing phase'. And it can also lead to the opinion that only a tiny number of women (the ones with a kink in their genes) have the potential to love and desire other women.

The 'born this way' explanation for lesbianism is popular with many heterosexuals because it reassures them that there is no danger of it rubbing off on them. I love the sense that I have chosen my sexuality. Rather than being ashamed or apologetic about it, as many women are, I can be proud and see it as a privilege.

Those who, like me, refuse to accept the crazy, unsubstantiated theory of the gay gene and innate sexual orientation are accused, by other gays, of playing into the hands of the enemy. When the actor Cynthia Nixon said to a journalist at the *New York Times Magazine* that she "chose" to be a lesbian following a perfectly happy heterosexual past, she was vilified and bullied into apologising. A few weeks later, she withdrew her comment and said she must have been born with "bisexual potential." Later still, she hit back against her critics saying: "Why can't it be a choice? Why is that any less legitimate? It seems we're just ceding this point to bigots who are demanding it, and I don't think that they should define the terms of the debate."

When lesbians are bullied into believing that our sexuality is written in the genes it results in a distinct lack of pride. In many ways it doesn't matter why a minority of women are exclusively same sex attracted, and our rights should never be defined by whatever people decide or believe on this matter. The truth is, whether we like it or not, lesbians have been at the forefront of both the gay rights movement in countries around the world, and we have always punched above our weight when it comes to fighting and campaigning for the liberation of all women. I think our track record is something to be tremendously proud of.

References

'1984–1985 United Kingdom miners' strike'. *Wikipedia* [online]. <https://en.wikipedia.org/wiki/1984%E2%80%931985_United_Kingdom_miners%27_strike>.

Bindel, Julie. (29 January 2009). 'My sexual revolution'. *The Guardian*. <https://www.theguardian.com/lifeandstyle/2009/jan/30/women-gayrights>.

Bindel, Julie. (8 August 2011). 'Why "fun feminism" should be consigned to the rubbish bin'. *New Statesman*. <https://www.newstatesman.com/politics/2011/08/fun-feminism-women-feminist>.

Pride. (2014). Directed by Matthew Warchus. [Film]. UK: Pathé UK/BBC Films.

Pathé UK. (28 June 2014). *Pride – Official Launch Trailer* [online video]. YouTube. <https://www.youtube.com/watch?v=vsFY0wHpR5o>.

Seeger, Pete. (n.d.). *Solidarity Forever*. YouTube video, posted by "Pete Seeger – Topic". <https://www.youtube.com/watch?v=R8eK9ZXf-Ow>.

Witchel, Alex. (22 January 2012). 'Life After "Sex"'. *The New York Times Magazine*. <https://www.nytimes.com/2012/01/22/magazine/cynthia-nixon-wit.html>.

The Labyrinth of Crooked Mirrors

Margherita Rubin

I'm a lesbian from Russia, probably the youngest among all the
participants of the anthology – I was born in 2004. My childhood
was during the golden noughties – the years of new winds of
freedom after the stuffiness of Soviet reclusiveness; my teenage
years were during the sanctions after the annexation of Crimea;
and adulthood started at the beginning of the world's far-right
turn. Growing up, I was influenced by the disturbing trends on
transgenderism that have long since taken over western society.
Despite the fact that Russian society differs significantly from
American and European ones, Russian youth after the collapse of
the USSR mostly support American-centricity and Euro-centricity,
which is why teenagers and young adults rebelling against the
conservative older generation easily fall under the influence of any
of the American and European trends. My story is no exception
to this.

I remember very little about my childhood. Incoherent
fragments of events play in my memory like a silent black-and-
white movie on a damaged film. There, I almost always see myself
from the outside.

I was an outsider. I didn't feel lonely though. I just didn't pay
much attention to connections with other people, and even within
my family I often felt like a stranger. Although it would be more
accurate to say that all people were strangers to me.

In other words, I had no preferences in terms of whom to socialize with. Perhaps it was only thanks to the policy of sex segregation supported in conservative Russia that I, as a girl, found myself in the company of other girls while growing up. It was easy to notice the opposition between women and men in society, and the girls around me, who had not yet had time to realize their belonging to the oppressed caste, were uniting against the opposite sex. Girls thought 'boys are dumb', and boys thought 'girls are fools'. But as we grow up, men maintain solidarity based on their hatred of women, and we – women – are immersed in the ocean of forced heterosexuality, and forced to forget our childish dislike of men.

And yet, in my child's mind, 'girls are fools' won. I knew that I was 'different', which meant that I wasn't a fool at all, so I wasn't a 'girl' at all (or at least not like other girls). This meant that if pink was for girls, then there was no way I was going to wear a pink-coloured thing. This meant that if the girls were playing with dolls, then I loved cars, and the dolls in the toy box would have their heads blown off. I hated all the 'girly' markers.

By my first decade of life, I could no longer ignore that I was being rejected, and I easily became the target of mockery or bullying from other girls who were becoming increasingly immersed in the practice of 'adult' femininity. I didn't want to have anything to do with them though, because I couldn't understand why they didn't feel disgusted that they belonged to a caste serving the dumb boys. I felt betrayed. Perhaps that's when I learned to dissociate.

By my teenage years, other people had become not only strangers but also hostile to me. I became frustrated with reality, and I started spending all my free time on the internet, socializing on online games or hobby groups. The internet was a completely different world for me, and unlike reality, it was not hostile at all. On the internet, no one knew me, and I knew no one, and it was all the easier for me to be 'not me', because no one liked 'me'.

By coincidence, the online communities I spent time in were mostly made up of women. Many of these women presented themselves as men, but they usually did not identify themselves as 'queer' or 'trans' – it was just the fashion of the Russian internet in those years, and those who pretended to be men almost always turned out to be women. Since there were many women, and there was zero female fellowship, 'yet another' woman was treated like a weed in a garden.

Being influenced by this neglect of me from being 'yet another' woman I decided to make a social network account under a male name and started to re-join all the communities in which I communicated as an adult male. I've never been close to any man myself, so I copied the images of male characters from fantasy novels (which were written by women). I became the embodiment of the illusory image that heterosexual women were fed. Of course, I became immediately adored.

The conclusions about how good it's to be born a man were self-evident. I saw that men had not only the benefits of women's attention, which I passionately desired, but also a generally simple life: no periods, comfortable clothes, and most importantly, the status of a human. It was evident to teenage me that men were the main characters. I was convinced that only men have deep thoughts and feelings, while women's feelings were shallow. That only men possessed humanity, while women were just empty vessels. Obviously, I, as an isolated teen prone to escapism, wanted to be a 'person', not a woman.

When I found out that such things as sex transition surgeries existed, I decided to save up for it. I dreamed of becoming a man one day. And since my dreams were far from reality, I was just jealous of other teenage girls who could successfully hide their breasts because I couldn't, and who looked like boys because I didn't.

But the women on the internet liked me, and that was the important thing. However, I faced a serious personal conflict when I, as the image of a heterosexual man, began to receive romantic attention from other women. I really liked the attention. I couldn't give myself the answer to the question: how should I feel about women's romantic interest in me, given the fact that I'm a woman in reality?

Well, it's always been hard for me to deny the material facts. That's how I came to the conclusion that I'm a lesbian. After all, what else can you call it when you've been falling in love with women all your life and yearning for women's attention, being a woman yourself?

Under the influence of queer culture, I was convinced that sexual orientation is an inborn quality and that, unlike sex, you can't change it, you can only get to the truth of who you are. In fact, I also didn't believe that sex could be changed (hard to deny material facts, yep), rather, I believed that one could be born in the wrong body, and that transitioning helped to put society's attitudes back where they belonged. Well, I was close to the truth.

At one point, I had my first internet friend. For the first time, I wasn't thinking about another woman romantically. We both chatted from male user accounts, but we didn't hide from each other that we were actually women. We talked a lot about our experiences of dysphoria, and she introduced me to radical feminism. By that time, I had already given up thinking about transitioning, just as I had stopped denying my sex. I just accepted this internalised misogyny: I saw myself as a loser born as a woman in this man's world.

Unfortunately, our friendship didn't last long, and soon I returned to my reflective solitude. As I immersed myself in reading a variety of online communities dedicated to radical feminism, I discovered that radical feminism is not just gender criticism, but an entire belief system that challenges every aspect of our lives as women in a world of male dominance. After a while, I joined one of these communities myself. I was determined to dedicate my life to the struggle for women's liberation.

It's important to note that Russian-speaking radical feminists were largely focused on western radical feminism five years ago, and they still are. Since Russia didn't go through the historical events that prompted the appearance of radical, revolutionary and finally lesbian feminism, the way America and the UK did, ideas such as 'radical feminism' are considered to be 'imported'. During the years of studying and spreading the ideas, experience and history of the western feminists, Russian feminists have made thorough work of adapting the western ideas to the Russian realities. They have also been developing their own ways of describing the mechanisms of phallocracy, how to survive in it, how to fight and destroy it.

During that time, lesbianism was not a very important topic to me. You can tell that in Russian radical feminism, lesbianism is segregated and put on the shelf, overshadowed by the 'female' problems, which are in fact heterosexual women's problems. Thus, lesbians end up being doubly invisible. Framing lesbianism as a politically important topic can get you accused of having an intersectional approach, which was bad because it was 'eroding our movement' and 'shifting the focus'. Lesbianism is considered to be a defect by a lot of Russian feminists, not a political force. At that time, I thought that I was just lucky to discover my lesbianism early enough before falling into a trap of relationships with men.

But it was shameful to be a lesbian. To even think that it's politically important to be a lesbian, or that lesbians can have their own vision. I started seeing sexual relationships with women as shameful and disgusting because everywhere the word 'sex' meant penetrative acts between a man and a woman, the mere thought of which was gross to me. And though there were a lot of lesbians among Russian feminist activists, nobody could talk about the force of lesbianism.

In that context, political lesbians were seen as the ultimate evil. In the community I was part of, the word 'political lesbian' always went hand in hand with the word 'misogyny': 'Political lesbians are straight women who force themselves to date other women and have sex with them, and who want to force others to do the same'; 'Political lesbians are erasing lesbians'; 'Political lesbians are aggressive misogynists and witch hunters who bully straight women'; 'Political lesbians establish a hierarchy among women based on their sexual orientation with gold star lesbians on top'. I estimated political lesbianism to be as harmful to women as trans ideology. Should it be said that I didn't know a single political lesbian personally?

For several years, I've been throwing rocks at straw women. I felt proud for defending the 'real' lesbians from political lesbianism when I could persuade them of my beliefs. During that time, I still didn't meet a single political lesbian on the whole internet. For me, it meant that I was successfully holding the line.

My world was turned upside down when I met political lesbians in my town. One day, I had a big argument with one of them about political lesbianism. I argued for the harm of political lesbianism and she said that what I said had nothing to do with reality.

With these arguments, a lot of things that I couldn't make sense of became clear. It was like all my life I was walking through a labyrinth of crooked mirrors and now these mirrors were shattered. The straw women were burned, and their ash fed the soil of identification with women. So, I joined political lesbianism. Finally, after feeling like an outsider all my life, I felt like I belonged.

I began reading the feminist literature. My understanding of how heterosexuality was historically constructed was aided by Gerda Lerner's *The Creation of Patriarchy*. I have found the answer to the question 'What is a lesbian?' in Marilyn Frye's essay 'To See and Be Seen'. 'Love Your Enemy' by the Leeds Revolutionary Feminist Collective has opened my eyes to the fact that political lesbians are still surrounded by the same myths as 50 years ago. Sheila Jeffreys' *The Lesbian Revolution* gave me hope that one day we will restore the lesbian culture: songs, festivals and events. I have read many other texts of western lesbian feminists experiencing many new feelings: anger, pride, grief, admiration, gratitude, solidarity. But most importantly now I could base my life on the experience of unity with other lesbians.

Sheila Jeffreys' *The Lesbian Heresy* was the key to understanding my teenage experiences. I was full of anger and regret now that I was reading about the culture of decadence, the industry of prostitution and pornography and the attack of sadomasochism, which I was enthusiastic about as a teen. I was angry at all the anti-lesbian i.e. queer activists for redefining love and sexuality through pain, violence and humiliation. I blamed them for the fact that I was growing up wandering among the crooked mirrors. Now, after so many years, I've finally escaped.

Lesbian feminism breathed new life into me. It's not just something that helped me escape the crooked mirrors, it also brings feminism to its logical conclusion and makes it a complete system by answering the question of what we should do. The answer is: we should choose women's interests every time, at every opportunity. I'm confident that we can fight back against phallocracy only by becoming lesbians – women whose life passions are centered around women.

Now I know that political lesbians do not 'erase' the 'real' lesbians, that we're not heterosexuals, bisexuals, asexuals or whatever else – we're lesbians in the feminist, not queer, sense of the word. We don't forcibly 'reject our nature' by loving women, as if women were something nasty, uninteresting, disgusting, undeserving of love, and as if we ourselves weren't women, but instead we do the most sensible thing a woman can do – we side with our own interests. Now I know why so many politically heterosexual women fear, avoid and reject us. Because they feel that the idea of being able to choose women threatens to destroy their identity. But if lesbians are destroying anything, it's only the things that support male interests.

Now I'm not ashamed to say it: lesbians are everywhere. Lesbians were a shaping force in women's movement in the west; lesbians have become that force in Russia as well. Lesbians are the ones behind women's aid networks, women's spaces, women's presses, women's culture. This is why we are so dangerous, attacked not only by proponents of male dominance, but also often by our sisters in the movement.

I want to end this story by giving thanks to my friends without whom it would be difficult to find the way out. Now I think at random moments in my life, 'How great that I was born a woman; How great that I'm a lesbian'. I consider the experience of lesbianism as healing and life-saving in a world that forces women to serve the interests of men. I want to say to every lesbian reading this text: thank you for being a lesbian.

References

Frye, Marilyn. (1983). 'To See and Be Seen: The Politics of Reality', in *The Politics of Reality: Essays in Feminist Theory*. Trumansburg, NY: The Crossing Press.

Leeds Revolutionary Feminist Group. (1981). Political Lesbianism: The Case Against Heterosexuality. In *Love Your Enemy*. London: Onlywomen Press.

Lerner, Gerda. (1986). *The Creation of Patriarchy*. New York, NY: Oxford University Press.

Jeffreys, Sheila. (1993). *The Lesbian Heresy: A Feminist Perspective on the Lesbian Feminist Revolution*. Melbourne: Spinifex Press.

Jeffreys, Sheila. (2018). *The Lesbian Revolution: Lesbian Feminism in the UK 1970–1990*. London: Routledge.

Women and Heterosexuality, a Lesbian of Color's Perspective

Daniela Medina

Maybe it's because it's been years that my life is the way that it is that I can't picture it differently. I am surrounded by lesbians. I wake up with her lying by my side every day, and I come home to her every night. I see my messages: lesbians, again, that I'm lucky enough to call my friends.

Sometimes, however, I remember myself at 17 or 18. Thinking of those years it's like touching a bruise. You know it's there; it hurts when you touch it, but you can almost completely dismiss it.

It's painful to think that I was once a sad young woman trying to deal with the fact that my relationships with men never truly fulfilled me the way they were supposed to. But it was the right thing to do, wasn't it? I could be as independent as I wanted to be. There were my male friends who swore to support and love me but then sexualized me at my most vulnerable moments. I was free to say no, though, because they were all about consent. And my boyfriend, with whom I could discuss anarchism and sometimes even feminism. The one so woke, the monogamy deconstructor.

All those supportive men in my life had one thing in common: they were sucking the life out of me. I was exhausted. I couldn't bear any more being treated like a pretty object that was fun to touch and look at but not to consider as a person. And especially I couldn't bear my non-monogamist boyfriend, who used that as an excuse to neglect multiple relationships with women while calling it freedom.

Some could say that perhaps I was just hanging out with the wrong men, or that non-monogamy must always be ethical. And to that I respond: the issue goes way deeper than you think.

While I was trying to make all these relationships work, I had almost no close female friends. Now I know this isn't a casualty. I started to have multiple deep friendships with women very late in my teenage years. When I started to get closer to women, it felt like I had found a missing piece. It's not like all my problems were fixed once I started to get closer to women. I must say, they are complex in themselves, but it was less likely that they would try to take advantage of me in my most vulnerable moments. With men, I had to try, and try, and try, and rip little pieces off myself. Did I like them? Maybe. But there was always something that triggered me. I felt, with men, like finding dead-end streets repeatedly. Even with the 'good dudes', there was always something: subtle misogyny every now and then, attempts to control, their disdain or their attitude towards the whole world, like they owned it.

This wasn't a political issue for me at 18 years old, even when I already used to call myself a radical feminist. I just thought that women in general struggled with men, like they were something we had to deal with. No one ever tells you that you can question what you're supposed to like, what is normal that you like. But fortunately, that's when I found them: lesbians, lesbofeminists.

I am from a country where 12 women are killed daily: Mexico. Yes, Mexico, widely known for putting the word 'femicide' on the map. Those femicides are usually committed by men who were close to the victims. That same country, nonetheless, also has a strong lesbian movement. Lesbofeminist critiques and analyses that lesbians from Mexico and Latin America have done have been mainly a necessity. When male violence is so close to us, we have taken action, observed the world, and built a strong women's network. Women are the only ones who are going to set women free.

In a territory like Mexico, which is considered a third-world country, intended to imitate economically and culturally white and/or European countries, feminists and lesbians also observed the different faces of male domination towards women and nature, known as the patriarchy. There are white men who will want to take advantage of women not just because we are women but also because we are poor and non-white. For example, the so-called maids of rich white families in Mexico will almost religiously be working-class brown women who are not paid enough. So, it's also a matter of race and class.

How is all this related to women's sexual preference for men? As a matter of fact, it is a deep political issue. We must think: what happens to women in relationships with men? In the worst-case scenario, as I mentioned before, those men who are trusted by women are the perpetrators of femicides. Does that sound too over the top? Too, the that-will-never-happen-to-me-my-boyfriend-is-the-best attitude? I understand where you're coming from. In this reality, women are expected to be with men. Yes, they won't always kill you, but maybe they will expect that you do all the domestic labor (doing the laundry, washing the dishes, preparing food) on top of your nine to five shift, doubling the amount of labor that you already do. Domestic labor, though, goes unpaid. He won't hit you, but maybe he will take the kids away when you divorce him and use them to manipulate you. Or perhaps he will just joke with his friends, saying, "My wife is crazy," or "You know how women are." Ask your female friends who have boyfriends. You don't have to go very far from your circle to see it for yourself.

Preference for men, heterosexuality isn't considered as the rule for no reason, it has a very targeted purpose. Let's say you find the good one (as if it was your responsibility to find that one non-misogynistic man!), but why is it so hard to find the ideal man who won't be a misogynist?

Heterosexuality starts to be uncovered or appear as something more than a sexual preference. That's why radical feminists and lesbofeminists name it compulsory heterosexuality. It is more than just liking men or wanting to be with them. Heterosexuality is a regime that is imposed on everyone under the patriarchal system, but that works very differently for men and women. For women, it has a very particular way of life: you grow up with the idea of being with a man who will take care of you and provide everything that you need, then you are expected to find that one man, marry him and have kids with him. Throughout that process, you also must raise the kids, do the laundry, satisfy his needs and so on. Things have changed, some might say, women now can have jobs and go to school. Unfortunately, I would disagree now that 'tradwives' are trending on social media.

Heterosexuality can take many different forms. It won't always be a traditional family, with a mom/wife that stays at home and a dad that goes to work. The successful modern couple where the woman also has her own career is another form of compulsory heterosexuality. The woman is always going to be pressured into being a good mother on top of everything. That micro world inside a heterosexual marriage is a replica of what the system wants. How can a relationship be free and balanced when the world outside, the system, privileges men? How can we be safe from the power dynamic when everything is made for and by men? And right now, I am not only talking about boyfriends, think also about your friends, your peers at work, etc.

Compulsory heterosexuality works very well with capitalism, racism, classism, imperialism, and so on. If women want to be with men, if they are raised to think that their role in life is to serve them and have children, it's going to be easy for men to have guaranteed domestic labor for free. This benefits the capitalists, owners of big companies, so they have future workers and women who will do their laundry and have food ready for them, even when they also must go to work. It's an endless cycle. If it isn't the wife, some other woman will do it. As I mentioned before, in rich white families, the one who will do the laundry, cook the food and take care of the children will be another exploited woman. White countries and white men – and women who benefit from being white and upper-class – will maintain their position. A very self-sufficient system.

Alongside all of this, we are told that our sexual preference is innate and genetic. Science tells us that heterosexuality is the sexual preference of most of the population and that we are born with it. That same science that has historically excluded women, especially women of color and lesbians, because we are not the model, and lesbians are very rare, according to science. We are not the main character for the big scientists.

These theories in Mexico and Latin America started in the late '60s, early '70s. They differ from the French materialists and radical lesbians in the Global North, we didn't follow their lead. For us, class and race are crucial to consider along with patriarchy. Those analyses are not found in texts written by white lesbians most of the time. My contention is also to highlight that being a separatist is not a privilege reserved for the rich, it's an urgency for lesbians of color.

At this point, I also want to be very careful. I don't intend to say that having a girlfriend or that women in general are an escape from men and patriarchy. What I want to pinpoint instead is that our preference isn't merely a preference because the patriarchy makes us believe that staying with men at all costs is the ideal. But giving our lives away to men keeps us disconnected from ourselves and other women. Have you ever ditched a female friend consistently because of a boyfriend? I bet either you have or you have been the ditched one. When women are constantly compared with each other for their looks, that tends to create rivalry between women. But anyway, what a joy it is to know a new woman who you can trust. Why is it that they want us so disconnected from other women? Because perhaps we don't hate each other, or because being among women could create different possibilities that don't imply giving our lives away for the well-being of a man's professional career.

What I can tell you is this, almost as a secret: she and I create different possibilities, different worlds, when I come home to her every night. Not as an escape but as a sanctuary I never knew existed.

References

Aldana-Castro, Mariana, César Jesús Burgos-Dávila, and Tania Esmeralda Rocha-Sánchez. 'La división sexual del trabajo reproductivo en México: experiencias, prácticas y significados en parejas jóvenes de doble ingreso'. *Revista Latinoamericana de Antropología del Trabajo 2*, no. 4 (2018): 1–34.

Blazquez Graf, Norma. (2008). *El retorno de las brujas: incorporación, aportaciones y críticas de las mujeres a la ciencia.* 1. ed. Colección Debate y Reflexión 15. México, D.F: Univ. Nacional Autónoma, Centro de Investigaciones Interdisciplinarias en Ciencias y Humanidades.

Escuela de Formación Política. Qué Es El Patriarcado? Adriana Guzman. 2021. 02:35. <https://www.youtube.com/watch?v=dBFxMWTNlwI>.

Morales Hernandez, Ma. Rocío. Feminicidio. First edition. *Opiniones Técnicas sobre Temas de Relevancia Nacional*, 24. Universidad Nacional Autónoma de México, Instituto de Investigaciones Jurídicas, 2020. <https://www.studocu. com/es-mx/document/universidadinteramericana-para-el-desarrollo/ derecho-penal/feminicidio-ley/51601681>.

Ngun, Tuck C. and Eric Vilain. "The Biological Basis of Human Sexual Orientation: Is There a Role for Epigenetics?" In *Advances in Genetics*, Vol. 86. Academic Press, 2014. <https://doi.org/10.1016/B978-0-12-800222-3.00008-5>.

Rich, Adrienne Cecile. (1981). *Compulsory Heterosexuality and Lesbian Existence*. London: Onlywomen Press, 1981. <http://archive.org/details/ compulsoryhetero00rich>.

Sánchez, Patricia Karina Vergara. (4 September 2015). 'Sin heterosexualidad obligatoria no hay capitalismo'. *La Crítica* (blog). <https://www.la-critica.org/ sin-heterosexualidadobligatoria-no-hay-capitalismo/>.

Tabor, Pamela Diane. "Vicarious Traumatization: Concept Analysis". *Journal of Forensic Nursing 7*, núm. 4 (2011): 203. <https://doi.org/10.1111/j.1939-3938.2011.01115.x>.

Toribio, Laura. 'Crece el feminicidio: Asesinan a 12 al día; una de cada 4 ha sido violentada en su relación'. Excélsior, 2025. <https://www.excelsior.com.mx/nacional/crece-elfeminicidio-asesinan-a-12-al-dia-una-de-cada-4-ha-sido-violentada-en-su-relacion>.

Whitfill Roeloffs, Mary. 'Ballerina Farm Controversy: What To Know About TikTok's Hannah And Daniel Neeleman'. Forbes, 2024. <https://www.forbes.com/sites/maryroeloffs/2024/07/25/ballerina-farm-controversy-timesprofile-hannah-david-neeleman-airline-fortune-epidural-trad-wife-tiktok/>.

Looking for Aliens

Syldys

I was born in a national republic in Siberia. My republic is infamous in Russia for the high rates of violence, birth rate and poverty. It is usually at the bottom of any social ratings of living conditions. The climate is severe, the roads are terrible, but the main issue is men, of course. I spent my childhood and teenage years there, dreaming of death or escape.

My family lived on the far outskirts of the town: when you looked around, you saw several small, old, shaky houses, the green steppe and distant blue mountains on the horizon. The steppe was full of grass, flowers, and the sounds of grasshoppers under the never-ending high sky. These are some of my best memories: the breathtaking blue sky, the infinite lively green steppe, the majestic blue mountains. The rest was not so nice. We had a skinny cow and garden beds with soil that had been carried by lorry because the steppe soil was not suitable for agriculture. One time, someone stole our cow and it was really sad, as we were poor. But despite everything, the landscape around me was something that touched me deeply in my childhood. I remember it: me, a small lonely girl, and the magnificent ancient indifferent nature – without borders and without people. We, people, were nothing in the face of the universe, and there was poetry in the sound of wind, and there was strange, eerie life in the eyes of spiders I could not understand.

Russian is my second language, and when I learned it as a child, I discovered the world of literature (almost all of the books were written in or translated to Russian, not in my first native language). I fell in love with reading. I devoured books like a worm in a rotten apple, like a fire burning in the steppe. What did I crave? I looked for new meanings, new words, new worlds. I gazed at the endless sky full of stars and wondered if life existed on other planets. I hoped we were not alone in the world. I looked for aliens. Because sometimes I felt like an alien myself.

I was a melancholic and thoughtful girl. When I was seven years old, I wrote:

> I am divided into two parts: the first one I called The Mask. This part of me was created because of my parents' expectations, because of the people around me. But the second part of me is just deep, unknown darkness. The Mask can smile, laugh, cry, interact with humans, but under The Mask I feel nothing.

It was, surprisingly (for a child), a clinically accurate introspection of how social pressure shaped my personality and what it was like: being a 'good' girl. Also, I faced sexual violence at this age (a boy neighbour and someone else) but my memory is too vague to see a clear picture of events.

When I turned nine, my best friend gave me one of the best gifts of my life – a diary. I liked making notes, it allowed me to analyze my feelings, my internal world. My first note in the diary was: "I wish to die." But why did I wish to die? I felt like an ungrateful person – so many people around me suffered, yet they seemed happy. I understood I had more than others: my parents worked hard to give me the best life they could, so we were getting out of poverty.

If I was a melancholic girl, as a teenager, I was truly depressed. Puberty is the time when the level of misogyny and male violence grew to a point that drove me insane. We moved to town; I had my first period. I went mad trying to comprehend the irrational rules of women's existence. You are supposed to be weak by nature, but if you push back too much you will be punished for excess of self-defence. My mother taught me that women should pretend to be silly not to offend men, and it was disgusting. The street taught me you can be a victim of violence – so be wary – or you are a slut and you wanted it. My father taught me that you cannot be safe even at home. I was sure every woman should marry a man and have children. Even if you do not, other women would marry and leave you hanging in a void because they would be too busy to see you. I saw pornography, and it was cruel and hateful. The vague and uncertain memory of sexual violence in childhood did not help (I had a terrible realization what some actions meant really but blurred memories did not allow me to talk clearly about the level of damage and it was another torture).

So, I learned on all levels: if you are a woman, you should be humiliated and hurt by men, you should serve and obey, and I hated being myself, being a woman. I wrote in my diary: "I am broken in many pieces, so many voices in my head, they scream opposite things." I was shocked by the sheer absurdity of everything.

And I still did not understand why I was so desperate. I thought something was wrong with me. If you feel the world is crazy, it means you are the real whack-job, right?

I thought about different paths in life, of course. I thought about transitioning, but it was not an option. I thought about relationships with women. The first time I learned that a girl can date another girl was when I watched the anime *Sailor Moon* in my childhood. There is a lesbian couple in the series, and part of the translations presented one of the lesbians as male. I was confused because I understood she was a girl, and she liked another girl. Why then was she called a boy? I liked poetry and I discovered Sappho in one of my family's poetry collections. I learned her poems by heart. Then, during my teenage years, I learned that there were some other lesbians (writers, musicians, poets), but they all were distant figures, totally detached from my daily life. It was as far and mythical as ancient Lesbos. Lesbians were a myth. They did not exist in this humble mortal life. I did not believe that someone would choose me over a man; lesbianism seemed something that women dropped for 'normal' hetero relationships.

So, I thought about killing my hypothetical future husband and living as a widow (and not marrying again because I was so 'heartbroken' by the loss). It was my backup plan. I felt no guilt thinking about murdering a husband – I hated him in advance for stealing my life. But there was a problem with potential imprisonment if I got caught. I decided suicide would be the best choice. Cheap, under my control, painful, but not as painful as living. I was scared of death, but I was far more scared of hitting 25 and getting married and living a 'common' woman's life.

I survived the attempt. To my surprise, my mother was very upset that I tried to kill myself (she found me floating in a bloody bath). I felt bad for my mommy – I did not blame her; she tried her best, and I always understood that. I went to therapy. My therapist was a good woman, but she convinced me that I was not normal if I did not fall in love with boys, and she even tried to set me up with her son. I liked my therapist; she influenced me a lot, and I tried to fall in love with someone. I felt attracted to a boy in a music band, and my best friend was delighted when I told her. I could read 'now you are normal' in her smile. I wanted to prove I was not a coward, so I forced myself to invite this boy on a date, but he rejected me. It was awkward and a little bit humiliating, but I was also relieved. I told my best friend that I had an unrequited love. It was also acceptable to her; she felt sorry for me and comforted me. I immediately forgot the boy's name after he rejected me. I still remember her laughter even ten years later. Ironically, I really had unrequited love – I loved her, not him. But I did not realise what it was. I avoided thoughts of love. 'Love' was ugly, it was cruel, it was for heteros. Men loved women and treated them like shit. I respected my friend, I cherished her, I valued her, I dreamed of her, I wanted to spend all my life with her, I did not want to fuck her, of course, it could not be 'true love'. 'True love' was a disaster, you'd better kill the male lover before he destroys you.

I was still depressed and wanted to take my life, but I decided to enter a university in another region in Russia and see what would happen. At least I still had my plan B (sometimes I did research lazily on how to avoid suspicions in case of murder).

I entered a university and moved to a female-only room in a share house. Then I discovered feminist groups on social networks. It shook my life completely.

The first groups I found were liberal feminist ones and it weakened my will and I thought about a compromise: I read all this stuff about open relationships and guest marriage and I thought – okay, maybe I could be with a man and be happy. I bargained with myself: let's imagine I date a man; how long can I tolerate him? Maybe two hours bi-weekly in my own apartment would be manageable – enough to endure his presence, not feel exhausted by him, and not murder him in the end. But I was sure that a man would want more, would demand more. Liberal feminist media insisted that everything was fine, that I had free choice, that I could be myself and so on, but I could not find any advice on how to eject a man safely from my life, and I had big doubts about other stuff. Liberal feminism did not explain things really.

I dug deeper and found radical feminism shaped by heterosexual women. It explained a lot of things, but there was an issue: all of their feminism was about how terrible the patriarchy was, about male violence, yet they still said 'we are heterosexual, we feel attraction to man – it is our nature', and it was very sinister. I saw these smart, experienced women whom I respected a lot, and all of them were in hetero relationships. I was desperate again.

It seemed like there was no escape, no exit – just fate, something out of your control, a curse. If even women smarter and more radical, more educated than me prioritized men in their lives, what hope was left for me? I did not date men, but I still feared that I might someday feel an attraction to them. I was terrified that this idea of heterosexual love would eventually consume me alive. The system was powerful, nature was cruel. I wished to be a lesbian, but how could I be if I was not born one? It felt like my genes were broken, that I was cursed to love men as most women did. It felt like an inescapable trap.

Then I discovered lesbian feminism. Of course, I first encountered its critics – discussions about 'conversion therapy', these false accusations that lesbians destroy hetero women trying to convert them to lesbians. I analyzed it, then concluded it was all nonsense, I went to the sources and realized that was the final piece of the puzzle. Everything finally made sense. I was not cursed – I could analyze how the system grooms girls and women into heterosexual relationships, how my life had been shaped this way. I could examine and rediscover my affection for other women. I believe all of us have had or have affection for women; the question is whether we recognise it as such or ignore it under layers of hetero-conditioning and hetero-propaganda.

I stopped wanting to commit suicide only when I believed that I could share my life with women, and women could share their lives with me. I can be chosen – even in this unfair, crazy world. Another woman can choose me for who I am. I can choose her. There was the mutuality I had always longed for! I am not in danger of losing my mind over some programmed attraction to someone I don't truly like. I want to dedicate my life to women because I am a woman, and I care about women. I place my faith in us.

What makes lesbian feminism unique and powerful, unlike other strands of feminism, is its vision – the idea of building a completely new society. Mainstream heterosexual radical feminism focuses on male abuse, how men harm women, and how women live with men (and suffer). But it remains centered on men. Lesbian feminism, on the other hand, is about women – about building connections between us, identification with women, lesbian power, dignity, will, autonomy: about positive things. It is truly gynocentric. Heterosexual separatism[1] (which I respect deeply, by the way) suggests running away from men. Lesbian feminism suggests returning to women. It is like coming home. I had felt like an alien, searching for other aliens, for an entirely different life, for other worlds – but I discovered a new world here, on Earth. I had felt so disconnected from women, from our history and culture, that it took a tremendous effort to turn around and understand that the answer had always been right here – with and within women.

I am alive, happy and as free as possible (at least not in prison for murdering a husband) thanks to the women who have loved and cared about me throughout my life. It was the best choice I ever made.

---

1   In Russia, there are lot of heterosexual separatists. Separatism is considered as the main core of radical feminism even for heterosexual women in our groups. Heterosexual separatists are women, who support radical feminist ideas, consider some men attractive, but refuse having heterosexual relationships. As a rule heterosexual separatists do not support lesbian feminism, but when they do, they have internalised the view that it cannot apply to them.

Does It Matter If They Did It?
A Return to the Debate

Sheila Jeffreys

Back in 1989, the London Lesbian History Group published an anthology of pieces on lesbian history called *Not a Passing Phase*. I had written two chapters in the book, one of which was called 'Does It Matter If They Did It?' It was about a controversy in the writing of lesbian history at the time caused by the publication of two books by the US lesbian historian, Lillian Faderman, *Surpassing the Love of Men* (1981) and *The Scotch Verdict* (1983). Faderman included in her fascinating and influential work on lesbian history, women for whom there was no proof that they had ever had genital connection but plenty of evidence that they had what she called "passionate friendships" with each other.

This evidence, from the nineteenth century, included the existence of passionate love letters in which they spoke of being all in all to each other, and the fact that they lived with each other for large parts of their lives. But some of the women were married to men because there was little chance of employment outside domestic service, and they required men for financial support. The women in her book who had married spent every moment they could with the women they loved, including, in one case, taking their passionate friends on their honeymoons for moral support, and it seemed clear that they would have been with them for life if they could have.

Faderman's work was controversial with some lesbians because she included these women in her history as well as women who, though they lived together their whole lives, like the ladies of Llangollen who lived together in Wales in the late eighteenth century (Mavor, 2011), did not make it clear that they were sexually engaged, and may just have kissed and cuddled every night.

The lesbians of the 1980s who were critical of Faderman's work and that of the Lesbian History Group, used a definition of the lesbian that came from sexology and had little relation to women who loved women in the eighteenth and nineteenth centuries. If we had accepted those definitions there would have been no lesbian history at all. Lesbian feminist historians at that time understood that we needed lesbian history to bolster our pride and create a foundation for the culture and community we were creating. Conventional history was determinedly heterosexual and took pains to exclude love between women.

At the time of the Women's Liberation Movement in the '70s and '80s, feminists, both lesbian and heterosexual, discussed who and what lesbians were with huge energy and read everything we could get our hands on. There was lesbian feminist theory and ethics then, something hard to imagine now. We saw lesbianism as revolutionary, a form of resistance to male domination (I write about all this in my book *The Lesbian Revolution*, 2018).

The theory and history that we created has mostly been expunged from memory and the spaces, bookstores, discos, festivals and culture have been erased or disappeared. The idea that sexuality was not biologically constructed and that women could leave men and become lesbians was the most revolutionary product of lesbian feminism. It was hugely liberating and the vital basis of the huge, international lesbian community that we created. Out of this ferment came the Political Lesbianism paper in 1979. This paper is repugnant to many lesbians today who had no experience of the joy and excitement of that time and are offended by the idea that women could choose to be lesbians.

Political Lesbianism

I was one of the lesbians who wrote the paper 'Political Lesbianism: The Case Against Heterosexuality' back in 1979, as a member of the Leeds Revolutionary Feminist Group. Today that paper is seen by some lesbians as insulting because it suggests that lesbianism is not biological and women can choose to be lesbians. Five decades ago, however, this idea of choice was not controversial. Many thousands of women chose to leave men and become lesbians. The members of our group saw themselves as having made this choice.

The paper explains why we thought that feminists who were involved with men should leave them and become what we called political lesbians. We thought that feminists should become lesbians because this created a closed system for women's energy. Instead of working with other women in the daytime for the downfall of male domination and then returning at night to put all her best energies into a man, a political lesbian directs both her emotional and political energies into other women. She experiences the joy of luxuriating in women's love at the same time as creating culture and doing activism with women. All parts of her life are in harmony.

We also considered that feminists should leave men because, as lesbian feminists were arguing in the US and the UK at that time, heterosexuality was a political institution on which male domination was based, and the sex of heterosexuality served to subordinate women to men.

We described political lesbians as women who left men, joined the community of women and directed all their love and energies towards other women. We wrote,

> We do think that all feminists can and should be political lesbians. Our definition of a political lesbian is a woman-

identified woman who does not fuck men. It does not mean compulsory sexual activity with women.

The idea that lesbians did not have to engage in compulsory sexual activity has turned out to be the most contentious idea in the paper for a new generation of lesbians. I shall focus on that point here.

How the Paper was Received

The paper was very influential at the time. It was given as a conference paper, then published in the feminist newsletter *WIRES*. It was then published by Onlywomen Press as a pamphlet accompanied by the thoughtful responses that were published in *WIRES* under the title *Love Your Enemy* in 1981. The paper was discussed in women's groups up and down the country and is likely to have increased the considerable numbers of women who were leaving men and rising in love with women at that time.[1] Some of the responses were critical, mainly from heterosexual women objecting to the idea that heterosexuality was a problem, but very few.

Today, the objections are mainly coming from lesbians who say that their love for women is the result of biology and could never be anything to do with choice. It is a narrow, sexological definition. These lesbians say that women who say they chose or that they ever had any sexual contact with men, are not 'real' ones. They are really bisexuals or pretendbians. I have been a lesbian for nearly 50 years now but I am told by some in a new and much younger generation of lesbians that I am not a lesbian and should not dare to call myself one because I had relationships with men in my early twenties. I am now 76.

---

1   I use the term 'rise' rather than 'fall' in love to convey the joy of lesbian love. Fall suggests a negative experience and is more suited to heterosexuality.

Biology and Homosexuality

The argument that some lesbians are making very loudly today that there are real, biological, lesbians and pretendbians who are fakes or bisexual takes lesbianism back to the late nineteenth century. At that time, the medical profession took over from the Church the task of adjudicating on correct sexual practice. They called themselves scientists of sex or sexologists.

Sexologists such as the British medical doctor, Henry Havelock Ellis, understood heterosexuality as natural. Homosexuality, on the other hand, was a form of innate sexual deviancy, which caused men to be feminine and women to be masculine. The masculine lesbians would seduce women that sexologists called 'pseudolesbians', with their hypnotic allure. Pseudolesbians were supposedly really heterosexual women and they were feminine (see my book, *The Spinster and Her Enemies*, 1985). This established an early form of butch/femme roleplaying as biological lesbianism. These ideas resemble what many lesbians are, unfortunately, saying today, about the innateness of real ones and the inauthenticity of pretendbians.

Other sexologists, such as the psychoanalyst Sigmund Freud, believed that homosexuality was the result of something going amiss in childhood, such as problematic relationships with parents. They did not believe that sexuality was socially constructed.

These ideas of biological or early childhood causation were challenged by the development of the social sciences. Anthropologists such as Margaret Mead in her *Coming of Age in Samoa* (1928) argued that female and male behaviours differed between societies as a result of differing social norms, i.e. social construction. By the 1950s, sociologists were arguing that sexual behaviour too was socially constructed. Ford and Beach in *Patterns of Social Behaviour* (1951) argued from their research that sexual norms were formed by culture and not biology and differed markedly across societies. By the 1960s, the sociology of sex was an established discipline and sociologists John Gagnon and William Simon in their book *Sexual Conduct* (1973) developed the idea of the 'sexual script' to explain how sexual interests and behaviour were learnt.

The ideas of these sociologists freed up thinking about the formation of both what were called in the 1970s 'sex roles' and the formation of sexuality too. The Women's Liberation Movement was created by women who understood that women's oppression was not natural or biological but founded upon culturally and politically enforced requirements called 'sex stereotypes'. This knowledge enabled us to throw off our oppression. We could not have had feminism without it.

But we also understood sexuality to be socially constructed, so that women's sexuality was based upon eroticising our oppression in masochism and for men, sexuality was based upon the eroticisation of dominance, aggression, and the objectification of women. We understood homosexuality and heterosexuality too as socially constructed. Gay men were more likely than lesbians to see their sexuality as biologically constructed because men tend to become sexually interested at an earlier age i.e. puberty, but still back at the time of gay liberation many gay men did understand homosexuality as socially constructed. At that time of hope and revolution in social attitudes, the idea that human behaviour was limited by biology was being overthrown by those involved in progressive social movements. The belief in the possibility of social transformation powered the times we lived in.

The way in which women explain to themselves how they come to love women has changed over time. Lorene Gottschalk did a PhD in Australia in the 1990s on how this changed. She interviewed three cohorts of lesbians. The first cohort became lesbians before 1970 and the majority of these women said that their lesbianism was biological. The second cohort became lesbians in the 1970s and early '80s and these women said that they chose to be lesbians.

The majority of the third cohort who became lesbians in the late 1980s and 1990s said that their lesbianism was biological. Women explain their lesbianism to themselves through the ideas that are available to them at the time, and in the '70s and '80s, lesbians were influenced by the ideas of the Women's Liberation Movement which were based on the notion of social construction (Gottschalk, 2003).

No evidence has ever been produced to suggest that lesbianism is the result of biology. Some sexologists, though, have argued that genes or hormones or special areas of the brain cause male sexuality, and have adduced fingerlength or the existence of gay male relatives as proof of biological causation. All of this is fiercely disputed. There is a desire now among some lesbians to believe this, but it is a matter of belief. The interesting question is why the lesbians who believe their lesbianism is innate so strongly wish to believe this, because it is a matter of belief or faith, rather than fact. It must offer some advantage but I am not sure what that is.

'Compulsory Sexual Activity'?

The most contentious line in the paper today is the statement that "political lesbians" are not required to have "compulsory sexual activity with women." We did envisage that some women would leave men and love and relate to women even though they may not have genital contact, though the vast majority in fact rose in love with women and dived enthusiastically into sexual relationships.

Some lesbians today, however, identify authentic lesbians only as those women who have never related to men, who say that they are biological and reject the notion of choice, and can demonstrate ongoing sexual attraction to and activity with women throughout the lifecourse. Such lesbians may call themselves or others who they see as fitting the category 'gold star' lesbians (Lesbian Lens, 2024). In this way they show that they see lesbianism as significantly different from heterosexuality or male homosexuality, neither of which have such strict definitions.

There exists, for instance, the category of spinster in heterosexuality, but there is no category of lesbian spinster. Women are assumed to be heterosexual if they move in heterosexual society even if they never engage sexually with men.

Women who love and relate to women and not men, though they may not sexually engage with women, or do so for not very long, are not seen as 'lesbian spinsters'. Lesbians are understood by those who believe in authentic lesbianism as sexually active women who relate to women from puberty and have no sexual contact with men. Many women in the heterosexual world may choose not to relate sexually to men for large parts or most of their lives, certainly when they are older, but they are likely to be seen as heterosexual. This is not so simple for lesbians who may have to prove sexual interest in and activity with women from puberty to death if they are to be seen as 'real' ones and not pretending.

The determination to restrict the category 'lesbian' to women who see themselves as biological and have never related sexually to men is specific to lesbians, and lesbians in very recent time. Gay men do not tend to wield the category of 'real' or 'gold star' male homosexuality to distinguish themselves from all the other men who relate sexually to men in the same way. We need to understand why these is such a difference. Many men do, of course, relate sexually to women before they settle on just being gay. Many marry women before leaving to pursue a gay life. I have never heard any suggestion that they are less authentic, or indeed any concern about authenticity at all.

Historically, when living openly with lovers of the same sex was socially censured, lesbians would marry men as cover or to provide financial support, as did the UK 1930s artist Dorothy Hepworth, who continued to live with her long-term lover, Patricia Preece. Sometimes, these men were themselves gay. There were terms in gay slang to cover these situations. The female companion of a gay man who sought to hide his sexuality was called 'a beard'. A marriage between a lesbian and a gay man, such as that between Vita Sackville-West and Harold Nicolson in the UK, was called 'a lavender marriage'.

Today such subterfuge may be less necessary but it is unlikely that Dorothy or Vita would be accepted as lesbians today by the biological determinists. They would certainly not be 'gold star'.

The result of questioning the authenticity of women who make a decision or choose to become lesbians, is that lesbianism can no longer be a form of resistance to male domination. It keeps our numbers small and positions us as deviants. It offers women no way out of heterosexuality. It also divides us amongst ourselves by setting up a hierarchy in our ranks. It signifies the very unrevolutionary nature of our times.

References

Faderman, Lilian. (1981). *Surpassing the Love of Men: Romantic Friendship and Love Between Women from the Renaissance to the Present*. New York: William Morrow and Company.

Faderman, Lillian. (1983). *The Scotch Verdict*. London: Quartet Books.

Ford, Clellan S. and Frank A. Beach. (1951). *Patterns of Sexual Behaviour*. New York City: Harper and Brothers.

Gagnon, John L. and William Simon. (1973). *Sexual Conduct. The Social Sources of Human Sexuality*. Abingdon on Thames, Oxfordshire, UK: Routledge.

Gottschalk, Lorene. (2003). 'From Gender Inversion to Choice and Back: Changing Perceptions of the Aetiology of Lesbianism Over Three Historical Periods'. *Women's Studies International Forum*. 26 (3): 221–233..

Jeffreys, Sheila. (1985; 1997). *The Spinster and Her Enemies. Feminism and Sexuality 1880–1930*. London: The Women's Press; Melbourne, Australia: Spinifex Press.

Jeffreys, Sheila. (2018). *The Lesbian Revolution. Lesbian Feminism in the UK 1970–1990*. Abingdon on Thames, Oxfordshire, UK: Routledge.

Leeds Revolutionary Feminist Group. (1981). Political Lesbianism: The Case Against Heterosexuality. In *Love Your Enemy*. London: Onlywomen Press.

Lesbian History Group. (1989). *Not a Passing Phase: Reclaiming Lesbians in History*. London: The Women's Press.

Lesbian Lens. (29 October 2024). 'Why It Is important For Lesbians to Reclaim the Goldstar Lesbian Term'. *Medium*.

Mavor, Eleanor. (2011). *The Ladies of Llangollen: A Study in Romantic Friendship*. Ludlow, Shropshire: Moonrise Press.

Mead, Margaret. (1928). *Coming of Age in Samoa*. New York City: William Morrow Paperbacks.

Gender Dysphoria:
A New Manifestation of Compulsory Heterosexuality in Modern Years

Charlie May

"Mum. At this point, just forget I am a girl. Just pretend I am a boy. Anything you would buy a boy, buy me."

We had been in the shops for just over an hour, and we were exasperated. I can't remember her exact response, but I remember studying her eyes as I tried to figure out how she was feeling. I imagine I felt like I could see disgust in her eyes, and understand now that she would have been feeling fear. She was already aware I was different to her other daughter, and the other girls at school. It was probably the first time I had so bluntly communicated my wish to be a boy, but it didn't come as a shock to the family. I was already 'girling' incorrectly. I didn't have photos of boy bands in my bedroom, and looked visibly uncomfortable in most clothes traditionally associated with femininity, and would keep my head down at the pavement as I walked to school. I would try to wear make-up, but would lose interest quickly, and it always came across as awkward. I had been demanding my hair to be cut short; I was more interested in video games and science than I was in the boys at school. I was angry, and had violent outbursts, I didn't want to shave my legs, or lose weight, or wear feminine clothes (aside from a hypersexualised punk era a bit later on in my teenage years).

This should have been the start of my journey to radical feminism. This should have been the moment I rejected compulsory heterosexuality and refused to conform to the ideas of what it means to be a woman. Instead, I took the only narrative I had been given – I feel wrong, because I am wrong. I was born innately wrong, and I was meant to be born a man.

For my mother, none of this was a chapter in the parenting books she had around the house. We were standing on the ground floor of the clothing store Primark overlooking Margate beach – the 'new' Primark, having been moved from the high street to the road overlooking the sands, already with its peeling paint blending into the row of abandoned shop fronts. Above the Primark sat an old bar called Sundowners which smelt of alcopops and stale smoke when we had walked past the entrance. It had opened in 2003, and was – at the time – the only gay bar in Thanet. And my heart was longing to be old enough to walk my Doc Marten boots over the sticky beer-stained floor.

If you have visited Margate over the last few years, your view of the town would be very different. An article informed me this week that, "once a rundown seaside town, this relatively small coastal resort has blossomed into one of the country's most exciting queer hubs." One of the comments referred to the town as 'British Ibiza' and 'Camden of the South East' underneath a photograph of Tracey Emin's neon light mounted on the Droit House on the seafront at Margate – *I Never Stopped Loving You.* We have a lesbian bar now in Ramsgate, off limits as it is owned by an ex-girlfriend's ex-friend's new friend's ex-girlfriend, but still, it is a lesbian bar, even if that comes complete with the lesbian personal-politics. Maybe that makes it more authentic. And it is nestled within vintage shops, art galleries, escape rooms, chip shops (the sort with big chunky chips wrapped in paper designed to look like newspaper while not being actual newspaper), and an array of bars owned by Londoners who have relocated next to the sea. Even today, Sundowners survives, of course. As does the influence of Tracey Emin.

At the time of our trip to Primark, before the gentrified queer renaissance of Margate, the area was known as 'The Armpit of Kent', or 'Skid-Row On Sea'. As I stood convincing my Mum that she shouldn't buy skirts for me anymore, and instead I wanted the plaid trousers an older boy in sixth form wore, I didn't know anything about Tracey Emin. But I knew enough about the world that I knew I *should*. I knew there was culture outside of my home town. There were people who spoke languages I didn't understand, who played instruments I had never seen, who cooked meals I couldn't pronounce with ingredients I had never heard of, grown in lands on the opposite side of my home, and – importantly – there were people and communities who had very different ideas of gender and sexuality. I had heard of two-spirit people from America, 'ladyboys' in Thailand. So different from the town where I had learnt quite young what it meant to be a girl.

As I looked around Primark, I tried to think of a way that I could appeal to gender stereotypes. Pink is for girls. Maybe I could buy something from the boys' section, if it was pink. It was a fair compromise that worked, and I left the shop ecstatic, clutching a black and pink checkered hoodie, and immediately took a selfie (the old-fashioned kind where you turned the lens of the digital camera to face you as you fumbled to press the button).

There was a girl at school who I was particularly hoping would see the photo and fall out of love with her horrible, lanky boyfriend, Peter, and want me to be her boyfriend instead.[1]

I had been aware of my sexuality for some time, and told my friends I was a lesbian in the summer holidays between Year 8 and Year 9. I was nervous, but I was certain. I knew I liked girls, and

---

1   For more info on lesbian boyfriends see: <https://www.tyla.com/entertainment/celebrity/lesbian-boyfriend-lily-rose-depp-070-shake-292656-20250107>.

I knew that would not change; neither did I want it to. The idea of being transgender hadn't been introduced to me yet. I wasn't ashamed of my body hair until other teenagers started reciting 'Hairy Maclary' after seeing a little bit of stubble under my armpits. Of course, I started to shave.

That was a pattern that continued. At school, and at home, I was not enough. I wasn't girly enough, straight enough, social enough, smart enough. I didn't feel particularly *liked* by anyone. And with every rejection, with every knock of enforced compulsory hetero-sexuality, I stepped slightly further back into the closet.

So, by the time I was 14 going into 15, my confidence was entirely shot, and I was filled with self-loathing, but I had figured a way to find some acceptance at school – entirely abandon myself, and use drink and drugs to numb the abandonment. I'd hang around Camden, bunking the train to London to not pay the fare. I didn't think too much about my gender or sexuality anymore. I had figured it was easier to say I was bisexual. It satisfied the boys because the door was open for their desire, and for the girls, the door wasn't entirely closed to being 'normal'. Not only is heterosexuality expected, but it is demanded, and I had fallen into its grasp.

On one of those trips to London, I met the 28-year-old man who would become my 'boyfriend' shortly after my sixteenth birthday. Going to London to visit him had become a regular visit on my rotation of bars and nightclubs, along with a new gay bar in Canterbury called CO2, which sold us one pound sambucas all night, and Sundowners who would let us smoke out of the windows of the toilets.

I don't really want to write too much about him. He lived in a council flat in Surrey, was addicted to sleeping pills and had been unemployed since his bachelor's degree. He believed he would make it rich and famous one day when he published his book, and – when he was awake – he would sit at his computer and chainsmoke, a horrible, greasy stain growing on the ceiling above his chair.

Of course, I thought he was the coolest person in the entire world, with his 'Midnight Blue' dyed long hair and his talk about university and *real literature*. He understood my interest in the world: that I had wanted to spend my birthday at The Globe to watch *Macbeth*, that I had questions about sexuality and gender. He believed I could be a doctor and travel the world. He encouraged me to explore my gender, and I quickly developed the answers I had been craving. I was a boy, born in the wrong body. He bought my first 'boy mode' bracelet (a silver chain) and first binder from T-Kingdom, and he showed me how to use it. It was horrible and uncomfortable, but it felt right. Men stopped cat-calling me as much. I used to get called 'he', and it made me feel powerful and protected. But it only offered a short-term fix. I became fixated on 'passing'. If people used the 'wrong' pronouns, I would feel an internal, horrible sense of betrayal. And identifying as trans meant I slipped past any other forms of intervention that could have helped with the trauma.

Of course, my relationship with him came at a price. He felt entitled to sex with me because he had 'saved' me. He felt entitled to my money because he 'made' me. He used to say I "owed [him] everything." He also identified as transgender, but said, "I would only be a second-rate woman, so I wouldn't transition." He described our relationship as heterosexual because he was a woman, and I am a man. He would photoshop his face onto nude photos of my teenage body. I'd confronted him recently, and his now wife (who was also 16 when they met) replied, "We hardly think of you at all." This makes sense. The axe doesn't think of the tree.

When I reflect on this now, I can see the crystallisation of the entire structure of compulsory heterosexuality: an older predator casting himself as the liberator (while being the oppressor). It took years to get out of the relationship. Seven years, specifically. The last time I saw him, I gingerly brought up the topic of gender by saying, "Do you think maybe Kathleen Stock has some good points about gender?" He slammed his hands onto the table, and I felt the eyes of every customer watching as he threw my thesis down and stormed out. I followed him, crying and apologising. I said he was right, I was brainwashed by Terfs, and an idiot. A few months later, I marched with Get The L Out at a protest at Manchester Pride, and he blocked me on all socials.

You'd be forgiven at this point if you are reading and wondering what any of this has to do with political lesbianism. So, I will get to the point.

All of this journey – meeting that man, wearing a binder, alcohol, and drugs – stemmed from one key belief. There is something innately wrong about me – mismatch, an incorrectness, a biological reason that I am not an appropriate woman – and I was born like this, and could not change it. My gender dysphoria could not be healed; I could only change my body to fit society. My 'bisexuality' was also innate. I was fated to terrible sex and shallow emotional connections – which at best were dull and at worst deeply harmful – with men for the rest of my life. Forever doomed to raise children and maintain the house to support a male partner's career, and remind him that it is his mother's birthday tomorrow. What a brilliant trick of the patriarchy to keep women in line and keep the nuclear family that is so necessary for capitalism to work. They've even made it a slogan now – 'Being straight is proof that sexuality isn't a choice.' Posted by feminists, and appropriately keeping in line with their heterosexual followers. The belief that one is born a lesbian, and that gender non-conforming girls are born in the wrong body, are intrinsically linked and both serve the job of acting as an oppressive force on women and girls. One ideology props up the other.

This was an attempt to chronicle what created a child who identified as transgender, and experienced a very real 'dysphoria' around her sexed body. It was a web of different issues: a child who experienced sexual exploitation, a teenager desperately in love with her best friend, a young woman who was rejected by her family and school, and who found an ideology that explained all of the 'symptoms' of her 'wrongness'. *I was born in the wrong body.* I felt wrong because I *was* wrong.

I am sure this is behind the 'detrans to radical feminist' pipeline. We were looking for answers to explain anything, and when the idea of being trans slipped away from us, we were able to confront all of the issues that were actually underlying. What we had experienced was misogyny. But when the definitions of woman and man are blurred, how can we see our oppressor? How can we describe what is happening to us accurately? And if we cannot see it, and we cannot speak it, we cannot action change against it.

It has had a lasting effect. I am still unable to touch my vulva; each period feels almost unbearable, I can't wear tampons or have smear tests, even buying underwear causes almost complete breakdowns, and maintaining a free and intimate sex life is challenging. What has changed is the belief that this is an innate discomfort because I have been 'born in the wrong body'. It is the right body; what has happened to it has been wrong. But my discomfort comes from trauma, forced gender stereotypes, bullying, and internalised misogyny. A whole host of issues that I haven't fully understood yet. But it is not *me*. It is not a genetic glitch, a disease, a condition where my sex and gender identity didn't align. Not my sexuality, and neither my 'gender non-conformity'. Understanding this has meant understanding what patriarchy does to women, and with that understanding means I am able to work on healing. For me, this has been activism, living a partially separatist life, creating women-only spaces, decorating my home with postcards and photographs, surrounding myself with other feminists, as well as the usual hot baths and long forest walks, new hobbies, and friends who accept me.

And I am happy. Happier and more healed than I have ever been. I have learnt to nurture my inner weird kid, and I finally cut my hair into the short, shaved mullet I have always wanted. I've grown out my armpit hair and my leg hair, and though I have kept one dress out of nostalgia, it has been many years since I forced myself into something that feels uncomfortable. I have found my style finally: vintage clothes, bold prints, Levi jeans, and of course – still – the Doc Marten boots. I wear the men's uniform at my merchant naval job as it feels better for me. I am the only woman on board wearing a bow tie and waistcoat, and on a new ship, I feel the nerves of how well I will be accepted, but I know there is no other way to live than being authentic. I will not abandon myself for the comfort of others again.

And for the first time, when I look in the mirror, I no longer see a failed woman, a second-rate man, a misfit – I see the woman looking back at me as strong, radical, loving, and powerful. A woman who has the words, who knows she is a woman, who knows what happened to her was male violence.

And when we find that language, we can find that we do have a choice. We are not fated to heterosexuality. We only need to escape its grasp for long enough that we can come home to ourselves. And I can show up in the world in a way that means I can show other women and girls – womanhood can look like *this* too.

A Political Awakening

Alima

When I was six years old, it was still possible to see lesbians on television in Russia – whether in music videos on MTV or in numerous Hollywood films. I was certainly aware that a woman could love another woman, but I had yet to fully grasp what that meant for me personally or what lesbianism truly was. By the time I was 11, I had a 'boyfriend' who was a couple of years older than me. We repaired bicycles together, built shelters out of branches and leaves, and held hands at every opportunity. Maybe I even loved him? But that didn't matter. One day, as he was walking me home, he tried to kiss me on the lips as a goodbye. I think that moment became one of the most repulsive memories of my childhood. Later, this very memory would become one of the things that made me believe I was simply born a lesbian.

At the age of 13, I discovered the internet. It was already 2008. I could spend entire nights chatting with my online friends – it was a whole secret life, unknown to anyone. And eventually, I grew so close to one of them that, of course, I fell hopelessly in love. Contrary to my own expectations, I felt no disgust when she confessed her feelings for me. I felt nothing but an incredible, uncontainable happiness. It may have lasted only a few months, but those feelings were what opened my heart to all the women who would come into my life afterwards. My love for women had awakened – and after that, it rushed beyond the confines of online chats and the internet.

As a teenager, I had a lot of lesbian experiences – whether it was a couple of relationships that lasted one or two years or short romances that stretched over a few weeks. I enjoyed my lesbian identity, my ability to have both physical and emotional intimacy with women. But unfortunately, due to the overwhelming pornographic discourse surrounding lesbians, my love was often reduced to sexual desire. I believed that being a lesbian meant having endless erotic encounters with other women. Now I realize that, all too often, this has become a substitute for real intimacy. As if I wasn't truly a lesbian but merely playing the role of one.

I was the kind of lesbian that men had probably imagined lesbians to be. All of this led to a terrible anxiety about my own appearance. I became obsessed with being conventionally attractive and feminine. Despite having short hair, I tried to dress as revealingly as possible and wear makeup as boldly as I could. I wanted to prove to everyone that I wasn't a lesbian simply because no man wanted me, but because I was truly, inherently drawn to women. Yet despite my genuine interest in women, I was constantly too focused on conforming to male standards. The way lesbianism was defined by society seemed to stand in the way of me realizing my full potential — both personally and politically.

It is important to note that I grew up in a very liberal environment, especially by Russian standards – my mother was not particularly lesbophobic. I was allowed to date girls and even invite them over. She believed I would inevitably grow out of it (by the time I reached 20, she began to suspect she had been wrong, but by then, she had already grown accustomed to my lesbianism). So, during my adolescence, I felt relatively safe as a lesbian. There was no situation that made me reflect on larger, more complex political issues, but there was an environment where I was allowed to love women.

Among lesbians who are far removed from [radical feminist] politics, women like me are commonly referred to as 'gold star' lesbians. This label kept me especially firmly on the side of essentialism. It allowed me to take pride in being 'special'. No, I wasn't blind to what was happening in heterosexual relationships or to how men, in general, treated women in society. I saw everything and felt an immense sense of relief that I had, by nature, absolutely no need to interact with men more than occasionally. Heterosexual women were simply unlucky; they were doomed. One could pity them, but there was no way to help them. I held this same belief during my first years at university, when I was just beginning to acquaint myself with feminism.

I came to the idea that sexual orientation could be socially constructed when I was around 24 years old. Now, in retrospect, it is much easier for me to analyze exactly what led me to this realization. My turn toward radical feminism provided me with a theoretical foundation to understand just how systemic the oppression of women is – and how it is undeniably linked to heterosexuality. As I began theorizing my own life through the lens of radical feminism, I eventually encountered lesbian feminism. At that time, most radical feminists in the Russian-speaking internet were also political lesbians. At first, I strongly resisted their ideas because their experiences shattered my own understanding of myself and of what it meant to be a lesbian. The nature of sexual orientation was like an elephant in the room – something I kept avoiding eye contact with, over and over again, for a very long time. Around the same period of my life, I was going through a very painful and difficult breakup. My ex-partner once firmly insisted she was exclusively attracted to women (naturally, of course). So when she found herself a boyfriend, it completely broke me. I couldn't comprehend how a woman who had once confided in me about her deep disgust toward men and her strong attraction to women could suddenly change her mind. Of course, at first I wanted to explain it away as so-called bisexuality, but deep down, I already knew the truth.

Women, throughout their lives, from the earliest age, are taught to experience romantic feelings toward men. A culture saturated with heterosexual role models surrounds us everywhere, including children's books and cartoons. Even if, for some reason, a woman identifies as a lesbian, societal pressure does not diminish for even a moment. Reality itself is essentially structured to guide women into relationships with men.

When men learn that a woman is a lesbian, they often attempt to push her boundaries. This may include inappropriate jokes, persistent invitations on dates, or even direct harassment. Older colleagues or relatives regularly inquire whether she has found a boyfriend yet. The media portrays lesbian relationships as marginal stories that inevitably end tragically. Heterosexual female friends occasionally suggest trying relationships with men. Society continuously promotes the belief that true love can only exist between a man and a woman.

It seems to me that when a woman who identifies as a lesbian or bisexual enters a relationship with a man, often her choice is motivated less by genuine attraction to the specific man and more by the pursuit of societal approval and validation, along with the accompanying illusory privileges and relative sense of security.

Over time, I became increasingly interested in lesbian feminism. I met women who had previously identified as bisexual or heterosexual but now, without a shadow of doubt, called themselves lesbians. The more I learned about their lives, the less internal resistance I felt. I was happy to love women, and suddenly, I fully understood that no one is destined to love their oppressor. My understanding of lesbianism changed significantly – it was no longer confined to a set of sexual practices; instead, it took on a profound political, cultural, and even philosophical meaning. This was my political awakening. Lesbian feminism gave me the ability to rethink my entire life through the lens of social constructivism; it gave me a new vision.

There was a time when I truly believed that I could intuitively sense which women were interested in relationships with other women. Because of this, I had no hesitation in approaching even those who identified as heterosexual. Now I realize that my genuine interest in them unintentionally gave them the opportunity to consider, perhaps for the first time, whether they could choose women. There was no built-in lesbian radar in me at all.

At times, it can be excruciatingly painful to endure waves of aggression from lesbians who see lesbianism as an inherent trait. Yes, I was once in their place. I know that to them, political lesbianism feels like it is taking something important away from them, looming over them with the threat of conversion therapy, and invalidating all the struggles they have faced in relation to their orientation. But in the end, for men, it makes no difference how we conceptualize lesbianism – their priority is ensuring that every single woman fulfils her 'sexual duty' to the phallocratic system. The supposed protection that essentialism offers lesbians is, in reality, an ideological shield for the exploitation of the vast majority of women.

Yes, it is unbearable when your heterosexual friend accuses you of 'pressuring' her into being a lesbian simply because you shared ideas of lesbian feminism with her and once dared to say that you wished all women were lesbians. But for every dozen women – lesbians, bisexuals, and heterosexuals – who get angry at me when I speak about my beliefs, there is always, from time to time, one who shows genuine interest. Now, I know quite a few women who have made both a heartfelt and political choice in favor of other women. And that makes me much happier.

I am happy to have the opportunity to make my own small but meaningful contribution to women's liberation – whether by moderating a small chat for political lesbians or running a reading club for those who want to engage with radical feminist literature. Because beyond leading me to a conscious struggle against oppression, lesbian feminism has truly opened me up to gyn-affection[1] and allowed me to understand the importance and value of women's friendship. It has also taught me to appreciate myself without viewing myself through the male gaze.

It's fascinating how political lesbianism can transform the life of a woman who once saw herself as merely a 'biological lesbian'.

References

Raymond, Janice G. (1986). *A Passion for Friends: Toward a Philosophy of Female Affection*. Boston: Beacon Press; (2001) Melbourne: Spinifex Press.

---

1   The term gyn-affection, coined by lesbian radical feminist theorist Janice Raymond, denotes "woman-to-woman attraction, influence, and movement" and articulates a form of relationship in which personal affection between women is inseparable from its political significance (Raymond 1986, p. 9).

The Joy of Choosing to Become a Lesbian[1]

Renate Klein

When I was about 17, my best girlfriend who was annoyed with me for some reason, yelled at me: "You are so stupid, you don't even know what a lesbian is and that our headmistress is one." It's true, I did not know what a lesbian was. I can't remember how I found out (a lexicon in my parents' bookshelves?). But somehow, I learnt that being a lesbian meant being a woman who has girlfriends. That didn't bother me at all, I had always had lots of girlfriends. What did bother me a lot was when I learnt that our headmistress' girlfriend was our horrible drawing teacher: a woman I could not stand (it was mutual). How could our nice headmistress have such bad taste?

I did know what a gay man was. My godfather was one and it was openly talked about. He was an artist and so was his boyfriend. My mother said being a gay artist was okay. Sadly, his boyfriend killed himself walking into a river with pockets full of stones. It was Easter and his death was explained as something to do with religion. I was very sorry for my godfather who had stopped smiling.

But anyway, knowing what a lesbian was had nothing to do with me. Like all my girlfriends I had boyfriends who at times came in

---

1   This is an edited version of the article I wrote for Julie Bindel's blog in 2024.

handy: they carried my schoolbag, ran all sorts of errands and had books at home that my mother forbade me to read. When the time came, I got married like everyone else.

I had finished my MSc in Natural Sciences at Zürich University and was teaching biology and chemistry to high school students in 1975, when I saw an announcement of a talk at the university by Alice Schwarzer who was going to discuss her just published book *Der kleine Unterschied und seine grossen Folgen* (The small difference and its big consequences) which was about men's violence against women. When I mentioned to my close group of friends that I was thinking of going, I was astounded by their unanimous response: "Why would you do that? Alice is stupid, she is a feminist. And she is really ugly and a lesbian."

Not being someone who likes to be told what to do, I went to the talk on my own. I came away very impressed with book in hand: not only had Alice Schwarzer's talk been really interesting, she was highly articulate, even entertaining and charming – and I found her rather good looking. I shared the good news with my friends, but from memory, they remained unimpressed. As a consequence of hearing Alice Schwarzer talk, I started to read the few books about feminism in German available at that time, Marielouise Janssen-Jurreit's *Sexismus* (1976) among them.

I found what I read very interesting: the violence against women, all the inequalities, men's dominance. But I shrugged it off; it was nothing to do with me who had such an equal relationship with my husband and was certainly not discriminated against.

That view changed rather rapidly when I found myself sitting in Garran (a suburb of Canberra in Australia) in 1977 where my husband had a one-year post-doc appointment at the university. And me? For the first time in my life, I was not treated as an intelligent independent human being: I was his 'wife' and relegated to the women's corner in events after work where they talked about babies, a topic that I found incredibly boring. So, I re-read

Sexismus (which for unexplained reasons I had brought with me from Switzerland) and had to admit to myself that boy oh boy Das Patriarchat had a lot more to do with me than I had thought ...

While this made me angry, it also made me determined that things had to change. As my clever husband had already secured himself another post-doc at a plush university near San Francisco. I gave myself three months to find something worthwhile to do, or else I would return to my teaching job in Switzerland.

With some chutzpah and a lot of luck, a month later I found myself happily ensconced in the Women's Studies Program at the University of California at Berkeley where they needed a feminist biologist (me!). I was co-teaching the seminar Theories of Women's Studies and, as I had discovered my ignorance about social sciences and humanities, I had enrolled in a BA in Women's Studies. I was happy as Larry, kept incredibly busy with teaching, studying and writing essays and becoming more of a radical feminist every day.

I was also meeting lots of lesbians – half of Women's Studies teachers and students fit into that category – and quite a few were in relationships. I found myself thinking more than once how good it would be to share one's erotic attractions with one's best feminist friend ...

And then a student said to me that she had a crush on me! I panicked and told her of course nothing could come of this as I was the teacher, she the student ... but what really annoyed me secretly was that I was not in the slightest attracted to this gorgeous woman with a big mop of black curls. I assumed, with a great deal of regret, that I must be hopelessly heterosexual. That made me sad.

A few weeks later, a friend convinced me to come with her to a party in downtown San Francisco on the weekend. It was a long drive and I had essays to finish but eventually I gave in and went with her. It was a beautiful hot summer evening.

When I entered the room, I immediately locked eyes with a woman standing opposite me. And then, before I knew what was happening, I felt this incredible tingling down my spine. Like moths attracted by light, we started moving towards each other. My life was about to change irrevocably and I couldn't have been readier.

I didn't drive back with my friend that night. Instead, I experienced the most perfect lovemaking possible. How could I have missed out on the intimate touch of a woman's body for 33 years? It was ecstasy and gentleness combined.

The next day, as I was taking the train back to Berkeley, I couldn't stop smiling. I wanted to shout from every rooftop so that the whole world could hear: "I am a lesbian; my new life starts now."

And, indeed, it did. The San Francisco fling did not last very long, but I never looked back. In 1981, when I moved to London to start working on my PhD, I defined myself as a lesbian radical feminist. The relationships kept coming … and going … bringing the most radiant of joys and the depth of sadness, but one thing was sure: all my lovers were fascinating artsy and bookish types – some wonderfully crazy – and all were of course feminists. Never a dull moment in our lives. Such a positive change from my rather boring relationships with (good) men. I never looked back: men were my past, women my future.

And thus it came that after I moved to Australia in 1986, I met my life partner Susan Hawthorne with whom I have now been together for 39 years. More than a lifetime during which we had so many great feminist adventures that it would be easy to fill a whole book with them. Over the years, our love and appreciation for each other has only increased and we both count ourselves incredibly lucky to be in each other's life.

I shake my head when I hear people pontificating that same-sex attraction is genetic and that women like me should call ourselves 'bisexual'. I absolutely reject that: since I fell in love with a woman for the first time, I have not been even remotely attracted to men.

Perhaps, if I had been born 30 years later, I might have become attracted to women earlier. As it was, I had to wait until I was totally surrounded by a feminist and lesbian environment for that to happen.

I find it very sad (well no, actually quite annoying), that some so-called 'gold star' lesbians are trying to tell me that I am a 'fake' lesbian; I know the stories of hundreds of lesbians like me, and in fact there are millions like us around the world. The search for a gay 'gene' or even worse, a 'gay brain', has been completely abandoned. I understand that some gay men find it easier to explain to their families that they can't help themselves ... 'it's in our genes' (god-given, so to speak). But lesbians should be braver and proud to declare that we are attracted to women's bodies, hearts and minds, because we want to be.

I don't use the world 'choice' very often, but I do use it to describe how I became a lesbian. I *chose* to be a lesbian and that was the best decision of my life!

An Approach to the Myth of Sexual Orientation

Ananda Castaño

Sexual orientation is a ubiquitous concept. Imbued with a scientific aura that makes it appear uncontested and indisputable, it is far from being any of those things, including scientific. Radical feminist theory has long understood heterosexuality as a patriarchal institution which works to keep women in line so they continue to service men with sexual, reproductive and emotional labor. This makes heterosexuality a keystone of patriarchal domination. So when feminists started to rebel against its basic principles, the agents of patriarchy needed to act fast to save their system. The 'sexual orientation' concept is the newest tool for this.

This essay aims to analyze the concept of sexual orientation from a radical and lesbian feminist perspective.[1]

What Is Sexual Orientation?

This term has been recently adopted to convey both the essentialist element of the pathological model of homosexuality as deviance and the individualistic element of what Celia Kitzinger called the "humanist liberal model" (Kitzinger, 1987).

---

1   This essay is a summarized and updated visit to some of the topics of a two-part essay I published in 2019, called 'El mito de la orientación sexual'. The original articles can be read at <https://existencialesbica.wordpress.com>.

This essentialism aims to divide women, making those who see themselves as heterosexual think they can never be like those with another 'sexual orientation'. They cannot aim to engage in certain kinds of relationships or activities with women, nor develop feelings for them that are reserved for men. The individualistic element aims to conceal any political significance of sexuality. That way, lesbian existence would be seen as posing no threat to the social system and heterosexuality couldn't be understood as an institution.

This new conceptualization integrates the basic aspects of two theories that were originally contradictory to maintain the institution of heterosexuality. It does so by deceiving, resorting to vague notions that are mostly fallacies, and by using well-established patriarchal narratives to sustain itself.

The concept of 'sexual orientation' is founded on the unsubstantiated idea that it is something fixed and immutable. Since the research on 'homosexuality' has never found evidence of it being innate, new theories had to be developed to keep an essentialist view of what is now seen as 'sexual orientation' (usually divided into heterosexuality, homosexuality and bisexuality).

Despite continued claims to the contrary, no genetic or biological evidence has been found to distinguish people of the same sex labelled homosexuals from those labelled heterosexuals. Unlike the characteristic of sex, which is checkable by observation or by genetic tests, no biological causation or predictive traits have been found for this so-called sexual orientation. A radical feminist (social constructionist) view suggests that there is more evidence for social, cultural, and political factors – rather than biology – shaping why people believe they have this 'sexual orientation'.

Current definitions of sexual orientation always include the same word: *attraction*. Attraction is a vague concept. It refers to perceived persistent desires towards something. The American Psychological Association defines sexual orientation as "an enduring pattern of emotional, romantic, and/or sexual attractions to men, women, or both sexes" (American Psychological Association, 2008). But attraction itself also seems to refer to a pattern or at least to an inferred principle, not to anything checkable by itself. The only potentially verifiable phenomenon would be that which leads a person to believe they are attracted to someone or something when it occurs repeatedly: desire. To stay within a positive scientific approach, we shouldn't use desire as reference but *sexual arousal* (leaving aside that what we consider 'sexual' is socioculturally conditioned): what makes us identify something as object of our 'sexual' desire. 'Sexual' arousal is the only measurable phenomenon in the social construction that is 'attraction'. As we can observe, 'sexual orientation' is a concept with many layers of ambiguity. We'll try to operate with the parts of it that can be used for reasoning.

The Fallacies at Work

Indeed, the 'sexual' arousal an object or person provokes in us is real and experiential. It can be somehow measured by neuroscience, in all its ambiguity, but it does in no way present itself as fixed or immutable – it is only a phenomenon, with spatial-temporal limitations. This arousal starts occurring, and it can stop occurring in the same way. Nothing makes us think that the fact that it was produced implies that it should inevitably recur, or that it will always occur in the same way: there's no underlying factor that makes that particular arousal 'necessary' instead of merely accidental/contingent. This is easily contrasted because we don't always feel this arousal in the presence of the same person, it begins and it can be sustained for some time until it ends; it can also be intermittent or only occur under certain circumstances.

How did the empirical fact of mutable and contingent arousal – or its subjective interpretation as desire – lead to the construction of the supposedly fixed and immutable 'sexual orientation'? The inductive fallacies came into play.

The notion of a 'sexual orientation' is inferred from the fact of 'desire', which is an arbitrary operation. Psychologists and sexologists assert that if they can see a pattern where a person supposedly only feels desire towards people of one sex or another, or even both, then there must be something in them that makes this happen, something that is conditioning this supposed pattern. This is a logical leap. We cannot establish a law from a pattern of occurrence. We cannot presume there's something (organic) modulating the pattern of occurrence of our desire, even less so if, despite every effort, nothing of this kind has been found.

There is another logical leap: even though desire is a contingent and mutable phenomenon, the particular desire towards a person of a certain sex is regarded as a sign of desire for the group of people of the same sex. This doesn't just essentialise a single experience of arousal or desire – it also misattributes causality. The arousal one person elicits in us is interpreted as if a specific characteristic of theirs is what necessarily triggered it. And that characteristic is precisely that of sex.

Desire occurs due to a variety of causes, even though our arousal is organic, our arousal ability is in no way dependent on the object of arousal. The sexual orientation concept implies there's something in us that turns on or off our ability to feel aroused when in contact with an object (person) based on the presence of certain sex characteristics. If we are meant to extract a pattern out of these arousals, which would supposedly define ourselves, it is convenient for the patriarchy that we do so based solely on the characteristic of sex.

This is the big set-up of the sexual orientation concept.

In order to infer this supposed modulating factor for arousal – one that is also fixed and immutable – sexologists and psychologists have used psychoanalytical strategies that amount to confirmation bias. They ask people to look into their childhood, in search of moments that can now be interpreted as sexual desire towards the sex they suspect they are 'naturally and immutably' attracted to. People are expected to find a clear manifestation of desire towards one sex but if they acknowledge any shifts in what they experience as desire across sexes, they're swiftly diagnosed as bisexual. Therefore, the thing that conditions their desire towards each sex ('sexual orientation') is still there – even though it is not conditioning it as much as it does for others.

Does not having a sexual orientation mean we're all 'bisexuals' then? No, the conceptualization of bisexuality is just another part of the theory of sexual orientations. It also relies on the naturalization of heterosexuality to establish itself as a model for sexual behavior and 'identity'. Bisexuality serves as the safety net for the essentialization of sexual desires and behaviors that is sexual orientation. When a woman considers the possibility of being a lesbian because she finds herself loving a woman or feeling desire towards one, the narrative of a bisexual sexual orientation prevents her from conceiving herself as unavailable to men. Instead, it keeps her emotionally dependent and sexually accessible to men even though she might be only interested in women at that moment. The slippery slope which is bisexuality also makes women keep seeing this heterosexual relationship scheme as the norm.

By including bisexuality in this model that constantly seeks validation through confirmation bias, they'd leave no space for exception, no way in the very theory of sexual orientation for the disproving of itself. This is called 'unfalsifiability', and it is a common criterion for regarding a theory as unscientific.

The Foundations of Patriarchal Narratives

Even feminist women resist renouncing the idea of 'sexual orientation'. This demonstrates how well ingrained it is in the patriarchal machinery. Some will claim to see a rigid pattern of desire and to 'feel' they *are* heterosexuals or homosexuals, and, if not, bisexuals.

Most will see themselves as heterosexual and claim this is due to evolutionary and reproductive reasons, a patriarchal deterministic viewpoint. As feminists, we can easily explain this by pointing to the institution of heterosexuality, which acts as a distorting lens through which desire, sex and human relationships are seen. We'll take a look at these distortions by answering common questions regarding sexuality.

1. Why Do Most Women See Themselves as 'Heterosexuals'?

What we have found as a constant modulating factor for desire (and sexual behavior) is social intervention. Many feminists have explained the way heterosexual desire is promoted in the patriarchy through fairy tales, role models, sex role stereotype, pornography, education, the family institution and so forth.

Along with this modulation of desire, we can also find an intervention of how desire is interpreted, which plays a key part in the assumption of having a 'sexual orientation'. A woman might feel the kind of arousal she would label sexual, but only if inspired by a man; she might feel something intense toward a female friend but dismiss it, because the dominant narrative has never taught her to recognise that as romantic. Much of this 'lesbian continuum' is rendered invisible, erased by the male-centred framing of who we're 'supposed' to feel what for.

From a young age, girls are encouraged to perform the roles patriarchy has scripted for them, so they learn to interpret almost any emotional or physical response as 'liking' a boy. Even attraction to distant older male celebrities becomes retrospectively framed as 'evidence' of heterosexual orientation. The result is that many women confidently and unquestioningly identify as heterosexual.

Heterosexuality also has a lot of short-term or merely ostensible rewards for women who comply with it. This makes women not just think of themselves as heterosexuals but (consciously or unconsciously) want to stay faithful to the institution.

2. If 'Compulsory Heterosexuality' Exists, Why Are Some Women Lesbians?

Under the sexual orientation narrative, women understand the lesbian existence as proof of some essential difference that makes lesbians avoid the patriarchal influence because 'they just can't help it'.

The simple answer to this question is: social norms don't mold the totality of human experience. Since we can't go over everything in this 'approach', I'll merely list the ways in which the institution of heterosexuality is challenged (willingly or unwillingly).

a. By a deficient learning of the social norms.
b. By bearing a critical consciousness towards social requirements.
c. By a conscious rejection of it (this is the feminist stance).
d. By the random occurrence of arousal or encounters that elicit feelings or behaviors that challenge heterosexuality.

More than one of these can be present. Most of the time, more than one is necessary for us to take the step of seeing ourselves as something other than heterosexual. The last one, the random occurrence of arousal (due to our bodily ability to feel aroused) is, as we said, usually dismissed as meaningless when it appears in the company of other women. But if we're also someone who didn't learn the cultural requirements very well (we didn't quite get the message that we're supposed to feel something else or only feel this with boys) or we're critical towards what we've been taught ('Why must I do what society tells me?' 'Why cannot I have this kind of relationship with another girl?'), then we may be able to give that occurrence some relevance and meaning in our lives, thus seeing ourselves as lesbians.

The idea of being a lesbian doesn't require the concept of sexual orientation. We might consider ourselves lesbians after a/b and/or d happens and not believe it to be because of an immutable and fixed conditional element over our desire.

But there are other ways to conclude that we're lesbians without falling into the narrative of sexual orientation. When we gain feminist consciousness, we reject the heterosexual institution and all its implications. Overcoming the heterosexual institution also means that we can start appreciating the value and possibilities of our relationships with women, against what patriarchal conditioning has taught us to expect and desire. Once we're experiencing our relationships from this place, it's only natural to become lesbians, which means to center women in our lives (individual women, not the idea of women) and keep our primary bonds with them and not with men. This can translate in 'sexual' relationships and other forms of intimacy which the patriarchy has reserved for men and understands as the foundations of their labelling women as lesbians. But we have historically known that being a lesbian is much more than this, contrary to what sexologists have reduced it to.

3. Why Do Some Lesbians Feel They've Always Been Lesbians?

Let's go back to the fallacies to answer this one. Remember, we cannot establish a law from a pattern of occurrence. This is an empirical principle; we might see a white swan once, twice, even ten times, that doesn't mean all swans are white. If we keep looking, black swans may appear. When the patriarchal narrative tries to assume and essentialize a pattern, it's important to realize it also deceives by deciding how and at what point the pattern will be established.

It is possible that women feel the arousal patriarchy uses to label them as homosexuals naturally, even if there's a patriarchal conditioning against it. In most cases, a single instance of desire towards a woman will be ignored as irrelevant when establishing a pattern for 'sexual orientation', especially if it is not understood as a 'sexual' desire. When desire towards women keeps happening, and it's also acknowledged, many won't want to 'close' the pattern: 'it's just a phase', a desire towards men will appear and break the pattern. But if the woman doesn't acknowledge any desire towards a man (or any desire as intense as those felt for certain women), she might start receiving the label 'homosexual' and she herself might start looking in her past for a 'sexual attraction' aligned with this new label, even if these desires only started appearing recently.

The reasoning for closing the pattern, for stopping counting, is only valid if it is founded on this essentialist, psychoanalytic understanding. But the experience of mutability and the spontaneous appearance of new desires is in clear contrast with this. This contrast might serve as a way to keep lesbians who believe in sexual orientation checking anxiously the meaning of their desires, making them doubt themselves and keeping the door open to men. This might make women want to believe in their immutable 'sexual orientation' just to feel calm over the possibility of the occurrence of a desire that would make them rethink 'who they are' and what they should expect from their oppressors.

Some women insist there must be something immutable in them since they have suffered social rejection for being lesbians. They assert they only recall moments of desire towards women and that they tried to feel towards men the same kind of desire they felt towards women, and failed. They also say they failed not to desire women. This could be because, being ourselves women, ceasing to appreciate women we already appreciate, goes against basic self-esteem and is alienating.

What has kept these women having recurring moments of desire towards other women and focusing on those moments as the meaningful ones is what has done the same for virtually all of us (old, new, political, pre-feminism, post-feminism …) lesbians: the fact that we're freer with other women. Being Seen (Frye, 1983), as Marilyn Frye would say, being regarded by someone else as a person, not as an object – in a way most society won't do because of patriarchy – is a totally powerful experience, and so is the feeling of being loved.

Sexual Orientation as Agency Erasure

We as lesbians feel free appreciating other women for what they really are, something that also speaks of appreciating ourSelves. A love that has transcended the alienating narratives about what we are as women is a reward much bigger than those crumbs the patriarchs might give us if we comply. We know this deep down even as we suffer their punishments and marginalizations. This would make us want more of this love and that would be enough to make many keep choosing women, in one way or another, never giving up to the patriarchal coercion.

This 'choosing' is the key to a feminist analysis of sexual orientation. The 'sexual orientation' narrative seeks to erase the possibility of agency over our sexual desires and practices (which are highly influenced by the patriarchy). We are lesbians not because we cannot help it; we are lesbians because we want to be lesbians, despite all patriarchal obstacles. Some of us might be less aware of this, but the fact is, they keep choosing lesbian relationships, which are more fulfilling for them. And by not doing so, they might be unhappy, not because they are going against their 'natural sexual orientation' but because they are acting against their best interest and renouncing relationships they have experienced as more authentic and positive than those imposed by the social system.

Radical feminist analysis has centered its efforts on reclaiming the agency of women over our relationships and sexuality. Embracing this new narrative of sexual orientation would mean turning our backs on the most basic points of radical feminism and thinking we lack any power over our sexuality, the very thing that men have used to get the most power over us. As lesbian feminists we consciously choose to reclaim our own power.

References

American Psychological Association. (2008). 'Answers to your questions: For a better understanding of sexual orientation and homosexuality'. <www.apa. org/topics/lgbt/orientation.pdf>.

Frye, Marilyn. (1983). 'To Be and Be Seen: The Politics of Reality' in *The Politics of Reality: Essays in Feminist Theory*. Trumansburg: The Crossing Press, pp. 152–173

Kitzinger, Celia. (1987). *The Social Construction of Lesbianism*. London: Sage Publications.

Choosing Women: A Working Vision for Political Lesbianism

Jesika Gonzalez

Though some deem political lesbianism a defunct relic of the past as an inoperative ideology, many of us are determined to resurrect it. Those of us who practice it are as committed as ever to its wide proliferation as a tool in the fight against patriarchy.

Defining Political Lesbianism

The most recognized definition of a political lesbian is "a woman-identified woman that does not fuck men." The term "woman-identified woman" emerged from the 1970 manifesto "The Woman-Identified Woman" by the Radicalesbians. It characterizes a woman who identifies herself independently of men, establishing her relationships, values, and sense of self in relation to other women. This challenges norms that define women by their relation to men, promoting autonomy and female solidarity.

Many reject that the term "lesbian," even with the qualifier "political," should apply to a woman that does not actually intend to partner with women. I am inclined to agree. For many, this distinction rests on whether there is a sexual relationship. It is my perspective that a sexual relationship is not essential. It undermines the goal of de-centering men to require that a patriarchal male-prerogative, specifically recreational sex, be the single and only requirement of a committed relationship between two women for that relationship to be valid.

Theoretically, a political lesbian relationship does not need to be romantic or sexual. However, given societal conditioning that requires recreational sex for relationship fulfillment, most political lesbian relationships will be sexual.

The Myth of Innate Sexuality

Political campaigns advocating for homosexual liberation have popularized the belief that sexual orientation is innate and immutable. Slogans such as "born this way" gained widespread acceptance, reinforced by scientific literature attempting to support the notion of a biological basis for sexual orientation. Due to these campaigns, it became widely accepted that sexual orientation is something one is born with and cannot change. Most people came to believe and repeat these slogans without much scrutiny. Alongside this, a deluge of scientific studies sought to validate the claim that sexual orientation is biologically determined. However, to date, no conclusive evidence has emerged to substantiate this idea. No genetic marker, hormonal balance, or other biological determinant of sexual orientation has been found, and the prevailing scientific consensus remains inconclusive.

Navigating Modern Challenges

The present liberal thinking around sexuality is that if sexuality can change, then religious zealots will seek to require all sexuality be changed to heterosexual. This fear is warranted. Most liberals are aware that churches have coerced members to undergo conversion therapy, usually understood as an attempt to reprogram a homosexual's sexuality to heterosexual. Many have endured being coerced into undergoing conversion therapy. This is an infuriating reality and one that political lesbian proponents of the notion that sexuality can change vehemently reject.

The fact that homosexuality is neither innate nor immutable does not justify punitive actions or coercive attempts to change it. Rather, we can and should embrace a more nuanced understanding – one that allows for both the protection of same-sex relationships and the recognition that sexual orientation, particularly for women, can be shaped by social, political, and personal factors. We can have both: the right to same-sex relationships and the right to acknowledge that lesbianism can be a choice.

Addressing Concerns and Misconceptions

Many feminists, especially born-this-way lesbians, reject the notion of political lesbianism based on the fear that political lesbians are liable to change their minds and revert to sexual and romantic relationships with men. The concern I suppose is that the defecting political lesbian will leave another woman heartbroken on her way out.

This evokes scenarios of straight, bi-curious, or bisexual women luring born-this-way-lesbians into bed under spurious circumstances. Perhaps having led a lesbian on in a way that suggested she was interested in a relationship, when in fact it was just a sexual experiment. Worse yet, maybe the whole engagement was pretextual and the straight, bi-curious, or bisexual woman was just posturing to eventually introduce that she had a male partner and was attempting to recruit the lesbian into a fulfillment of that man's sexual fantasy. These things can and have happened, but I would assume the women involved in this kind of sexual manipulation are usually not radical feminists.

Political lesbians are woman-identified. Women who use other women in sexually exploitative ways are anything but woman identified. Political lesbians, especially new ones, should be upfront about their intentions and should be honest about their pasts. That advice applies to anyone seeking to enter a sexual or romantic relationship. The other partner can then decide whether they believe being with a political lesbian is worth the risk. I reject the supposition that if political lesbianism becomes more widely practiced, a surge of straight and bi women would suddenly besiege born-this-way lesbians looking for opportunities to use and exploit them. Political lesbianism is predicated on the idea of finding women with whom to grow and collaborate. Unfortunately for romantics of all stripes, heartbreak, pain, and rejection are a by-product of relationship seeking regardless of the sexualities of those involved.

Redirecting Women's Devotion Toward Each Other

Political lesbianism can be a powerful tool to improve the lives of women who suffer for their romantic and sexual attraction to men. This vision is especially relevant for women who already identify as bisexual, as transitioning away from heterosexual relationships may be easier for them. However, all women-identified women, even women who see themselves as strictly heterosexual, should make an earnest effort to re-examine their heterosexuality. Radical feminists recognize that sexuality is a social construct, and thus, the possibility of evolving or changing one's sexual orientation should always remain open.

Much has changed since *Love Your Enemy* was published. In the United States, where I live, and in many other anglophone and even some non-anglophone countries, social progress has made it safer for women from diverse backgrounds to become out lesbians. Today, women pay a lower social penalty than ever before for choosing a woman instead of a man. For this reason, political lesbianism is accessible to more women than ever before.

At the same time, despite the spread of feminist ideas, heterosexual relationships remain a losing proposition for women. Among radical feminists, this is not controversial. It should be self-evident that dedicated radical feminists should avoid partnering with men. The disadvantages of heterosexual relationships are undeniable – from the orgasm gap to unequal domestic and emotional labor. Historically, these relationships have included marital rape, domestic violence, and other abuses. Even now, many women would consider it an improvement if their primary burden was merely an unfair division of household labor.

One significant reason why heterosexual relationships remain a losing proposition for women is male violence, which is the predominant force behind intimate partner violence (IPV). Numerous studies have found that men commit most domestic violence, with women suffering disproportionately as victims. Heterosexual relationships exist within a broader patriarchal framework that normalizes male dominance, making control, coercion, and violence more likely. In contrast, lesbian relationships lack this ingrained power imbalance, reducing the likelihood of physical, emotional, or financial abuse being used as a means of control.

Additionally, research suggests that lesbian couples tend to prioritize communication, emotional intelligence, and conflict resolution over physical aggression. Without rigid gender roles that reinforce male entitlement and female subservience, disagreements in lesbian relationships are more likely to be addressed through dialogue rather than coercion or violence. Studies indicate that same-sex female couples more frequently adopt cooperative strategies to manage relationship conflicts, leading to lower rates of IPV.

Furthermore, while domestic violence does occur in some lesbian relationships, it is often found to be less severe than in heterosexual relationships, with lower rates of physical injury, hospitalization, or fatal outcomes. When violence does occur between women, it is generally less extreme than male-perpetrated violence against women.

By choosing relationships with other women, lesbians not only gain emotional and financial benefits but also experience significantly reduced exposure to domestic violence, reinforcing the idea that women-centered partnerships provide safer and more equitable environments.

Women are kept the sex underclass primarily through socialization. We are conditioned to adopt behaviors that harm us or make us vulnerable to exploitation. Two of the most damaging are our socialization into prioritizing permanent coupleship and, inextricably, our conditioning to serve our male partners. Undoing this conditioning will take generations, and there is no indication we will begin this process soon. Given this reality, I propose we redirect these ingrained behaviors to serve us rather than harm us. It would be revolutionary to channel the effort and devotion women have been trained to give men toward other women instead. Not every woman must embrace this shift for it to be impactful – it has the potential to be genuinely empowering for those who do.

One key reason for this is the absence of traditional gender roles that dictate which partner should be responsible for certain household tasks. In heterosexual relationships, deeply ingrained societal expectations often assign domestic work and caregiving to women, even when they are equally or more financially responsible for the household. In contrast, lesbian couples tend to negotiate responsibilities based on practical considerations such as work schedules, personal preferences, and skill sets rather than defaulting to gender-based expectations.

Another factor contributing to the more equitable division of labor in same-sex female relationships is a heightened awareness of fairness and mutual respect. Many women in lesbian partnerships consciously strive to avoid replicating the inequalities they have observed or experienced in heterosexual relationships. As a result, they are more likely to communicate openly about household responsibilities and ensure a more balanced workload. Additionally, research suggests that lesbian couples value egalitarianism more highly than heterosexual couples, making them more likely to share duties like childcare, cooking, and cleaning. By working together rather than falling into predefined roles, same-sex female couples create partnerships that prioritize cooperation, reducing the stress and resentment often associated with unequal divisions of labor.

This equitable distribution of domestic work fosters healthier relationships and allows both partners to pursue their careers, personal growth, and leisure without the burden of disproportionate household responsibilities.

Beyond Romance: Marriage as a Feminist Tactic for Collective Well-Being

Marriage, even lesbian marriage, remains a contentious issue among radical feminists. However, I believe women should strategically use marriage when it offers tangible benefits. We should use whatever tools we have available for the advancement of women. If a legal union serves both parties, we should take advantage of existing structures to advance women's interests. Some argue that marriage should be avoided due to the challenges of dissolution and that its benefits should instead be replicated through individual contracts. While this is a valid approach, it can be time-consuming and costly, making it inaccessible to many women.

In a same-sex marriage between two women-identified women, feminism wins, regardless of which partner gains economic power. Even if one woman contributes more financially or through domestic labor, that effort is not being funneled into men but remains within a partnership that supports women. The benefits of marriage extend beyond financial security. In the United States, marriage provides access to healthcare, Family Medical Leave Act protections, next-of-kin rights for critical medical and legal decisions, and can yield potential tax advantages. For working poor and working-class lesbians in the US, marriage can be especially beneficial, allowing them to pool resources while maintaining a lower tax bracket.

Political lesbian marriage makes the most sense for working women. It is only logical that women would seek to invest their energy in themselves and each other rather than in relationships that reinforce male supremacy. Working class women may benefit more than high earning women from political lesbianism. Working-class women, often in a state of economic precarity, have the most to gain from political lesbianism. Partnering with another woman provides financial stability, cost-sharing, and a higher quality of life. If children are involved, they are statistically safer in the care of another woman. A higher combined income and cost-sharing will yield an elevated quality of life. Working poor, working class, and lower middle-class lesbians benefit from a higher household income than comparable heterosexual couples. When lesbians marry, they enjoy a 6% earnings premium over their unmarried cohabitating counterparts. Marriage also secures survivor benefits, retirement funds, insurance, and inheritance, ensuring that wealth remains in the hands of women rather than being redirected to other would-be next of kin.

A Call to Prioritize Women

Resurrecting political lesbianism offers a transformative path for women seeking to break free from the constraints of patriarchy and reclaim their autonomy. This vision is not just about rejecting men but about redirecting our emotional, intellectual, and physical devotion toward each other as women. By centering female relationships—whether romantic, sexual, platonic, or communal—women can forge new systems of support, security, and empowerment outside of male dominance.

The misconception that political lesbianism is an outdated or impractical ideology ignores the tangible benefits it offers. Women who disengage from heterosexual relationships not only free themselves from systemic inequalities but also gain access to more equitable partnerships. Lesbian relationships foster healthier dynamics, reducing the burdens of domestic labor, emotional labor, and the risks of male violence. Furthermore, political lesbianism provides a viable alternative to the economic instability that many working-class women face. By pooling resources and building women-centered households, women can achieve financial security and collective well-being in ways that are nearly impossible within traditional heterosexual structures.

As we continue to challenge the deeply ingrained socialization that binds women to men, we must recognize that change is not instantaneous. The reorientation of female devotion will not happen overnight, nor does it need to be universally embraced to be impactful. Even a small but growing movement of women choosing each other over men creates a ripple effect, fostering stronger, more independent female communities.

Political lesbianism is not merely a personal choice—it is a radical and necessary strategy for dismantling patriarchy. By investing in ourselves and one another, we can create a future where women's labor, love, and loyalty are no longer exploited for male benefit but instead serve to uplift and liberate women as a class. It is time to reconsider political lesbianism.

References

Leeds Revolutionary Feminist Group. (1981). 'Political Lesbianism: The Case Against Heterosexuality'. In *Love Your Enemy*. London: Onlywomen Press.

Radicalesbians. (1970). *The Woman-Identified Woman*. United States: Know, Inc. Reprinted in *Women's Liberation Movement Print Culture*, Duke University Libraries. <https://idn.duke.edu/ark:/87924/r3gx1t>.

The Birth of a Lesbian

Angela C. Wild

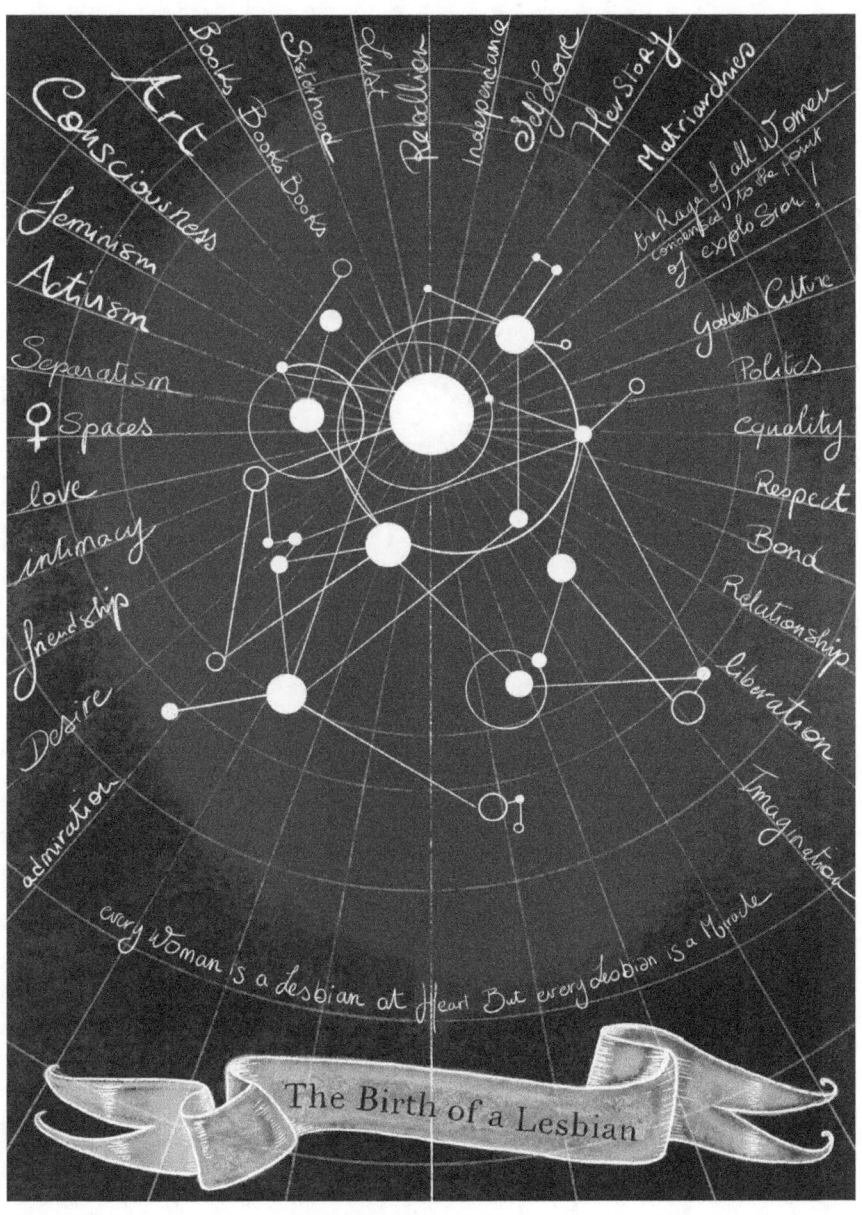

Solitude as Resistance and the Survival of Lesbian Feminist Communities

Frances Woods

One restless night, my eyes flickered across the scores of Facebook trivialities designed to hook me in and clickbait me. Cute cats and ridiculous memes and endless adverts trying to make me buy what I did not need. Then a quote about women and solitude. I stopped. I read more. And then a name. Susan Sontag. I had never heard of her. I researched more about her – she was an artist, an intellectual and she had relationships with women. I quickly shut Facebook down, drawn into a world that emphasised solitude, contrasting with the internet traffic that had just whizzed through my unwilling eyes. In that moment, I understood we can be entirely alone, browsing the net, and yet not be in a place of solitude.

I have long been fascinated by women in past times who, somehow, managed to escape hetero-patriarchy in their own ways and on their own terms, despite the vast economic, political and cultural obstacles thrown in their paths. Susan Sontag (2012) was one such woman. I would very much like to think that, had she been born slightly later, she would have chosen political lesbianism but there is no guarantee. She saw herself as an artist and intellectual first and foremost, viewing her relationships with women as private affairs. And yet her thinking was political in the sense that she valued unconventionality in relationships.

Her solitude was not merely the artist's retreat, but an act of quiet defiance against the hetero-patriarchal order. She viewed seclusion as a political space where she could be creatively autonomous and push intellectual boundaries. She thought of her version of solitude as a subversive act. She rejected the prescriptive narratives imposed on women by the hetero-patriarchy. Her kind of solitude represented a rejection of the stereotypical trappings of hetero-patriarchy such as the heterosexual institution of family life.

By contrast, for men, solitude has often been associated with intellectual rigour, genius, artistic creation and power. When men retreat from the world, it is rarely questioned. Instead, it is romanticised as a hallmark of greatness. For women, choosing isolation or living alone was often viewed as 'deviant,' 'selfish,' or even to be pitied, the sad spinster who can't get a man; a figure that continues to haunt female stereotypes. This is still true, even today.

Susan's idea about solitude aligns with Virginia Woolf's (1996) concept in *A Room of One's Own*. Virginia argued that women, historically, lacked the financial and social freedom to claim solitude, which limited their creative potential. Virginia's demand for "a room of one's own" resonates with Susan's belief that solitude is essential for intellectual work. Both women recognised the gendered expectations inherent within patriarchy where women should prioritise others over their own needs. Both defied such notions, in their own way. From a working-class view, this vision of solitude belongs to the privileged few. There is no doubt that money, class, time, are all privileges, not rights. Yet I vividly remember someone at college with me, explaining the struggle she had to get there. "I used to spend time slowly stacking shelves, thinking" she said, "The power of my mind led me here," suggesting that her concept of political solitude could take place at a busy job, doing a repetitive task.

Adrienne Rich (1980) and Audre Lorde (2017) also explored the concept of solitude in politicised ways. For Adrienne, it was a refusal to be shaped by men's expectations and a necessary step towards feminist consciousness. It was more complex for Audre who saw solitude as a refuge from racism, sexism and homophobia. She said: "Caring for myself is not self-indulgence, it is self-preservation, and that is an act of political warfare" (p.130). The concept of solitude was a necessary protective move in a world that was hostile to black lesbian women.

Yet in the absence of CR (consciousness-raising) groups of the '70s, politicised solitude can be a place for reflection, reading political works, and re-ordering our thoughts, away from male control. Understanding our trauma, with so many of us being rape survivors or survivors of domestic abuse, solitude can act as a space where we make sense of that traumatic past and decide what our present and future freedoms will look like.

But solitude as a politicised action by itself, for most of us, is not enough. Susan, Adrienne and Audre, in their different ways, understood that autonomy without community connection risks turning into isolation. The ongoing dismantling of lesbian feminist spaces has not only left individual lesbians more vulnerable but has erased the very networks that once politicised solitude and gave it meaning.

For some, the ability to build a stable, loving lesbian relationship within a hostile world is itself a radical act. I understand this. And yet, for me, the political significance of lesbianism has always gone beyond simply resisting heterosexuality in private. It is about dismantling the structures and dominating cultural pressures that seek to privatise and depoliticise lesbian lives; about forging something greater than the replication of coupledom, even when that couple is two women.

As a woman, a lesbian feminist, I am aware that my choices to live in solitude and claim space on my own terms are suspect to the world at large. For decades, I have watched lesbian feminists couple up and, to all intents and purposes, live lives that seem to imitate hetero-norms. I do accept that, for the most part, this is not actually what happens and conventional relationships between women are qualitatively different in all kinds of ways from those with men. Even so, the structure of those relationships where two women, and perhaps children, live together in family units, still fit within some kind of normative pattern, especially now women can marry legally in many countries. Some of the same corrosive patterns can emerge – silence, secrecy and coercive control. None of us like to think of it. All of us know it can happen in private spaces away from the political eyes of others.

What the word 'political' in the term 'political lesbian' means to me is not finding one relationship, living like swans with her for the rest of our lives. I shudder at such a thought. To me the word means questioning, challenging, understanding, that every aspect of our lives is eaten up by hetero-patriarchal expectations. For so long, it has been important to me that I have company along that politically conscious journey. Not the company of one woman. The company of many lesbian feminists – all questioning, wondering, exploring what it might mean to live beyond patriarchal shackles. Places like The Michigan Womyn's Music Festival (Michfest), the women's lands, and the scattered lesbian communities that developed over time. I want women who are newly out as lesbian feminists to know that coupledom is not the only choice available to them. For that to be realistic, though, alternative, lesbian feminist spaces need to exist.

When I first came out as a lesbian feminist, I read *Women of Ideas* by Dale Spender (2024). Her first chapter called 'Why Didn't I Know?' entranced me. I read with wonder when she explained how important it is that women are not cut off from our historical sisters. She could not believe that in 1911 there had been 21 regular feminist periodicals in the UK, "a feminist bookshop, a women's press, a women's bank run by and for women" (p. 4). When she made that discovery, she realised that the woman's movement of the past had been bigger, stronger and more influential than she ever knew. This led to asking herself, "How are women made to disappear?"

When I last read her words, somewhere in the 1980s or 1990s, little did I imagine that landmarks that I knew so well would also disappear in the blink of an eye. Sisterwrite, my local bookshop on Upper Street in London, Silver Moon, hundreds of London-based lesbian and feminist groups, a women's room at my uni. Space after space closed down because they were operating within a neoliberal, patriarchal world and could not survive. Now, much of the discourse has moved online, where visibility should be easier, but instead, a different kind of erasure takes place. Conversations collapse into factional disputes. The very idea of political lesbianism is derided, dismissed as appropriation, a relic of a past that some lesbians wish to forget. And so, without community, I retreat – not to isolation, but to a solitude that remains political, a space where thought still resists.

As hostility increased, many lesbian feminists I had known retreated into the safety of coupledom and family life and I lost touch for many years. Lesbian feminist spaces were not just community touchpoints. They were a way of connecting, of politicising life, whether we're lesbians or not, the malestream world dominates. Meeting together helps us find ways to fight back. Those spaces were essential to my lesbian feminist framing of what it means to be a political lesbian. Their existence meant going beyond what is known about relationships, finding new ways to connect with sisters. Crucially for me, politicising solitude so that I can expand my creative and intellectual understanding of being a lesbian feminist in a hostile world. A place where I can create strategies for resistance. The challenge of coupling up is that it is individualistic and often comes to an end or results in isolated retreat. Lesbian feminist communities, however, have the potential of lasting beyond immediate satisfaction of needs.

Herein lies the tension that Susan, Audre and perhaps Adrienne felt between a politicised solitude and a politicised community. They needed both. Both give political nourishment in different ways. For Susan, a pull between the obsessive romantic relationships she had and the need for solitude to fortify her intellectual and creative inner life, was palpable. It was a paradox for her that valuing solitude was in opposition to the deep, immersive relationships she longed for. Solitude was necessary for thinking and writing, but relationships provided fuel for her mind. She was drawn to women who expanded her intellectual world, but she also recognised that relationships could be distractions from the intense focus required for creative work.

Susan and I part ways on her position that relationships with women are private affairs. I don't see political lesbian feminist 'identity' as dogma. I see it as a way of freeing my mind, my beliefs, how I view the world. Encouraging me to think differently, to live unconventionally, and to find ways of supporting women in my everyday life. In subtle ways. In more obvious ways. In ways that centre women. I do know the passionate heady heights Susan strived for with one woman and it is an experience I am glad I had. However, I would not want it again. It was too all-consuming and stopped me from exploring other meanings in my life. And so, for someone like me, the survival of lesbian feminist community spaces, places to sink into for sustenance and connection, is life-sustaining.

I can't express any of this in the limited lesbian or feminist internet platforms that exist, and that I have known to be full of toxicity. So, I avoid them. I am not in a place of politicised solitude, even if no one is physically near me at the point I access them. There are chattering disembodied electronic voices that cry out in opposition to all my political thoughts, and I see no benefit or joy in battling with them. The most heartbreaking voices are those that oppose political lesbianism, seeing the politicisation of being a lesbian under hetero-patriarchal rule as 'appropriation'. They argue that if a woman once had relationships with men and, through a process of political consciousness, later found love and connections with women, her lesbianism is somehow less legitimate. The debates rage on, the attacks get voracious, and I retreat to my place of solitude where I think, read, expand the boundaries of my mind, while I sit in a vacuum of political peace.

In 2024, I journeyed from solitude to lesbian feminist community in a precious moment of needing connection. It was a rare experience. One I had not had for many, many years. I basked in the unspoken bonds of lesbian feminist connections and the desire to reach out in moments of rarity in shared unity.

But what struck me with overwhelming sadness was the feeling that this lesbian feminist community was under siege. Met in secret. Venue a secret until the last minute. Going underground like lesbians were forced to do in the 1950s so as to avoid lesbophobic attacks. And so it is today that our desire to be in lesbian-only communities provokes rage, hostility and backlash. Individual lesbians are threatened in their jobs, their lives, and, most of all, in their need for lesbian feminist spaces. I heard story after story of lesbian spaces being shut down, under attack, threatened by men who think (or pretend they think) they are lesbians and their 'queer' allies. Lesbian feminist spaces are under siege because defining lesbianism as exclusively female and rejecting male intrusion – however it is framed – is now seen as intolerable, in an era where personal and intimate boundaries are increasingly policed. Yet somehow small pockets of resistance remain. Underground, and under siege, but valued and fought for. I saw the look of hunger in the eyes of the lesbian feminists I met that day for a space they could call their own. Bigger than Virginia's room – a space where lesbian feminists could name their truths and exist in freedom, unrestrained by the calls of 'bigot' and 'transphobes' and the threat of protest and violence.

And so these hostilities block and control lesbian feminist spaces. Without a wider sense of community or movement, lesbian feminists may well retreat or choose conventional relationships. It is not for me. I mourn times gone by when how we could be free of the malestream occupied our collective thoughts and dreams. It was never about finding one woman through which to channel our hopes. It was always a bigger, politicised community where we could create alternative ways of living. But when those communities are dismantled or erased, it is as if they never existed – and future generations of women may never know how we fought for our own spaces to laugh, live and breathe. I cling to my politicised notion of what solitude is. I need it while also acknowledging the power of lesbian feminist communities and my unwavering bonds with them. I will wait in my space of solitude for them to multiply and diversify once more.

Opposition to political lesbianism shuts down these wider conversations and narrows being lesbian to an innate 'feeling', ignoring the impact of patriarchy on us all. I don't want to simulate a lesbian version of marriage and settle down with a good woman. I want to embrace my unconventionality. I want lesbian feminist communities to grow, be unafraid, and rise up against all opposition wherever it may come from.

And so, my version of solitude holds a political purpose. It keeps alive my lesbian feminist spirit; a place from which I can think, read, and reach out, tentatively, to others politicising the world as I do. In that solitude, I am not alone. It is a refuge until the hunger shared by other lesbian feminists ignites multiple community spaces that are filled with integrity, feminist values, and sisterly connections made in good faith. The more men tell us we can't create these spaces, and oppose them with violence, aggression and hostility, the more we will resist. And rise up.

References

Lorde, Audre. (2017). *A Burst of Light: And Other Essays.* New York: Dover Publications.

Rich, Adrienne. (1980). 'Compulsory heterosexuality and lesbian existence'. In *Signs: Journal of Women in Culture and Society*, Vol. 5, No. 4, pp. 631–660.

Sontag, Susan. (2012). *As Consciousness Is Harnessed to Flesh: Diaries 1964–1980* (David Rieff, ed.). New York: Farrar, Straus & Giroux.

Spender, Dale. (2024). *Women of Ideas: And What Men Have Done to Them.* London: Pandora.

Woolf, Virginia. (1996). *A Room of One's Own.* London: Vintage.

Woolf, Virginia. (1996). *Three Guineas.* London: Vintage.

The Door Behind the Wallpaper

Yana

I'm seven and I'm watching a comedy show. I want to be a comedian so I'm trying to understand what makes a good joke. Suddenly I hear the word 'virgin'. I have heard it hundreds of times before. Always the bottom of the joke, the virgin. Always said in the same context as sex, boobs, ass, wife, nag. And I realise: a virgin is someone who hasn't had sex. Obviously, I hadn't had sex, I didn't even know what sex was. Which means … virgin is me. Which means that sex boobs ass wife nag – is me. What is mocked, hated, disgusting, something that will never be me – is me. I realise that I will grow up and develop and each day that passes brings me closer to being all of these things. My vision darkens. The world around me is black. Inside me is a void, blunt pain. Static. Which means, I'm shocked. Virgin is me, virgin is me. I remain in a shocked state for several weeks. Detached, no joy, life passing by, jolting awake at five a.m., eyes wide. It passes eventually, but also doesn't. The shock is gone, but the knowledge isn't.

Same time, outside, hanging out with older girls and boys. An older boy says: "Go touch the boobs of that girl and I'll give you a cell phone!"

I'm five and I ask my mom what it means when someone says that a woman is pink or a man is blue. She says a pink woman is a woman who likes other women, the same with men. I don't know what it means to like someone.

I'm thirteen, we are in the park. It's late but I'm still in my school uniform because it's just too difficult to change clothes. I even sleep in it sometimes. One girl asks me if I want to be in her 'harem'. She asks me if I like girls. I don't know. At that point I only had the experience of liking boys I have never talked to.

I'm in my drama club. Break. Three of us. The new girl talks. And I don't care about people. Actually, they scare me and I hate them. I judge them, the way they look, the way they behave, they're ugly and stupid and just painful to be around. The new girl talks. In a matter of seconds, something happens. And I know it sounds corny but she becomes beautiful in a matter of seconds.

In the choir. Two rows of chairs for us, piano, our teacher. Break. They talk about *her*. They talk about the glowing angel with a shining halo from the sky. Nobody will ever talk about me. I don't even exist. I think that being talked about in a good way when I'm not around would make me the happiest person ever. It would mean … that I exist.

In the summer camp. Red, fire, sun. The girl with the head of fire-sun takes me out to the gazebo. She thinks that my weirdness is amusing. She tells me that I resemble a turtle and a giraffe at the same time. I make a stupid pun. She is the angel of fire.

I'm fifteen, in my room, with a lot of friends, we're talking, laughing. I'm saying all the right things, they laugh at my jokes, my crush admires me. Then I tell myself, listen, it's not real. The lights fade. I see the dark corners, the empty seats, the dirty orange sky.

Some dusty foot-wide dirt pavement. I know I will be forced to experience every single moment of the next three years. Going to school, being in school with the people I hate, going home, being home with the people I hate. I don't hate myself because I'm right and they're wrong. I enjoy making the teachers mad, showing that I don't care, that I don't respect them. They can punish me all they want because they cannot make my life worse. The thought of suicide does not occur, the thought of genocide does. But I know it's literally unbearable, banging head against concrete, screaming into the void, impossible to just *be*. I decide to put myself to sleep until I can be free.

Eighteen or nineteen. I officially date a male now. It feels like having an alien from *Alien* hatching in my chest. It feels like having soul cancer. It feels like rotting from inside. I act like it doesn't. It's what I always wanted, it's what I dreamed about all these years. I want him to fucking die or at least move as far away from me as possible due to unforeseen external circumstances. I was lucky that he learned enough liberal values not to rape or even nag for sex. But that came with the downside of him thinking that being depressed and not liking his life made him a woman. Soul cancer intensifies. You fucking never were a fucking woman. I act like I don't think so. He's smart and sincere and he wouldn't think that if it wasn't true. I once said to him: "I don't relate. I'm just a straight cis woman." After a couple of months we break up. He whines that sex is important and I'm still proud that I didn't give him any. Or even kissed him for that matter. Dumbass.

Watching YouTube I see a snippet of Ellen DeGeneres show. She's doing some move, dancing or something. She's in a suit with pants. I realise that it's the first time I see a woman on screen who is not dressed like her boobs and ass are the most important things about her. For the first time I see that they aren't shamefully hidden, or displayed, or playfully hinted at, or business-like hinted at, but just are. That they aren't detached, but a normal part of the whole. That a woman is whole, and just is, and has nothing to do with the magazine covers, advertisements and billboards; that she is human, and not a thing that consists of four sexy spheres and a mask.

Slowly dying in a ditch. I mean attending a university. I meet a feminist woman in my town. I've heard about political lesbianism once or twice before but I couldn't force myself to be aroused by random strangers' boobs and asses so I decided that it wasn't real.

I'm hard at work listening to the same phrases in English over and over, trying to turn them into text for further translation. I'm doing it because I hate the Russian language more than anyone else in the group. Sheila Jeffreys gives an interview about *Anticlimax*. It clashes with everything I think I know about reality. After listening to every phrase in the video for dozens of times I start to doubt what I think I know.

The pink-golden dusk of a million suns. The torn astral tether in stars connected again. Finding a door to the other world, hidden behind the old wallpaper. Just like I saw in dreams so many times. I see you, in the same plane of existence as me.

My Journey from lesbian to Lesbian

Anne Ehrlich

> I prefer to reserve the term *Lesbian* to describe women who are woman-identified, having rejected false loyalties to men on all levels. The terms *gay* or *female homosexual* more accurately describe women who, although they relate genitally to women, give their allegiance to men and male myths, ideologies, styles, practices, institutions, and professions.
>
> —Mary Daly, Gyn/Ecology, 1978, p. 26

My lesbianism hasn't always been what it is now. Even though I first fell for a girl when I was just 15, shared intimate moments with a female friend when I was 17, and came out in my early twenties – about 20 years ago – roughly only half of my open lesbian life has been shaped by a growing feminist understanding of my lesbian identity. I guess I was somewhat of the prototypical lesbian: a tomgirl who wanted her hair cut and her dresses exchanged for pants when she was only six years old, who only played with boys, who wasn't interested in any 'girly' activity but in running around, getting her clothes dirty, her elbows and knees scratched open. The girl who has been asked innumerable times if she was a boy or a girl and who later wondered if her mother might have been hiding an intersex condition from her, because she was really just not how girls were supposed to be – something, it felt, must be biologically wrong. The transition through my teenage years meant trying to fit in as best as I could – I gave in to my female friends' reminders to dress differently, to do my hair, to put on some make-up. The feminized version of myself got male approval, earned male courtship and ended with different trials on heterosexual relationships, the last and longest for four years. I am still grateful for him not pressuring me into being more feminine and for being nothing but kind. For most of my teenage/adolescence years, my longing for women had been half-anaesthetized, half-slumbering, half-awake, enough on the backseat to be ignored until I fell in love with a woman madly, but unilaterally. I knew that I couldn't go back to a heterosexual life, and I was so heartbroken that I had to come out to my friends and my mother. It took some time to heal and my first lesbian relationship until I came out to the rest of the world. A few weeks later I was thrown out of my favourite café by the same guy who had brought me coffee many times but who now didn't like that I was kissing a woman. What a warm welcome into the world of homosexuals. But no force in the world, I felt, could change the way I felt and lived now – I was happy, I was living in tune with myself. I didn't care what other people thought – because it felt right, end of story.

What seems like a true 'born-this-way' lesbian story, can also be seen as a story about how compulsory heterosexuality's tight grip is weakened when a girl is already set off to defy the roles and behaviors that are expected of her. A story instead about compulsory femininity – the pressure to be feminine, a story about how gendered roles and sexuality become inseparable around the teenage years when we all struggle to be part of a group. My pre-feminist self wouldn't know – and she wouldn't care. She would expect society to be okay with lesbians and that's it. She wouldn't understand the strength of her decision, the bravery even, she wouldn't feel proud but simply accepting of that little girl she was. She would still think that she is simply 'other', totally different from other women. She would still think that men are more fun, more interesting, more creative. She would still read men's books, listen to men's music. She would still think that sex work is work and that porn is totally fine, especially if it's queer porn. And she would still consume it – trying to navigate lesbian sexuality, struggling to find out what is her own. She would have no reluctance calling herself 'queer', feeling a heavy feeling when someone uses the word 'woman' in any given topic. 'Woman' – how alien that sounded. Mixed with feelings of making a Sunday roast beef for the husband and the two children, boy and girl, while putting on stockings and lipstick (which is weird because the women around me did not do this, so, hello society). She hadn't understood that being a woman and being a lesbian both have a political meaning in our world even though since childhood she thought that women should run the world because then there would be no wars and everyone would be happy. The split-mind of a girl/woman in patriarchy.

I know that this woman was me, and I do have a lot of empathy for her – and a lot of anger towards the society that purposefully hid all of that feminist knowledge from her. Knowing what I know now, I can see how different forces pulled, lured and dragged me through the course of my life – forces that wanted me to be how women should *be*, feminine, and love who women should *adore*, men. I can now see the strength, the resistance it took, to *not* cave in, or at least to not cave in for too long. To understand compulsory heterosexuality as a lesbian means to become aware of our own strength that lies in our decision to not cave in, to not be with men even though we might as well. The concept of compulsory heterosexuality has the potential to help women like me become women-identified and enable us to connect with women on many more levels than just romantically or sexually.

Born in the '80s, a child of the '90s, I spent my teenage years in post-socialist East-Germany, under the heavy influence of the capitalist west with its latest US-American pop songs and

Hollywood movies. We only had one well-known lesbian – and she was an anti-role-model, a parody of some kind. My music didn't have lesbians, my movies didn't have lesbians. Our school had one lesbian and she was an outcast. Luckily, my teenage magazine had lots of empathetic information about love and sexuality, so I knew, in theory, that homosexuality existed and it was supposed to be okay. Since I was born in a socialist country, the grown-up women around me were working, were divorced, didn't dress in the hypersexualized ways that capitalism requests of women. I have not yet understood how sexuality became such a central part of western culture, but the capitalization of female bodies – men making money through women – in pornography and prostitution surely must play a role in it. And it might be important in shaping society's views on lesbian women. To say it rather bluntly: loving women is not the same as fucking/having sex with women. As a lesbian feminist I feel connected to women on so many more levels than just the romantic or sexual.

When I was an adolescent woman, lesbianism was on one hand depathologized, but on the other hand depoliticized. It had no bigger meaning, but it also didn't mean that you were sick. We have experienced a strong shift in the last decade since lesbianism is now sexualized and mainly pornified. We have become the most searched porn category. It's easy to imagine that this plays its own role in the machine of comp het: it's yet another signal to women that they *cannot* escape male sexual aggression. You won't let us fuck you? We'll fuck you anyways. Some women have described how the pornification of lesbianism has led to the rejection of their own lesbianism ('If a lesbian is a porn category, I'm not it!'). If pornified lesbian sex acts is all we see – how can we identify with it, and why should we? Women in general seem to have become much more open to having sex with women – this might be a reaction to seeing supposedly 'lesbian' porn on porn websites, that women visit more and more. Since in porn women learn what men want from them sexually, they might as well learn that they can or should have sex with women as well. This seeming sexual 'openness', at least judging from what I saw on OK Cupid in Germany's capital (Try BDSM! Try kink! Try lesbian sex acts!), stands in stark contrast to the women falling in love with women during the western feminist movements in the '70s and '80s. Something so common, that there was a name for those women in Germany: Bewegungslesbe, meaning 'movement lesbian' – a woman who came to lesbianism, to loving women, through the feminist movement (to differentiate between them and the 'Urlesbe', meaning always-have-been lesbian). Even though I have no proof of it, we might as well have the 'porn lesbians' now – women who find interest in sleeping with women through porn. While others reject lesbianism because it is represented in porn as a male sexual fantasy.

I have heard lesbians say that they are annoyed by the emphasis on 'love' when lesbianism is really about sex – as in: who do you sleep with? I have witnessed debates on political lesbianism where one side overemphasises the connectedness between women and minimizes everything that is erotic/sexual, almost leaving sex out of the lesbian identity, while the other side claims that the only thing that matters in defining a lesbian is who you sleep with, putting sex/genital attraction at the center of lesbian identity, minimizing the political potential of woman-loving. The Political Potential of Woman-Loving. We might as well capitalize it as Mary Daly capitalized Lesbian "when the word is used in its woman-identified (correct) sense" (1978, p. 25) – which is an important differentiation to make.

When I look back on my pre-feminist self, even though I lived a lesbian life, I don't think I was a big help to women. I remember encounters and positions I am less than proud of, and I remember that as a lesbian I had a weird inner distance to the struggles women who lived with men were facing. Your boyfriend watches porn? Why judge him? It was almost like I wasn't part of the group 'women', I was only part of the group 'lesbians'. Since I was not a 'normal' girl or woman, 'normal' girls and women were alien to me, while 'normal' boys and men were my tribe – I just 'knew' them better after spending my whole life in close proximity with them. So no wonder that I loved consuming their music, their art, their books and no wonder then, that I had zero problems relating to them, understanding their perspective. In a very non-sexual, non-romantic way, you might as well say that I loved men, lesbian-style. Sometimes this still wants to get in my way, but I won't let it. I have turned off the male entertainment machine. I won't read their books and only rarely listen to their music. I refuse to identify with them. My deprogramming is an ongoing journey. I'm turning up the volume of female voices, whether I agree or disagree with them. I want to hear our stories, our thoughts, our pain, for I have learned that I am neither different nor separate from other women, whether they live a heterosexual life or not. I know that in a different time, a different place I could have been among them, having less fortunate circumstances, making it more difficult to live a lesbian life, maybe needing an amount of courage that I do not have. I am a very social creature but I can also be very hard headed, so who knows which side would have won under different circumstances: the need to fit in or the need to express myself no matter what.

When Adrienne Rich wrote her revolutionary text 'Compulsory Heterosexuality and Lesbian Existence' in 1980, society was a bit different. So, to look at the forms of comp het that apply today, 45 years later, seems useful. At a feminist camp where we did a lesbian-only consciousness raising group on compulsory heterosexuality, women – all under 40 – described that heterosexuality had been enforced in their personal lives in different ways. Some of these forces are patriarchal classics: the dependence on men, femininity, religion, male sexual violence or the pressure to do PIV (penis-in-vagina intercourse) but also by leaving us without words for what we feel. Other mechanisms were also not too new: the invisibility of lesbians or the bullying of out and visible lesbians, as well as the portrayal of lesbians as predatory. But some ways were rather recent male inventions: through the predominantly male view of lesbianism as something only to consume in porn and, especially crafty, through the now-common ideological pressure to accept men in lesbian spaces with the logical conclusion that we should also accept them in our lesbian beds. All of the pressures we discussed directed us towards a heterosexual form of life, much like Rich had explained it so many years ago.

What is different now is that the ideology of queer theory plays a sad role in (ab)using lesbians politically: just as the boundaries of women in general are routinely questioned under patriarchal rule, the sexual boundaries of lesbians are now questioned quite creatively – unfortunately with the help of our own lesbian sisters who politically insist that male lesbians exist. A linguistic trick that blurs who we are and how we define what we want. My lesbian sisters soaked in male ideology, forming allegiances with men, to the detriment of women. Maybe like me, like my old lesbian self, they have forgotten that during the past 5000 years of male rule that they, too, are women, that women deserve dignity, that the male view does not benefit us, that diluting women's sexual boundaries through ideological or emotional pressure only serves to ensure male access to women and ... that there is a woman-identified world out there which is – our home.

References

Daly, Mary. (1978). *Gyn/Ecology. The Metaethics of Radical Feminism*. Boston: Beacon Press.

Rich, Adrienne. (1980). 'Compulsory Heterosexuality and Lesbian Existence'. In *Signs*, Vol. 5, No. 4, Women: Sex and Sexuality, pp. 631–660.

Born That Way

Ann E. Menasche

It's just like a woman
To have a change of mind
To change her hair, her clothes, her furniture,
The way her heart's inclined
Change the way she's living
Add some getting to all that giving
It's a miracle but it's just like a woman.

—From song by Alix Dobkin, 1980

A Bit of My Herstory

If I was born anything (besides female of Sephardic Jewish heritage), I was born a feminist. My feminist instincts go way back to early childhood and frankly, there is nothing more intractable about me.

Of course, I don't literally believe I have a gene for feminism – my belief in the equality and dignity of women – any more than I have a gene for lesbianism – my passionate love and commitment to other women as sexual partners and life companions. Both are intertwined in my life, roots growing out of the same tree.

I first learned my feminism on my mother's knee, she, a smart gutsy tomboyish woman who resented her dependency on my father and subordinate status. She did her own gardening, not terribly 'feminine' work in those days. In the stultifying atmosphere of the 1950s and 1960s, she grasped whatever independence that she could, returning to college, becoming a teacher, earning her own money, and raising three daughters to follow their dreams.

Yet I didn't always believe my mother – that I was really okay and that being female didn't have to limit me. I saw how it constricted her own life. I cried when I first had my period and thought about 'sex change' after reading about Christine Jorgensen. I would have been a sitting duck for transgenderism if I was growing up now. I could have been easily swallowed up in female self-hatred *had it not been for my good fortune of coming of age during the rise of Second Wave feminism*. I wasn't weird or crazy after all. We were reaching our hands out to each other, truth-telling -consciousness raising – organizing, marching together, hundreds of thousands of us, in a revolt against the rule of men over women. That movement, aiming to do nothing less than change the world, turned my own life upside down, as it did so many other women.

But what has this to do with lesbianism? Plenty! Social context is everything, or almost everything.

Biologically, human sexuality is not solely about reproduction but also about bonding. We are highly social animals. Our closest relatives, the Bonobo chimps, who like humans walk upright and do not go through estrus, engage in virtually universal same sex behavior, *especially* the females.

No, I don't believe we are born with a blank slate either. A smattering of our ancestors' blood and bones, their DNA, perhaps their very memories, are in us. We are born with distinct personalities, certainly. Those personalities may tend to varying degrees to fit in or not fit into 'feminine' stereotypes. Mine wasn't a great fit. There is a documented correlation between pronounced gender non-conformity in childhood and homosexuality as an adult. But since 'femininity' is ultimately about the behavioral traits required of a subordinate, no woman really 'fits in'.

I recently learned that I come from a long line of rabbis. Is this why I wanted to be a rabbi as a child (not yet possible for a girl), and I later gravitated to the law that was just opening up for women? Rabbis in those days also argued and interpreted law; the thinking process is strikingly similar.

Do I also hold a genetic memory of the era before patriarchy? Do other women? I believe there was such a time.

Alas, there are no lesbians in my family tree, at least that can be recognized as such. Lesbianism as understood as a women-centered life involving sexual and romantic love between women, becomes impossible in the absence of the ability to support oneself independent of men. Female independence was exceedingly rare in the Sephardic orthodox Jewish communities of the Ottoman empire. Such highly patriarchal societies had strong prohibitions against male homosexuality. But since women weren't full persons and had no options to escape marriage to a man, what women might do wasn't taken as seriously.

My female ancestors were married off to men at young ages, had many children, and some died in childbirth. They had virtually no possibility of an independent life.

There is a famous Sephardic woman in the sixteenth century, Garcia Mendes Nasi, who broke that mold. She was from a very wealthy family, a Crypto Jew who was highly literate, and was married off to her maternal uncle. After her husband died, she became a famous businesswoman and philanthropist, helping to save Jews from the Inquisition. Her one daughter, whose husband died early, became a book publisher. Neither mother nor daughter remarried (Brooks, 2002). Were they lesbians? Who knows?

My maternal grandmother was extremely close to her women friends. As a small child, I saw the warmth and affection with which she related to them, which I never saw in her relationship with my grandfather. But whatever women may have felt in their hearts, or that there may have been some that engaged in occasional same sex behavior (Maimonides in twelfth century Spain warned husbands about their wives engaging in such elicit acts) there was no possibility of women making their lives together. My ancestors thus left virtually no trace of lesbianism.

I grew up not knowing what lesbians were or knowing any that I was aware of. The lesbians of the 1950s and early '60s, though there were a lot of them, were deeply underground. I had crushes on boys as I was supposed to. My burgeoning adolescent sexuality had to go somewhere, and that was where it was supposed to be directed. Indeed, having a boyfriend was a badge of respectability and acceptance for a girl, a necessary part of becoming a woman. I was without this 'prize' for most of high school and felt the stigma. The boys didn't consider me dating material because I refused to hide my intelligence. A few admitted as much when they signed my yearbook.

I also had crushes on girls in school and on female movie stars but didn't recognize their sexual element. I merely 'admired them' *a lot*. In college, as soon as I had a name for these feelings, they mushroomed. I had an intensely romantic relationship with a girlfriend, but we did no more than hug. I still had difficulty labelling these feelings as sexual. Meanwhile, I was deeply dissatisfied in my one heterosexual relationship. I could no longer tolerate the sexism. Soon, nothing was more exciting and important to me than my relationships with other women and the new world we were creating. This had everything to do with feminism all around me.

In law school, far from my boyfriend and parents, in the hotbed of feminist activism and lesbian culture in San Francisco, I made my first lesbian friend. She took me to my first lesbian bar and gifted me with an album from Alix Dobkin, *Lavender Jane Loves Women.*

Could I be a lesbian, I asked myself? Was it even possible? Alix sang, "Any woman can be a lesbian." Seeing women leave husbands and boyfriends and come out in droves all around me, I believed her. I jumped in with both feet, mind, body and spirit, and never looked back. I was 24 years old, half a century ago. There was an equality and mutuality in my intimate relationships with women that drew me and continues to keep me in this place. And, yes, plenty of passion.

Not that my lovers were saints – they weren't. Still, it was a homecoming. I remember a poem I wrote to my first lover that ended, "I found my lost powers in your strong sisterly arms." In the arms of another woman, I could be a whole human being.

But am I a 'real lesbian'? Some lesbians nowadays have accused me of being a fraud, a 'political lesbian', claiming that anyone who ever felt an inkling of heterosexual feelings is at most bisexual, or some acronym I can't remember, that it is not possible for sexuality to change, that feminism has nothing to do with lesbianism, and who would ever choose to be a lesbian anyway? That I have been with my current partner for 35 years was irrelevant, according to these women. I simply was lacking the distinct genes and/or brain required to be a lesbian.

This idea that virtually all women except a tiny minority who were 'born that way', can't possibly be or become lesbians is one way to ensure that no one ventures outside of heterosexual expectations. It is how the institution of compulsory heterosexuality, a bulwark of male supremacy, defines lesbianism out of existence for most women. It ties women to one-to-one relationships with members of the oppressor sex class, ensuring male access to our bodies and reproductive labor, or else confines women to a life without sexual intimacy.

Moreover, that position would have been laughed at in the vibrant lesbian community of the late 1970s. We virtually all believed that sexuality was socially constructed, whether we were life-long 'gold star' lesbians or not, and that being a lesbian was a wonderful choice that any woman could make. We all celebrated the nascent feminist rebellion involved in choosing women as lovers and life companions. We were proud of being lesbians and wouldn't have it any other way. Yes, we paid a big price for our difference, including stigma and ostracism from family and society, but it was worth it.

It is not surprising we felt that way. Though we were only in the early stages of the struggle for lesbian/gay civil rights with few legal protections, our community and movement were huge sources of support. There were women's bars, lesbian music celebrating love between women, feminist concerts, bookstores, newspapers, presses, coffee houses, lesbian hiking groups, lesbian theatre groups, music festivals – each weekend there were several activities to choose from. And our movement for women's liberation was growing. The end of patriarchy was near. We could feel it in our bones. No wonder there were more lesbians at that time and place than before or since.

Anti-Feminist Backlash and Resurgence of the Heterosexual Institution

But hard times returned, the radicalism of the 1960s and '70s receded, and the pressure to conform to the heterosexual norm and to secure male, familial and societal approval grew. Though subtle at first, these pressures as well as increasing economic insecurity, began to erode lesbian community. In the United States, the beginnings of the anti-feminist backlash, which has only deepened since then, was well-documented in Susan Faludi's book, *Backlash* (1991). However, it was marked a decade earlier by the apparent defeat of the Equal Rights Amendment when the deadline for ratification expired. The demoralization that set in among feminists was palpable.

Soon, my own personal life was negatively affected. I had been blessed with supportive parents, and I was self-employed, so I didn't experience the usual pressure to conform from family and employers. Rather, my partner of three years decided to leave our relationship and return to an old boyfriend who boasted, "I'm the man in her life, I'm it."

It wasn't just mourning the loss of this partner. I noticed that she was not the only one doing so. The lesbian community was shrinking before my eyes, which caused a panic to set in, that I might end up being alone, without partner or community, that women would always choose men over me.

I needed to understand why this was happening. So, I began a six-year long project of researching and writing a book on 'ex-lesbians'. That book was called, *Leaving the Life: Lesbians, Ex-Lesbians and the Heterosexual Imperative* (Menasche, 1999; out of print but occasionally you can find a used copy online).

I hoped to expand on Adrienne Rich's 1980 essay 'Compulsory Heterosexuality and Lesbian Existence' which analyzed hetero-sexuality as a political institution that crushes, invalidates, and forces into hiding love between women. Was my instinct correct, that decades after Stonewall, many of us were still not free to love other women, though this was where our minds, passions and politics led?

To get answers, I surveyed 64 'ex-lesbians' ('lesbians who left') and 147 lesbians who shared their stories through completing a questionnaire. I interviewed a number of these women.

The ex-lesbians waxed nostalgic about their former lesbian lives and showed considerable ambivalence about their current relationships with men. As one woman wrote, "Many times I wished Ed was a woman (and sometimes he wishes he was one too). This has not been easy for me."

They also revealed how much societal and familial pressures, social isolation, and internalized sexism and homophobia influenced their choices to engage in heterosexual relationship again, or sometimes for the first time.

One ex-lesbian described her lesbian life as both "very exciting" and "very scary." Why was it scary? "Because I was doing something that most of society really disapproved of and really misunderstood."

Another 'ex-lesbian' told me, "I remember that I went on a date with a man ... and I really liked feeling normal ... it's just harder to be in the world not following the program." Her mother was "excited" about her return to heterosexuality. "I was glad that what I was doing was helping her feel happy instead of contributing to her feeling awful." She said heterosexual attraction played *no role* in her decision to leave a lesbian life.

This surprising response was typical of the 'ex-lesbians' I surveyed. Only 28% listed falling in love with a man or heterosexual attraction as even one reason for their change; a mere 4% gave this as the only reason. Instead, or in addition, they listed a desire to fit in with society (48%), difficulty finding a satisfactory long-term woman love (42%); lack of role models for successful lesbian relationships (32%), or a desire to obtain family approval (24%), to avoid job discrimination (20%); or for economic security (14%).

The lesbians and 'ex-lesbians' I surveyed differed in several ways. The ex-lesbians had less family acceptance; were more likely to believe lesbophobic myths such as 'most lesbians hate men' and that traumatic experiences with men 'causes' lesbianism; more likely to have doubts about raising children in a lesbian household; more likely to feel uncomfortable around women who are overtly lesbian; and more likely to have difficulty saying no to men when they didn't want sex, and to believe they needed a man for protection and validation. In other words, they had less support as lesbians, were more likely to internalize anti-lesbian prejudices and were less assertive and independent as women compared to the lesbians.

I also interviewed lesbians who had left a lesbian life to return years or decades later ('lesbians who returned'). Many of these women had struggled with religious guilt over their lesbianism.

One Protestant lesbian described feeling "very guilty" after her first lesbian sexual experience. "And that was related to religious messages I was getting. When it first happened, I had to be hospitalized – I became comatose … I just didn't see how I could go on with life." She later married a man "in order to fit in" and because she was "damn tired" of being alone. However, she was excommunicated from her church for refusing to have sex with her husband and returned to a lesbian life.

Are We Free Yet?

In the decades that have passed since then, lesbians and gay men in the United States have won civil rights laws (though we still lack a federal gay rights statute). We have won marriage equality and employment protections through Supreme Court decisions. There is a greater level of tolerance than in the past. No one grows up, as I did, not knowing there is such a thing as a lesbian.

But they are still likely not to know any lesbians. The lesbian culture and community have been virtually destroyed, by the dual forces of the growing religious Right, and sex-denying transactivists. The status of women as a sex continues to be pushed back. The prejudice and stigma against a lesbian life remains deep and pervasive.

Yes, you can marry another woman but good luck finding any prospects.

Virtually everyone (except the hardcore religious right) believes in 'born that way' ideology – not only that sexual orientation is fixed at birth but that some people are 'born in the wrong body'. Girls and young women who don't fit into sex stereotypes or recognize same sex feelings are being convinced that they are really 'men' or 'non-binary' – they can't possibly be women. Most potential role models have 'transitioned'. Few young lesbians can escape unscathed, without at least a period of embracing trans identities, often causing permanent harms to their bodies and mental health.

So, was I born that way? Yes, I was born female. That's all the physical attributes one needs to be a lesbian. Nothing more. But to survive, we lesbians need women's liberation. Without freeing our sex, we lesbians will always be isolated islands with most of us disappeared just below the horizon.

References

Brooks, Andree Aelion. (2002). *The Woman Who Defied Kings, The Life and Times of Dona Garcia Nasi*. St Paul, MN: Paragon House, 2002.

Dobkin, Alix. (1973). *Lavender Jane Loves Woman*. New York: Women's Wax Works.

Dobkin, Alix. (1980). 'Just Like a Woman', in album XX. New York: Women's Wax Works

Faludi, Susan. (1991). *Backlash: The Undeclared War Against American Women*. New York: Crown Publishing Group.

Menasche, Ann E. (1999). *Leaving the Life: Lesbians, Ex-Lesbians and the Heterosexual Imperative*. London, Onlywomen Press.

Rich, Adrienne. (1980). 'Compulsory Heterosexuality and Lesbian Existence', In *Signs*, Vol. 5, No. 4, Women: Sex and Sexuality, pp. 631–660.

A Return to Lesbianism: This Time It's Political

Michelle Kerwin

When I found radical feminism in my 30s, I consumed as much theory as I possibly could. I listened to hours of podcasts, watched YouTube videos of first- and second-wave sisters, and discovered lesbian feminists. I had no idea that women like this existed. I became involved in radical feminist groups and grassroots activism. In 2018 I joined FiLiA as a volunteer. I was in a relationship with a man 'sleeping with the enemy', which was a conflict I felt heavily. My consciousness was being raised by decades' worth of feminist analysis. I began to deconstruct heterosexuality and understand this as a patriarchal mechanism to control and oppress women.

I came out as a lesbian for the first time around age 19, then went back in the closet again. I had no real understanding of why I had gone back to heterosexuality in my late 20s, beyond the usual rhetoric of 'lesbianism is a phase, everyone experiments when they are young.' I began to wonder why I had lost that lesbian label, and could I ever claim it again as my own? Could I escape compulsory heterosexuality? Was political lesbianism the way forward?

My experience of compulsory heterosexuality and sexuality within a patriarchal world began at an early age, as it does for all women, though we are mostly unaware of it. Many women remain in (somewhat blissful) ignorance throughout their lives. Thanks to feminism, some of us, like me, choose to leave heterosexuality behind.

As Dworkin (1976) wrote, "Many women, I think, resist feminism because it is an agony to be fully conscious of the brutal misogyny which permeates culture, society, and all personal relationships." I would extend this to say that many women in heterosexual relationships do not want to connect their own life experiences to an analysis of compulsory heterosexuality, because it is too painful – not only to understand the theory of compulsory heterosexuality, but to actually confront it and recognise it throughout all of their life experiences.

Once I saw it, I couldn't unsee it and was suddenly exposed to all of these huge, raw emotions causing physical and mental agony. It felt to me as though I had been conditioned to enjoy pain inflicted by men, coerced into situations that forced me to participate in my own abuse, to go along with the heteronormative life that women are trained for. I drew comparisons with the way the armed forces break soldiers down mentally, only to build them up in a way that they follow orders without question.

I was raised in poverty on a council estate in the early '80s, and at this time, homophobia was rife. During the AIDS pandemic, there were horrifying TV adverts in the UK as part of the 'AIDS: Don't Die of Ignorance' campaign. These adverts depicted gravestones with voiceovers talking about a deadly disease that affected gay men. Leaflets were sent to every household, not only terrifying a generation but giving the public reasons to be openly homophobic.

I grew up under Section 28, a clause in the Local Government Act of 1988 that prohibited local authorities from promoting homosexuality. It was repealed in 2001 and 2003. During her speech at the Conservative Party Conference on 9 October 1987 Margaret Thatcher said, "Children who need to be taught to respect traditional moral values are being taught they have an inalienable right to be gay. All of those children are being cheated out of a sound start in life." This speech contributed to the political climate that led to the introduction of Section 28. This clause gave permission for people to openly say being gay or lesbian was perverse and abnormal. Akin to having Donald Trump in power in 2024 and men freely saying things like 'your body, my choice'. Men would make comments about lesbians such as 'she just needs a good shag, she's not had the right dick yet'. Section 28 also meant that in school, we were only taught about heterosexual couples in sex education, reinforcing the idea of heterosexuality as the sole option.

As a child in the early '80s, all I wanted for Christmas was a Liverpool FC kit and a Mr Frosty machine. Instead, I was presented with baby dolls, every single year. In reception class, we would play house; 'mummy' would stay in the playhouse holding the baby and pretending to cook while 'daddy' went out to work. Teachers encouraged this kind of play. I was being conditioned to believe marriage to a man and motherhood were the only way forward for a working-class girl like me.

During my teenage years, I was expected to look after my infant niece and nephew, getting up during the night at weekends to help give bottle feeds, change nappies – because one day it would be my turn to raise children. I often had comments from family members like, "It suits you having a baby on the hip."

In my Catholic high school in the early '90s, girls weren't allowed to wear trousers! So unfeminine, so not what god wanted. I would constantly be asked, "Have you got a boyfriend yet?" And in the same breath I was told not to get myself pregnant. I didn't care about boys, or relationships of any kind. I cared about science, music and football. Yet I would write my name in a heart with some boy's name all over my school books, decorating my bedroom with posters of male pop stars, because it was the expectation.

There was never any suggestion that there could be a different option to heterosexuality. Somewhere along the way I had read *Tipping the Velvet* by Sarah Waters, a seductive story of lesbian love set in Victorian England. I remember thinking that sounded much better than the hell of men and babies. During my teen years I kissed a couple of girls, all very secretly and with a bit of shame. But due to compulsory heterosexuality, religion, growing up in poverty and the pressure to get a job, have babies and make a home for a man, lesbianism seemed like a fantasy life and any thoughts of women were put away in a box. It was very clear to me that I did not want the trad wife and kids' life and certainly not with a bloke who was going to damage me and eventually abandon me. I also knew this wasn't something to be vocal about. I had to internalise all of that.

I was raped by an older man at age 14. He had bought alcohol and cannabis for me and my friend and allowed us to use his flat to hang out. In my mind, I had said yes, so that meant I had consented. It took me until my 30s and finding feminism before I recognised what had happened as child rape. A few years later, I started to go out clubbing and would go home with random blokes, having what I perceived to be consensual sex. This was right in the middle of '90s ladette culture and Spice Girls-influenced feminism. We were being sold the idea that women can and should have casual sex the same as men, with no thought or feelings.

I now view those experiences as rape, because I was groomed into heterosexuality, and being raped at such a young age reinforced heterosexuality. All subsequent sex with men felt very similar. It was not casual and consensual sex, even though I had said yes. I wasn't fully informed of my choices, therefore it was never true consent. I can see now it was me attempting to control the way men used my body, trying to avoid the violence by being compliant to their wants – the good girl behaviour that I had been trained into.

As an older teen and with the introduction of home internet, I found some online spaces and began to talk to other girls, and eventually met one to go on a date with. I began to think of myself as a lesbian, and wanted to reject men entirely from my romantic life.

One night I had several whiskeys and plucked up the courage to tell my mother, who turned out to be my first lesbophobic bully. She told me I was dirty and disgusting and I had to leave immediately. I was full of trauma and confusion about life. She insisted it was "just a phase" and didn't speak to me for many years.

Where I lived at that time there was one pub that once a month held a LGB night. It was advertised as a 'private party' and I felt a mix of excitement and shame to be in attendance, like loving women was shameful and something to be hidden from sight.

I made the decision to move to Manchester as I had heard it was a wonderful place to be gay! And perhaps it is for men … I regularly visited Canal Street and a lesbian bar, which should have been fucking wonderful! Except the lesbians in this bar where treating women like men did, objectifying women, emulating Shane from the L word and her treatment of women as disposable and to be used for sexual gratification. The bar would regularly hold traffic light parties, where you would wear a green, amber or red wristband depending on how available for sex you were.

I felt uncomfortable in this place, the constant judgement based on my appearance. I felt uncomfortable being a lesbian; I could not understand why women would treat other women the same way men did. I was labelled a 'lipstick lesbian' despite never wearing lipstick – but I did occasionally wear dresses and had long hair. I played the part of a femme, despite being confused by the butch/femme pairings that seemed to be required. I questioned what was the point in being a lesbian if I was expected to conform to heterosexual relationship standards.

After a year in Manchester, I met my first girlfriend. We were together for a couple of years. We were often followed out of Canal Street by men offering us money to watch us in bed together or asking for a threesome. She upped and left one day leaving me heartbroken. At this point I gave up on love and relationships entirely.

The grooming into heterosexuality, and the shame that had come with labelling myself a lesbian, led me back to a heteronormative lifestyle. I was working in the NHS at the time, in a highly traumatic role, surrounded by misogyny and constant sexual harassment. I was being fucked by men I worked with and men I met online, all of whom treated me as a masturbatory aid. To re-enact the violent porn they were consuming, they would strangle me, spit on me, degrade me verbally. All the while I was telling myself it was what I wanted. Like the rape in my teens, it took me years to identify these men as my rapists too. A man I had met online said to me, "You shouldn't let strange men into your house. Anything could happen." I laughed the comment off, but of course I complied with what he wanted to use my body for, out of fear he was going to kill me. If you say yes because you are terrified to say no – this is not consent. I couldn't see this at the time; I felt I was playing men at their own game. Yet, every time a woman has sex with a man, she is risking her life.

We are gaslighted as women from such an early age to accept male power over us sexually, to the extent we truly believe we enjoy the BDSM aspect, even when they draw blood and leave marks on our bodies. I was a liberal feminist during this period in my life – 'love is love', 'don't kink shame', 'what is the harm if no one is getting hurt?' I would ask. Yet I was getting hurt, physically and mentally damaged repeatedly. Through radical feminist analysis, I learnt how violent sex creates and reinforces a trauma bond with men, and that explains to me why I kept saying yes to the violence.

The combination of the sexual violence and the traumatic experiences I was exposed to in the NHS, both from the sexual harassment and exposure to verbal and physical abuse, all led to a diagnosis of borderline personality disorder, and I was then put on various medications by psychiatric doctors.

Radical feminist analysis helps women to deconstruct beauty standards imposed on us by patriarchy. I spent my late teens and twenties performing femininity, trying to be slim, wearing a push-up bra, shaving my legs, styling my hair. Through consciousness raising I had the realisation that wanting to be attractive to men did not mean I was attracted TO them – this was an absolute lightbulb moment for me. By this point, I had already been rejecting the malestream beauty standards for a good few years. In fact, it was one of the things the psychiatric doctors recorded in my notes: "poor basic hygiene, patient has not shaved legs."

In 2021, I volunteered at the FiLiA conference in Portsmouth. I walked away from Portsmouth determined my life would change and become my own. As Adrienne Rich wrote, "Change is not a threat to your life but an invitation to live." When I arrived home from Portsmouth, I almost instantly stopped taking the medication. I could finally see that BPD was equivalent to the hysteria diagnosis doctors had given women for centuries. After dropping the medication, I dumped the man, and made the decision that there would never be another man again.

For a while, I didn't mention my sexuality at all. The word lesbian held such negative connotations to me evoked from the disgust it caused my mother, alongside the sexualised view of lesbianism from the porn sick men I had been with. I had also seen ex-straight women being bullied online for not being 'gold star lesbian'. Women calling themselves gold star believe they are born lesbian, yet sexuality is not innate, we are not born gay or straight. I was more than a little wary of that happening to me too.

I have been told by some women that I shouldn't call myself a lesbian because I have had sexual relationships with men in the past. They have asked, "Why not call yourself bisexual?" I would counter that with "Would there be bisexuality if women weren't oppressed by patriarchy and forced into heterosexuality?" Then like a fire had been lit in me, I stood up and claimed political lesbianism.

Lesbianism has been a non-linear journey for me. I was not 'born this way', the decision to be a lesbian is closely tied to the radical feminist theory of political lesbianism. It was a conscious decision made after much internal fighting. It was not an easy process, and at times was extremely painful to dismantle every sexual experience I ever had.

For me being a political lesbian means to centre women, to love women romantically and sexually, and to provide other women with the space and time to find a way through enforced heterosexuality. One particular quote that resonates with me is from Adrienne Rich: "The lesbian existence is not an 'alternative' to heterosexuality, but a means of resisting compulsory heterosexuality." ('Compulsory Heterosexuality and Lesbian Existence', 1980).

I do wonder what my life would be if I had found radical feminism earlier, if I'd had older lesbians in my life as a teenager. I feel a lot of anger at the fact that I experienced compulsory heterosexuality, and grief for the life I could have had earlier. I am grateful to feminists for helping me through it, and I feel lucky to have met my incredible girlfriend who supports me, encourages me and makes me laugh every single day.

References

Donegan, Moira. (13 November 2024). 'Your body, my choice: MAGA men'. *The Guardian.* <https://www.theguardian.com/commentisfree/2024/nov/13/your-body-my-choice-maga-men>.

Dworkin, Andrea. (1976). *Our Blood: Prophecies and Discourses on Sexual Politics*. London: The Women's Press.

Rich, Adrienne. (1980). 'Compulsory Heterosexuality and Lesbian Existence'. In *Signs*, Vol. 5, No. 4, Women: Sex and Sexuality, pp. 631–660.

Thatcher, Margaret. (9 October 1987). Speech to Conservative Party Conference. <https://www.margaretthatcher.org/document/106941>.

I Wish I Was a Lesbian

Tabata Spinster

Any Woman Can Be a Lesbian – And It's Never Too Late[1]

Cris Walker

> First principle: I speak only for myself
>
> Second principle: I do not try to get other wimmin to accept my beliefs in place of their own
>
> Third principle: there is no 'given'
>
> —Joyce Trebilcot, 1988, 'Dyke Methods',
> *Hypatia*, Vol. 3, no 2, p. 1.

I am about to turn 60. For over 50 years, I thought heterosexuality was the only way of life for me. Then came the pandemic, and everything changed, including that.

2020 is when I woke up; I first opened my eyes to feminism, and then my heart to lesbianism. Anna Prats, a young lesbian I met online who would later become a dear friend and colleague, told me I could actually escape and *choose* to be a lesbian. I didn't hesitate for a second. It was immediate. She was right, it felt right, and made perfect sense.

It was a liberation, like a backpack full of stones had been taken off my back. I felt light, happy, free.

---

1 My title is inspired by Alix Dobkin's song 'View From Gay Head', 1973.

It was then time to remove the mindbindings, to tear down what had been my way of life until then, and to realize I had been lied to, brainwashed, swindled, deceived, abused, and coerced to serve and please a series of men who never deserved, much less reciprocated, all they received. "I was a perfect example of successful social conditioning into heterosexuality," says Cathy Avila in *NOW is the time, not the place* (Avila, 1990, p. 56). Yes. Me too.

Dismantle the structures that have sustained you for 54 years, and everything will tremble, everything will crack. And, as it gradually falls apart, you rebuild yourself, you recover, you re-member, and you return to your origins. In my origins, I had felt love and attraction for a very dear girlfriend. I believe life spirals, so what had been interrupted in pre-adolescence had remained almost intact in my guts. Try as they might to take it all, they never could. There was something very intimate, which I discovered decades later among the ruins and debris: my desire and love for women.

As Micheline Grimard-Leduc says in her wonderful *The Mind-Drifting Islands*:

> It has been such a long exile away from our island that when we get in touch with our lesbian identity, it is the same as reaching a longed-for country … I knew that I had come to my coherent self, mind, heart, body, all of them blending into one emotion. I felt I had reached the land I had been traveling towards, delayed by so many detours. At last, I was coming home! I even remember the physical feeling of landing on an island. There would be a lot to discover in this island, but there I was! The wandering had come to an end (Grimard-Leduc, 1988, p. 499).

And of course, there was still a lot to discover. With the help of many readings and conversations, I have gradually defined the woman I am today. Learning about the life stories of other women who at some point in their lives have chosen lesbianism (see, for example, Renate Klein and her splendid 'The Joy of Choosing to be a Lesbian' (2024. See her essay in this volume.) I am reaffirmed every day as a lesbian. I know there is a lot of controversy around political lesbianism. I know many feminists think (and will tell you) that you can't choose, that sexual orientations are innate – even if no one has discovered the famous gene so far. I've heard it several times: "I wish I liked women" or "I tried but it didn't work" or the definitive "I just really like men, what can I do?" I have also heard from 'born-this-way' lesbians that lesbianism is essential, innate. Either way, political lesbians are disregarded. I believe lesbianism is a choice, if anything else because I made it itself, but one thing I do know: heterosexuality is not.

My DHP[2]

I didn't choose heterosexuality. It was quite literally and forcibly imposed on me. For decades, I didn't even know that another way of life was possible, that I could choose to prioritise and love women rather than see them as competition in the struggle to find 'the ideal man' (like beauty, it is ideal because it doesn't exist). As a child growing up in a small Spanish town during Franco's dictatorship, and attending a catholic all-girls school, my models were the classic male/female relationship: in my family, in my family's circle of friends, later in my own friendships. The whole world was heterosexual and my destiny in life was to find a good husband and give him offspring. Growing up, my brothers would get 'Madelman' or 'Geyperman' for Christmas, scale little toys that replicated the action men they would eventually become. They also received toy cars for frantic racing that could and did run over the baby dolls I got, the prophetic gifts I was supposed to care for until

---

2   My dark heterosexual past, inspired by Uma Conti's words: *OPH: Mi oscuro pasado heterosexual.*

I produced my own creatures. And girl, did I do that. I remember fights with my eldest brother when he would behead my dolls or cut their hair (a clear attack on the prevailing femininity). So I progressively internalised what my role in the world was, what my future would be. When I was ordered to set the table while my brothers watched TV, I protested, I rebelled. I received answers like: "Don't talk back and obey." But no one gave me a good reason why I should do the housework while my siblings were exempted and allowed precious leisure time that I was denied. In my heart, this was an injustice, but I had no tools to fight it because what I was risking was precious: the love and approval of my mother and father. I had to please, I had to please everyone, I had to comply, smile and kiss when required. As much as I hated those impositions.

When I was 16, I was raped by one of my eldest brother's friends. Despite the violence he used, it took me more than 20 years to recognise it as a sexual assault. Forty years later, I read Janice Raymond in *A Passion for Friends*:

> Virginity, for example, is attractive to men because it presents the lure of untamed womanhood. More than this, virginity also signals a woman who still resides in the world of women … When a man deflowers a woman, he takes her out of the world of women while also depriving her of a future with and for women.

It all clicked. I read Jane Caputi's 'Take back what doesn't belong to me'. (2003, pp. 1–14). Click. I read Andrea Dworkin's *Pornography* (1981). Click. Click. Click.

Men had taken me out of my world, and enforced hetero-sexuality on me to ensure I would serve them all my life. They couldn't possibly know I would seek my way out eventually and go back. I didn't even know it myself until much later.

After two boyfriends, and shortly after finishing university, I got married, as I was supposed to, and became a mother at 23. I hadn't even considered the possibility of being a mother and I already had a baby in my arms. It didn't seem strange to me though; it was not so long ago that I had been looking after my baby dolls. Then came another child, a divorce, another relationship from which a third child was born, another separation. My body was a battlefield, battered by three pregnancies and three c-sections. And yet, I kept thinking that somewhere out there my Prince Charming was waiting for me.

For almost 20 years, I was what Marcela Lagarde called 'madresposa' (a portmanteau for mother and wife). I devoted myself to child-rearing and housework while first my husband, and then the father of my last child would go to work and have their own lives. I belonged in the private sphere: the house, the children, the family. It wasn't until I was 40 that I decided to enter the job market, with a CV that barely mentioned my studies and a sporadic job as a private English teacher. Between 2006 and 2020, I had about 20 different jobs, in which my body continued to be a battlefield. In 2020, I had my last paid job as a teacher of Spanish as a foreign language. A chronic illness took me out of the labour market for good, and largely out of the social life I had had until then.

And I Finally Woke Up

Fortunately, that was when feminism came into my life. I felt I had lost precious time, so I began reading everything I could, going from liberal feminism to separatism in a matter of weeks. It was also when I cleaned out my library and removed all the books written by men. Five years later, my shelves are overflowing with works written exclusively by women.

In 2021, I had my first contact with a consciousness-raising group, which continues to this day. That was crucial. In 2022, I met a woman who would be pivotal in my life. Uma Conti, through her project Hiladas: Escuela de Libertad Femenina introduced me to Carroll Smith-Rosenberg and The *Female World of Love and Ritual*, to the women who made *Sinister Wisdom*, to Sally Miller Gearhart and *The Wanderground*, to Elizabeth Gould Davis and *The First Sex*, and made me dive into Mary Daly and her whole Amazing Shimmering World. Within that community, I met two Mexican lesbians who would change my life for the better: Las Desobedientes, Marianella Villa and Liliana Papalotl, whose podcast I have listened to from episode one until now.

It cost me nothing to take my 'eyes off the guys', as Sonia Johnson recommended; to put men out of my thoughts, to stop giving them credit, to stop caring about their opinions or the way they acted or lived.

When I read Sheila Jeffreys in *Trigger Warning* saying,

> In my group, theory is developed out of experience. Ensure never to use a book or male system of thought; never assume a man can be helpful' and 'We do not use a single man's thought. We are feminists; we do not use men', everything came together again (Jeffreys, 2020, p. 135).

I had completed a Mister-ectomy, a wonderful concept conjured by Mary Daly in *Gyn/Ecology* (Daly, 1978, p. 239).

Living as a Lesbian

My main occupation since then has been reading and translating, listening, prioritising, talking and relating to women, especially lesbians. When I learned that lesbians had always been behind the Women's Liberation Movement, creating an extensive and very rich culture, I focused mainly on their texts: Adrienne Rich, Susan

Hawthorne, Sheila Jeffreys, Kate Millett, Andrea Dworkin, Mary Daly, Janice Raymond, Julia Penelope, Jeffner Allen, Bev Jo, among many others.

I have also translated some of their work into Spanish. Anthologies such as *For Lesbians Only* (1988) and *Finding the Lesbians* (1991) have been a turning point.

I have observed that lesbian culture is almost invisible: most of the theory is not translated, books are out of print and/or sold for next to nothing, or lesbian authors find it difficult to publish. That's why I translate. I want those voices to reach more women. I want to contribute to lesbian culture.

I define my position in the world as a radical lesbian existence, which I understand as feminism, put into practice by my conscious exercise of separatism as much as I can.

For the past few years, I have been running an online feminist consciousness-raising group with my friend and colleague Ana María Iborra, via Zoom. I participate in activities organised exclusively by and for women; if they accept men or there are mixed spaces, I don't participate. Ninety-nine per cent of the people I relate to are women. And of these women, more and more are lesbians. I participate in the creation of women-only, sometimes lesbian-only networks or spaces. I put women in contact with each other. I facilitate meetings among women, I help when needed. I only read women. I listen to music made by female singers; I go to female artists' exhibitions. When it comes to films or TV series, I prioritise those directed by or starring women.

I like women. I love women. I am a woman.

We women are the best thing going. We are warm and passionate; we cry, and we live! Let's celebrate.
—Margaret Sloan-Hunter

I am a woman.
I am a lesbian.
I live.
I celebrate.

References

African American Registry. (2025). *Margaret Sloan-Hunter, Black Feminist & Publisher*. African American Registry. <https://aaregistry.org/story/margaret-sloan-hunter-born/>.

Avila, Cathy. (1990). *NOW is the time, not the place*. In Penelope, Julia, and Sarah Valentine. (1990). *Finding the Lesbians: Personal Accounts from Around the World*. Crossing Press Freedom, CA, p. 56.

Caputi, Jane. (2003) 'Take Back What Doesn't Belong to Me': Sexual Violence, Resistance and the 'Transmission of Affect'. *Women's Studies International Forum* Vol. 26, Issue 1, January–February 2003, pp. 1–14.

Daly, Mary. (1978). *Gyn/Ecology: The Metaethics of Radical Feminism*. London: The Women's Press Ltd.

Dobkin, Alix. (1973). *View From Gay Head*. On: *Lavender Jane Loves Women* [LP]. New York: Women's Wax Works.

Dworkin, Andrea. (1981). *Pornography: Men Possessing Women*. London: The Women's Press Ltd.

Gould Davis, Elizabeth. (1972). *The First Sex*. New York, NY: Penguin Books.

Grimard-Leduc, Micheline. (1988). 'Mind-Drifting Islands'. In Hoagland, Sarah Lucia, and Julia Penelope. (1988). *For Lesbians Only: A Separatist Anthology*. London: Onlywomen Press, pp. 489–500.

Hoagland, Sarah Lucia, and Julia Penelope. (1988). *For Lesbians Only: A Separatist Anthology*. London: Onlywomen Press.

Jeffreys, Sheila. (2020). *Trigger Warning: My Lesbian Feminist Life*. Mission Beach: Spinifex Press, p. 135.

Klein, Renate. (2024). 'The Joy of Choosing to Become a Lesbian'. *Julie Bindel Substack*.

Lagarde y de los Ríos, Marcela. (2016). *Los Cautiverios de Las Mujeres: Madresposas, Monjas, Putas, Presas Y Locas*. México: Siglo XXI Editores.

Miller Gearhart, Sally. (1985). *The Wanderground: Stories of the hill women*. London: The Women's Press Ltd.

Penelope, Julia, and Sarah Valentine. (1990). *Finding the Lesbians: Personal Accounts from Around the World*. Crossing Press Freedom, CA, p. 56.

Raymond, Janice G. (1986/2001). *A Passion for Friends: Towards a Philosophy of Female Affection*. London: The Women's Press; Mission Beach: Spinifex Press, p. 62.

Smith-Rosenberg, Carroll. 'The Female World of Love and Ritual: Relations between Women in Nineteenth-Century America.' *Signs*, Vol. 1, No. 1, 1975, pp. 1–29. *JSTOR*. <http://www.jstor.org/stable/3172964>. Accessed 4 Jan. 2025.

Star, Susan Leigh, Harriet Desmoines, Julia Stanley, Ellen Marie Bissert, Catherine Nicholson, Jan Millsapps, Deena Metzger, Elsa Gidlow, Mandy Wallace, Kris Gray, Merril Harris, Cathy Cruikshank, and Monique Wittig. (1976). *Sinister Wisdom,* Vol. 1, No. 1. Sallie Bingham Center for Women's History and Culture, Duke University. Independent Voices. Reveal Digital. <https://jstor.org/stable/community.28044729>.

Trebilcot, Joyce. 'Dyke Methods or Principles for the Discovery/Creation of the Withstanding.' *Hypatia*, Vol. 3, No. 2, 1988, pp. 1–13. *JSTOR*. <http://www.jstor.org/stable/3809948>.

Choosing Life, Six Acts

Elizabeth Vigo

1
My conditioning began at birth,
my mother's apology to my father:
"It's a girl …"

From that first moment,
I learned to orbit around men's existence,
to measure my worth through their approval.

As I grew,
I became fluent in male desire,
bending against my own instinct,
mistaking their control for affection.
Never once pausing to contemplate
the life-giving connections with women
that lay neglected in the shadows.

I gave men trust they hadn't earned,
unaware of the indoctrination
they had received under patriarchy.
Oblivious to the unspoken pact
that bound their love and loyalty
exclusively to one another.

2

Centering practically my entire existence around men
should have been sacrifice enough,
but the mandate was relentless.

So, I starved my body
to conform to their ever-shifting standard,
painted my skin and nails,
tore the hair from my entire body by its roots,
all of it striving to be pleasing to their gaze,
and still they demanded more.

I attuned my ear to their unspoken wishes so acutely
that my own became a distant echo,
then disappeared entirely.
The silence grew so complete
that I didn't notice when my true self stopped calling out
and gave up trying to reach me.

With my voice gone,
I got used to dampening my intelligence
so as not to constrict their comfort.
Diverted most of my talents
toward their convenience
bordering on forgetting I had needs of my own.

Shouldered their shame,
sugarcoated their violence,
handled what they couldn't be bothered with
while my own world and dreams
nearly withered into emptiness from neglect.

All these thousand daily deaths of self,
for what?

3
I didn't see the cage,[1]
but it was there.

Heterosexuality, with bars of thin lies,
threads so fine we can't touch them,
so carefully interlinked we confuse them
with being free.

Most of the lies become our second skin,
so familiar we can't feel them.

That if born female,
then we exist as incomplete halves
until we're 'fortunate enough' to find THE man.

As if our significance in the world hinged on male selection,
as if our mere existence were insufficient,
as if our creations held no inherent worth.

All of it, plainly, is a lie.

4
Men name it love:
the relentless sacrifice women make,
uncompensated devotion flowing one way.

What they demand of us,
they never intend to return,
taught from birth that women's service
is their 'well-deserved' right.

Men have been trained to parasitize women.
That ruthless. That simple.

---

1   This insight emerges from the work of Adrienne Rich ('Compulsory Heterosexuality
     and Lesbian Existence') and Marilyn Frye (*The Politics of Reality*).

What happens when we realize
that men don't protect, don't provide,
but rather, it is we, women, who sustain their very lives?

5
In turning toward men,
I turned my back on women.
I almost forgot to treasure them,
though it was always women
who kept me whole.
Not just mending what men shattered,
but constantly breathing life into me.

While I chased men,
women wove safety nets beneath my steps,
and illuminated paths I couldn't yet see.

While I spent years trying to be enough for men,
women waited for me, with open arms,
patient, knowing
they had already traversed the same hell,
and emerged triumphant.

They knew the world of men was never ours.
It only allows us in as long as we serve.
It extracts our life force,
never giving anything valuable back.

Not fate or destiny,
just a system designed to consume us.

They knew freedom has its own gravity.

That each woman who moves away from men
creates a ripple, a possibility,
a force that draws others,
a magnetic current of liberation.

Men, and women still bound to them,
still parasitized by their misogyny,
claim we are resigned to this path out of bitterness.
They don't comprehend that choosing is possible,
that we can step away from their world,
and choose life.[2]

6

Unlearning, for me, came in stages:
first glimpses of truth,
then small choices to see more.
Each glimpse making the next choice easier ...
First the mind saw through the lies,
then came the body.

Letting myself feel again
what they had trained me to reject.
Unlearning the revulsion the system planted,
uncovering the desire it buried,
each cell remembering its own wisdom,
how to feel authentically
after years of faking pleasure,
and pretending contentment.

There is a particular joy
in spaces shared only by women,
where laughter flows without
self-censorship or fear.

Where we tell the stories
of trusting ourselves again:
our rage, our bodies,

---

2   This understanding of life over death grows from Mary Daly's *Gyn/Ecology* and her
    concept of biophilia.

our intuition, other women.
Where our creativity burns freely.

Where we reclaim our energy:
love, admiration, respect,
first for ourselves, then shared,
free and furious,
toward and from other women.

Indisputable, vast:
not only in lovers' touch,
but in hands that hold,
in the quiet power of women's bonds,
woven through space and time,
real without male witness.[3]

Choosing women,
ourselves and others,
is not a consolation prize,
it's reclaiming our existence.

This is my testimony:
there is life beyond men,
beyond their fetish for submission,
their cult of manipulation, dressed as romance.

There is power in recognizing
the difference between love and conditioning.

We have never been halves.
Our wholeness has built the very world we inhabit.

Since the beginning of time,
we have been creators:
not just of what men allow us to claim,

---

3   The awareness of the power of women's relationships awakens from Janice G.
    Raymond's *A Passion for Friends*.

but of knowledge, of science, of culture …
buried by stolen credit, deliberate erasure,
and the endless labor of heterosexuality.

For so long, I saw myself
through the eyes of men,
filtered through their contempt.

But when I looked at myself
through the eyes of women
who had chosen themselves and each other,
who had built lives where men were inconsequential:
in their words and art,
their analysis and vision,
for the very first time,
I could see myself
not as something to be consumed,
but as someone who belonged to herself.

You can choose too.

If these words sound strange,
let them rest like seeds in the dark.
Truth takes root in its own time,
We'll be here waiting for you.

References

Each of these books made visible what had been invisible to me, changing not only my understanding but my actual lived experience.

Daly, Mary. (1978). *Gyn/Ecology: The Metaethics of Radical Feminism*. Boston: Beacon Press.

Frye, Marilyn. (1983). *The Politics of Reality: Essays in Feminist Theory*. Trumansburg: The Crossing Press.

Raymond, Janice G. (1986/2001). *A Passion for Friends: Toward a Philosophy of Female Affection*. Boston: Beacon Press; Melbourne: Spinifex Press.

Rich, Adrienne. (1980). 'Compulsory Heterosexuality and Lesbian Existence'. In *Signs*, Vol. 5, No. 4, Women: Sex and Sexuality, pp. 631–660.

Global Foundation to Eliminate Heterosexuality and Other Forms of Male Diseases

Yağmur Uygarkızı

Depression,
Anxiety,
Boredom...

You've tried
everything, but...

Have you tried

Lesbianism?

Global Foundation to Eliminate Heterosexuality   Promoted by the Global Foundation to Eliminate Heterosexuality and other forms of male diseases

Political Lesbianism:
A Revolution of the Imagination

Lynn Alderson

As a Second Wave feminist, everything in my upbringing during the '50s and '60s was geared towards a future of marriage and motherhood. We did know there was something called lesbianism; there were unmarried female teachers at our girls' school, well, nothing was actually said but … And close relationships between the girls were noticed. Though one day I remember, almost the only specific day at school I do remember – it was summer, hot, and the end of the afternoon. I felt the girl sitting at the desk behind me gently stroke the back of my neck with one finger. I looked around and realised there was a whole row of girls, all of us clad in yellow gingham dresses, each stroking the neck of the girl in front. So I did too. It was lovely. We never spoke of it.

By my early 20s, I felt, in an almost obligatory 1970s way, an impulse to try pretty much everything. I had been a visitor to the straight gay world of London clubs (and by 'straight' I mean pre-feminist, non-political) which was still the 'underworld'. Seen as deviant, exciting, taboo and dangerous, this hidden community also encompassed drugs and various forms of unorthodox sexual expression. Lesbians were either butch or femme, signalled by men or women's clothing and stereotypes of masculine and feminine behaviour. All the good stuff was 'masculine', of course. You could be dashing, assertive, stylish in your suit, Chelsea boots and short hair. And you could ask someone to dance. The 'femme' side was unappealing to me, way too much like my mother to be in any way either attractive or how I wanted to be. It's still the case that if you reject feminine stereotypes then you are viewed as 'masculine' whether that's about not deferring to men or what is actually non-gendered clothing. Today's 'non-binary' seems to be a bit of both rather than neither, not exactly defying the binary but similar in some ways to what we would have called androgynous.

In the early '70s, I found the Women's Liberation Movement which changed everything. Feminist analysis exposed the power structures that underlay those stereotypes, and we tried to think through the lives we actually lived, using our experience to expose the lies we had been seduced and conditioned by. The heterosexual part of our indoctrination relied heavily on romance and the notion that a man would, quite literally, sweep you off your feet, look after you and your kids, be a rock you could rely on for the rest of your life, and in return you gave your body, your labour and your life. It was very powerful, and woven into that mixed blessing of a sexual revolution where women often wore fussy dresses, and were long-haired, earth mothers – though a space was also created for the 'chick' who was up for sexual adventures, on the pill so always available to men, sexy and naughty, and maybe even a comrade in the struggle – but who still made the tea and slept with the long-haired hero.

The feminist revolution made us the heroes of our own stories.

Falling in love with women as women was a heady experience. Listening to women talk, fiercely and passionately about our lives, remaking the world with a radicalism that redefined us and the politics we were making with our own intellect and actions. It unleashed our imaginations – we became writers and poets, printers and woodworkers, plumbers, electricians, playwrights and politicians, activists, artists and revolutionaries. You may have assumed you would become a wife and mother, maybe working too, but in 'acceptable' ways – supporting his income and career. Then here you were, a lesbian poet living in a squatted house with five other outrageous, courageous women and a number of cats. We found strength in each other, working together, in the way our world made sense to us now, as it hadn't before. It gave us agency and empowered us to act. We believed in revolution. Yes, we really did.

One of the questions we asked was what kind of relationships do we want? Heterosexuality defined not only sexual practice but an entire existence of life *in relation to men*, as wife, daughter, sister, mother, girlfriend, and along with that, servant, cook, cleaner, sex object, prostitute, care-giver … And, as had been said elsewhere, a mirror in which the man could see himself reflected, at twice the size. Women who continued to be heterosexual challenged many of those things. Lesbians said no! We doubted that we could create a relationship of friend, lover, political comrade – an equal with whom we shared mutual respect and trust – with a man. A very different model was emerging from our relationships with other women. Without implying that our relationships were without problems, they seemed better suited to mutuality and women's autonomy.

We wore 'How dare you assume I'm heterosexual' and 'A woman needs a man like a fish needs a bicycle' badges. The two intertwined women's symbols became three as we questioned coupledom and the nuclear family structure.

And yes, a lot of this was cerebral, in our heads. Our minds were spinning with possibilities, futures we hadn't imagined before, and we jumped – with the excitement of reimagining one's life, – not knowing where we'd land. The mind is, after all, one of the most powerful erogenous zones. It is hard to be what you cannot imagine. And it is hard to love women if we see ourselves as inferior, objects, as the submissive stereotypes imposed on us.

Working out a sexual practice, pretty much from scratch, is not a straightforward path. All relationships have a framework historically formed by men's desires and power. Endlessly reproduced over generations, relationships in that framework were largely lived out in ignorance and indifference to both the mechanics and importance of female sexual fulfilment. Lesbians questioned those patterns. My brief history of sexual encounters with men did not meet the expectations that had been relentlessly implanted in me. At one and the same time we were meant to be fulfilled by the romantic notions of being mate and mother and also indifferent to the lack of actual sexual and personal fulfilment many women experienced in such pre-determined lives. I am not saying that women never found happiness in relationships with men or in having children but it is perhaps worth remembering that the number of women then on prescriptions for Valium to enable them to 'cope' turned into a national scandal.

With women it was different.

The Hite Report was published in 1976, the first research to actually ask a great many women about sex; what they liked, and what it was like from their point of view. It was clear that clitoral stimulation was the most effective orgasm-producer for many women. With books, exploration and persistence, we learned how our bodies worked. When our bodies knew how to orgasm, it became much easier to achieve a much more fulfilling sex life. For us, learner lesbians, when you understood your own body, you understood much about another woman's body too. Good sex didn't just happen naturally, with the 'right' man. The experience of working things out, exploring together and discovering our sensuality seemed much more possible in a woman-to-woman relationship. 'Wham bam, thank you mam' really didn't appeal.

In general, women don't choose to separate sex from relationships. It matters who we admire and love, want to spend our days with as well as our nights. We had our share of one-night stands at the end of drunken nights at the disco too, but more commonly the boundaries between friends were porous, for most of us, exploring our bodies and feelings required trust and respect.

Women are not raised to love our bodies, whatever shape they are, whichever community we come from. We have been schooled to judge ourselves by the 'male gaze', and socially determined standards of what is beautiful and desirable. This is still so. In fact, the porn aesthetic has become an overwhelming influence on both current notions of sexual practice and mainstream culture. As feminists we tried to rethink what we valued and found pleasing. We largely abandoned the conventional in dress and appearance. We wanted to look different, make our rejection of the hetero establishment visible. Many refused to use make-up or shave, preferred the natural, and evolved a jumble-sale fashion of everything from school blazers and ties to dangly earrings. The passionate, critical engagement that hallmarked our feminism burned through the whole of our lives, from perceiving the world to perceiving ourselves. We became beautiful to one another, and for the first time for many, to ourselves.

Feeling embodied, deep desire didn't really evolve in me until my mid-20s. The maturation of physical passion is often assumed to be part of early sexual activity, but I wonder how often that is true. It seems to me that growing up, becoming your own person is fundamentally connected to how we experience sex and relationship. My generation of women were stepping away from being 'other' and object towards full personhood, demanding respect across our society. Political lesbianism meant understanding that our sexuality did not exist in some culturally isolated box, determined by immutable nature, but that how it was lived out in our lives reflects our changing selves and our choices.

What political lesbianism wasn't was denying oneself the joys of a 'natural' heterosexuality. It wasn't a directive either. It was an invitation to explore who we might be as women not in relation to men and their purposes. We wanted to make possible woman-centred sexuality and lives, creating families and communities that we chose. We wanted different ways of being lesbians too, not bound into masculine and feminine stereotypes and imitation marriages.

Significantly our bodies changed to become powerful in ways we hadn't known before. Hands, tongues became erotic. The varieties of touch required new words and images, which is partly why we grew so many poets. The 'lesbian body' was not the female body as object that had been defined and drawn by men. As our capacity for the erotic expanded, our bodies and minds learned new ways of responding. Once, when I was in my mid-20s, I was in a pub and a woman I didn't know came in. I was so immediately physically attracted to her that my teeth chattered. That would not have happened to me at 18 but I am in no doubt as to the authenticity of that response and the changes that had occurred in me. We learned to love ourselves as women, for our female bodies, to give each other pleasure, for our capacities for courage and commitment, for our dreams of revolution, for our failures, and for what we could become together.

Some of my friends had always been attracted to women. Some had married early, had children and chose women later. Others grew to love women as I did. And a few could not find a way through and remained celibate. A few parted company with us and went down the rabbit-hole of sado-masochism, immersing themselves in forms of dominance and submission that most feminists had long rejected. One or two chose to have relationships with men again in later years.

Most of us went on to create lesbian communities. We came together as groups of friends who supported one another through hardship and illness, made a social life together, with discos, walking groups, film nights or Saturday football. Some choose to have children, learned the intricacies of self-insemination together and shared motherhood. For many years, we still had to fight for the right to live the lives we had chosen, have our families respected, be out at work, adopt and foster children, be recognised as life partners. Over time, we won those things. My own struggle to adopt as an out lesbian took us through the High Court and to a victory which established the right for lesbian and gay adoption in England and Wales.

One of the later arguments made for equal rights, mostly by the gay movement, is that we are 'born this way', our sexuality is not a choice, sometimes even 'god made us this way, we cannot help it'. It amounts to saying that sexual orientation is genetic, although the 'gay gene' remains elusive. There was always a stronger impulse towards acceptance and assimilation in the 'straight' gay communities, those that sought parity not radical change. And indeed, gay men have done very well in business, in the media, in parliament, while lesbians have always also experienced the sexism and misogyny extended to all women. The argument for natural and uncontrollable sexual impulses has been used to repress and blame women, and excuse men's abuse, across many cultures and times. Women's freedoms have been greatly limited for fear of provoking such 'natural' expression. We know, however, that how sexuality is regarded and expressed varies greatly historically and according to culture and circumstance.

Heterosexuality, as it is expressed in our society and many others, is defined and policed, determined by men and their desires. The way the human impulse to have sex and relationships is made real in the world is not a shared, mutual endeavour. We are living in a culture poisoned by violent and abusive porn, where young women have demands made upon them from strangulation to gang and anal sex as part of 'normal' heterosexual relationships. Recently we witnessed the Pelicot case, in France, which concerned the insensate body of an older woman used by many 'normal' men as though it was a piece of meat. An internet site recently

243

recorded hundreds of men queuing to stick their penis in the body of a 'consenting' young woman for whom no care or concern was shown. Violence to women is increasingly being expressed as part of men's sexuality and normalised in heterosexual culture. Porn both responds to that demand and fuels it to greater and greater extremes. The objectification of women is increasing – from the sex industry, to the rapidly growing surrogacy industry – the commodification of women's bodies is taking new forms and will take more. The undermining of women's rights, personhood and control over our bodies is necessary for those industries and technologies to thrive. The subjugation of women in Afghanistan, child marriage reasserting itself in many countries – these abuses are taking place with little or no international opposition – a global diminution of the state of being female and the power of women.

Rape and sexual violence have become widespread and go increasingly unpunished. They are, ever increasingly, used as weapons of war, to intimidate and control, not just individuals but communities and peoples. The formation of men's sexuality is taking place in this context. For many men, porn will be their principal form of sexual activity. What passes for heterosexuality is increasingly a hostile and dangerous, masculine world where women have little agency.

More recently, the sanctification of men who want to identify as women and/or lesbians has worked to change the very meaning of those words, our words for our sex, our bodies and our experiences as women. It is a deliberate destruction of women's fundamental rights to describe our reality, to private space, to women's collective space, to safety, and to choose separate, autonomous lives. Supported by profit-oriented health and porn industries, and preying on the vulnerabilities of children emerging into this troubled, hyper-sexualised culture, men's sexual fetishes and fantasies shape its defining images. The recent widespread acceptance of gender identity ideology has damaged the common/

shared understanding of what we are as a female sex, denies our existence as lesbians and our right to self-determination as women. It is profoundly anti-feminist and anti-lesbian.

Were I a young woman today, I would choose, as I did many years ago, to centre women in my life. I would say no to men's power over us, for, far from simply a sexual practice or choice, that is what the institution of heterosexuality is. The control of women's bodies is essential in maintaining patriarchal power; claiming our collective autonomy threatens it. Patriarchal power is a force that has a catastrophic impact not only on women but on our existence as a species, on this planet. Choosing to be a lesbian is a revolutionary act and like all revolutions requires courage, working together and the imagination to know that we can make change, both personal and political.

Is Lesbian Political Potential Impacted by the Doctrine of Born-That-Way?

A structural analysis by the WDI USA Lesbian Caucus

The authors of this article are the members of the Lesbian Caucus of Women's Declaration International, Inc. (WDI USA). We're writing collectively because women's liberation will require collective strategies, and because we think pooling our experiential data strengthens our database and deepens our analysis.

In this article, we intend to discuss the following:

  I. Defining lesbianism, born-that-way, and why it matters.
 II. How and by whom is the born-that-way doctrine implemented?
III. What do we think is true about (women's) sexual orientation? Why?
IV. What is the political potential of lesbianism under the belief that sexual orientation is innate versus not innate?

Defining lesbian, born-that-way, and why it matters

The Lesbian Bill of Rights (the LBOR) defines 'lesbian' as "a human female homosexual; or, a woman or girl who is exclusively same-sex attracted." So it's about desire, but also more than desire: A lesbian doesn't share her bed with a man. In fact, many lesbians do not live with a man as head of household. This has significance in patriarchy, whose most fundamental unit is the heterosexual couple having a dominant man and a subordinate woman.

Living as a lesbian subverts patriarchy at its root, making lesbians inherently subversive, intentionally or not. To avoid unnecessary risk and to maximize effectiveness, we think it's best to be intentional about our subversion of patriarchy. This leads us to consideration of 'political lesbianism', or the notion that lesbianism has the political potential to topple patriarchy, provided we get our strategies in order. Such strategies might include consistently avoiding submissive behaviors and questioning all assumptions as to what it innately means to be female.

The doctrine of born-that-way (BTW) holds that lesbianism (as well as 'gay male' or 'bisexual') is innate and immutable; and some believers also insist that butchness and femmeness (i.e., the lesbian gender identities that track masculinity and femininity) are innate and immutable.

BTW is fundamentally a defensive position: "Being lesbian is not my fault!" The negative value is clear. **Furthermore, the question of lesbian origin comes from patriarchy, which benefits from the distraction and division among lesbians caused by the very raising of the question.**

The LBOR intentionally does not take a position on the BTW doctrine, focusing instead on rights:

> RESOLVED, that as we do not yet, and may never, fully know the origin of sexual orientation, lesbians have the right to be protected as lesbians regardless of how their lesbianism arose – whether inborn, socially influenced, or chosen …

The doctrine of BTW runs into problems when faced with the common occurrence of women who arrive at lesbianism long after reaching sexual maturity. The BTW explanation is this: Given that heterosexuality is presented as both natural and compulsory (but which is it?), and that lesbianism is both said not to exist and punished outright (but which is it?), the BTW narrative concludes that most women would assume they're heterosexual unless/until they can no longer deny or resist their innate lesbianism.

The logical fallacies become apparent when BTW is faced with a woman who used to believe she was a lesbian, behaving accordingly, but now is with a man. Contradictory explanations become strained:

1. She succumbed to compulsory heterosexuality ('comp het'), despite being a lesbian.
2. She is bisexual, and always was.
3. She is heterosexual, and was experimenting.

One problem is the contradiction between asserting that lesbianism is innate/immutable, and nevertheless being unable to predict whether a woman's behavior will remain lesbian. Each time a woman partners with a man, or again with a woman, her past is re-written; but her future remains unpredictable. This problem undermines the doctrine of immutability, and seems to annoy adherents of BTW, who, rather than re-examining their doctrine (or moving their focus from lesbian origin altogether), may instead vilify the poor woman for being disloyal or dishonest. The woman may be ostracized from her lesbian community. This is not the best process or outcome for lesbians.

However, it may be a desirable outcome for patriarchy: Ostracism from lesbian community supports the narrative that lesbianism is not a viable life. The heteropatriarchy generously welcomes her back and may point to her as a warning to all women. Sadly, the lesbian community is less likely to be forgiving should she return. She's a fallen woman. More importantly, if lesbianism is innate/immutable, there is no room for structural analysis that could threaten patriarchy.

How and by whom is the born-that-way doctrine implemented?

As we stated earlier, heterosexuality's most fundamental enforcement unit is the heterosexual couple, consisting of a dominant man and a subordinate woman. Dom-sub is in part played out by the assumption that the man acts and the woman is acted upon. He has agency, she doesn't. Lacking sexual agency, whether or not a woman has a sexual orientation usually has no public relevance; women married to men are presumed to be heterosexual. Anecdotally, many gay men have described their sexual encounters with married men, and there is no reason to disbelieve how common they say it is. But any woman in a heterosexual couple is presumed to lack sexual agency, so heterosexual status is the default assumption. This assumption is supported by lesbian erasure (e.g. "There are no lesbians, only women who haven't yet met the right man.").

Born-that-way works for men because it reassures them that their wives won't turn lesbian, no matter what. It also works for men if their wives believe that if they were ever heterosexual, they will never be able to be lesbian, even if they wish they could be.

For heterosexual women, the doctrine works as a signal of their loyalty to men – not voluntary loyalty, because that would signal female agency; but involuntary loyalty: "I can't help being loyal."

And it works against lesbians, who build barriers not only between would-be lesbians and established lesbians, but between 'gold-star' lesbians and lesbians who have histories with men, even if those histories are decades old. The doctrine keeps lesbian communities small, defensive, suspicious, unwelcoming, fragile, and (most crucially) apolitical: "Of *course*, we're not coming for your wives and daughters! They can't become lesbians! We are no threat. Please don't hit us now?"

Lesbians might consider coming for the wives.

What do we think is true about (women's) sexual orientation? Why?

Born-that-way (BTW) is appealing for a couple of reasons. For one, it is an uncomplicated narrative that requires no deep analysis. If something simply *is,* as the existence of the sun *is,* then it is beyond question. In the present tribal, dogmatic era, a tribal, dogmatic explanation for our sexuality appeals.

For another, it benefits male sexual violence: BTW has been used not just in relation to loving, adult-oriented sexualities, but also in relation to sadism and pedophilia. These are primarily male behaviors, and men have often succeeded in mainstreaming and decriminalizing them by claiming it's wrong to shame 'who they are'.

But this simplistic and politically expedient narrative doesn't benefit or even relate to lesbians. Certainly, there are lesbians who have felt strongly from childhood that they are lesbians. But there are also countless lesbians with a range of differing experiences: from those who have experienced their sexuality shift involuntarily at some point in their lives, to women who feel that their interpretation of their sexuality (or their relationship to it) has changed toward lesbian, and to lesbians who are certain that they were able to choose their sexuality. Women describe a variety of different processes for these shifts: no known cause, losing attraction to men because of previous experience or feminist awareness, discovering love for women through a close relationship. There is no reason to think they are lying. They certainly don't benefit socially from challenging BTW in the current climate of queer ideology, which is hostile toward such challenges.

And while we could argue, correctly, that there's no scientific proof for BTW ideology and that fluidity is statistically common in women, in our opinion, it doesn't matter. **The idea that lesbians should have to expose their feelings for dissection by a male-dominated institution, or justify them so that a jury may debate** their legitimacy and worth, is, as we have indicated throughout this article, a fundamentally patriarchal one meant to keep women divided, distrustful of each other, and unable to work together.

We cannot see into the souls of others and know for sure what they are feeling for us. But we can listen, and we can observe. There is still a possibility of heartbreak, and this possibility remains regardless of the perceived 'legitimacy' of a woman's sexuality. Parts of the lesbian community still cling to the patriarchal idea that the dissolution of a relationship is a personal failure of the two women involved, and not a normal occurrence that can happen between caring people for countless reasons.

The scariness of admitting the diversity of how women arrive at lesbianism is perhaps that it requires us to trust each other, which is something all women are methodically trained out of from childhood – 'not like the other girls' is alive and well in the lesbian community. But the only benefit from this paranoia flows to men and patriarchy.

When we don't trust or believe each other, or we care more about dogma than community, our visible numbers decrease, morale crashes, and we are politically divided and weakened. Now is not the time to be weak, given the nearly total loss of public lesbian spaces. A woman who would be happier as a lesbian, but doesn't feel she has the 'right' to be one due to her history or age will remain trapped in heteropatriarchy at worst, or simply isolated on her own at best, when we make the process of coming out as lesbian fraught with exclusion, hierarchy, and suspicion.

Women's lives stubbornly resist one-dimensional patriarchal narratives, and their journeys to lesbianism are no different. We have nothing to lose and everything to gain by valuing women's experiences over men's dogmatic institutional narratives. And all women have everything to gain from knowing that they can leave heteropatriarchy, and that many women have done so, for decades.

We're arriving at a moment of sexual awareness among women that is unlike anything we've seen since the 1970s. The combination of the 4B movement,[1] lesbian visibility in pop culture, and the resurgent awareness of the importance and greater depth of female bonding in this time of rising misogyny is creating an interest in lesbianism that is straining the bonds of BTW ideology. We'd do well to let them break and welcome all women who find love and desire for other women, no matter the path they took to get to us, with open arms.

How does a belief that sexual orientation is innate versus not innate affect the political potential of lesbianism?

When we think about the behavior of patriarchy, or male domination, we observe that men habitually tell women what we are 'by nature'. Women are gracious, women are kind, women aren't interested in math, women are risk averse – all 'by nature'. Women are 'just naturally better' at cleaning, child-rearing, and self-abnegation. That's just how women are, didn't you know?

With this long history of gender (i.e. sex-based roles that force women into subordinate positions), the idea that we are 'naturally' anything is reflexively regarded with skepticism by many women, as it should be. Women of the second wave of feminism, in fact, chose to deliberately assume that any given characteristic of women is a product of socialization, because that starting point allows all behavior to be analyzed. Perhaps some behaviors are innate to our sex; but in any given scenario, is it useful to assume that? **The idea that we are 'naturally' or 'biologically' or 'born *any* way' serves as a thought-terminating device, creating sealed boxes that nobody thinks can be opened.**

---

1   The 4B movement is a radical feminist movement from South Korea that has made its way to the US in light of Donald Trump's second election. In Korean, the prefix for 'no' starts with a 'bi-' sound, so 4B translates to choosing the four nos – no sex with men, no dating men, no marriage to men, and no birthing children.

A key facet of male supremacy (and of any system of domination) is that it requires, to varying extents, the cooperation of the oppressed group. Men's expectations for women shape us – and also shape our own expectations of ourselves and other women. As a result, women police ourselves and each other. This socialization creates warped, male-identified perspectives, as in the Margaret Atwood quote from *The Robber Bride,* where she writes of "the ever-present watcher peering through the keyhole, peering through the keyhole in your own head, if nowhere else. You are a woman with a man inside watching a woman. You are your own voyeur" (Atwood, 1993, p. 441).

Women's history of socialization (as well as the fact that we're human, and fallible) means that women are suspect: our judgment, assumptions, reasoning, and conclusions. We must especially be careful of applying male patterns of thinking onto our own lives. Therefore, if we would be skeptical of a man's assertion that 'women are naturally X' or 'women are born Y,' then we should also be skeptical of that assertion coming from women, including ourselves. And why would we not extend that skepticism to lesbianism?

As we have mentioned, it's also not politically useful for lesbians or for all women, to take a BTW position on sexuality. It's not useful to reinforce patriarchal tropes of female helplessness. It's not useful to terminate thought around any subject that concerns or affects us. It's not useful to create the habit of justifying our agency.

Furthermore, our thought processes do not have to be limited by patriarchal assumptions of causality and relation. Something often heard in discussions around the origins of sexuality is women saying, well-intentioned and concerned for the rights of lesbians to be free from conversion therapy, that *If sexuality isn't innate, if there is any influence at all of socialization or choice, then we open the doors to making conversion therapy acceptable again.* And it's true that arguments against conversion therapy have relied on the idea that conversion therapy is unethical because sexuality is innate, and attempts to change the unchangeable amount to torture. One may just as well try to stretch a short woman to make her taller. This, again, is a fundamentally defensive argument, which makes sense considering that women have been on the defensive for a long, long time. But what if we were to argue that **conversion therapy is unethical not because it won't work, but because women have a right to decide how they wish to live for themselves,** whether or not other options are available, or would appease men more?

This argument – *If sexuality isn't innate then conversion therapy would become acceptable again* – is like the gotchas men create around women's rights. Men say things like *If women are equal, then it's ok for me to hit a girl, right?* Why is it that their first metric of equality is whom they can hurt? Both arguments are disingenuous in the same way.

If lesbians are born that way, we will remain a small oppressed group begging for a few more rights from men under the present system of male domination and female submission. But if lesbians stop participating in all the lies that disempower us, so that any woman can choose to be a lesbian, and so that lesbian communities enthusiastically welcome newcomers, **lesbians will have created the potential to increase both our individual agency and our collective political power.** We would be living proof that patriarchy doesn't define us, but that we define ourselves. How could any woman resist joining us? How could patriarchy remain intact when there are welcoming lesbian communities that contradict its most basic tenets of women's nature?

Can a woman who feels that she was always a lesbian be telling the truth? Can a woman who feels that she chose to be a lesbian be telling the truth? If we believe women (and we do), the answer to both is yes; and we also think both affirmative answers should be irrelevant in law and in culture.

And when a woman says she wishes she were a lesbian, our response as lesbians should be that she is welcome to become one of us whenever she is ready.

The WDI USA Lesbian Caucus:

KC Bianco

Mary Ellen Kelleher

Katherine Kinney

Lauren Levey

References

Atwood, Margaret. (1993). *The Robber Bride*. New York: Bantam Books.

WDI USA Lesbian Caucus. (2022). 'The Lesbian Bill of Rights (LBOR)'. <https://womensdeclarationusa.com/lesbian-bill-of-rights/>.

Reject Performance, Start Be-ing

Tabata Spinster

> Just as we no longer tolerate physical abuse, we must also reach the point of not tolerating cultural abuse, which has not changed, which has only refined this aesthetic vision of domination, implied and twisted in the beauty of femininity.
>
> —Pisano, 2001, p. 170

Since childhood, I've been fascinated by images. They seemed to me the closest thing to truth, to security; the idea that images could lie didn't fit into my mind. I was aware that some could be edited or taken with malicious intent, but images of the intimate life of a group of people united by a blood tie and what they do 'for love' seemed to me an exception to the rule.

Later, I learned there was always something to fix before I could be worthy of transcending time through an image. For me, photographs were memory and evidence; for those who photographed me, they were a way of showing the world the girl who would be a member of this society and culture. And under patriarchy, culture is heterosexuality. The images that were accepted were where I reflected femininity. "See how much prettier you are when you smile?" my grandmother would tell me every time we looked at family photos. Constant – not so subtle – conditioning. I lived in that reality curated by my family and the images they gave me access to (at least until the internet arrived). As my body changed, the images and my environment became more rigid, and so did the voices in my head and my decisions.

Pre-adolescence is this crucial and mammalian period where your survival depends on the acceptance of the people who make up the environment in which you develop; socialization deepens and internalizes. As adolescents, we do not understand the transcendence of our actions or words; most of the time, we do not understand the meaning of what we imitate, and we repeat it until we think and feel it is our own. What better target for indoctrination than a bunch of teenagers seeking acceptance and individuality, while not yet having the capacity to effectively understand, articulate, and communicate their emotions and thoughts? This becomes a conducive environment for internalizing heterosexuality, femininity, silence, submission, and violence, while being reinforced through all institutions (and relationships) with which one is in contact: from family to school, to media and the internet.

I keep many photographs of the friends I cultivated during my school life. It was clear that my deepest bonds were with women. My relationships with women never went unnoticed by my family, who insisted that friendships – with women – were not real, that 'support and love' existed only within the family nucleus. At that time, I did not interpret my deep and intimate bonds with my friends from a sexual consciousness, but it was bodily security and emotional affinity that drew me towards them. And for my family, this was already sufficient reason for scandal, repression, and vigilance. The first time I heard the word lesbian was in a pejorative and lascivious way, in the context of school bullying and subsequently from my grandmother's mouth questioning me "what kind of woman I was" and casting upon me the most disturbing gaze I had received until then.

From a very early age, I lived a double life, pleasing with make-up, boyfriends, and social aspirations. The desperation induced by inhabiting an insecure environment makes it very easy to confuse it with decision, and for everything that unfolds afterwards to seem solely your fault for making 'bad decisions' and not the result of a heterosexual socialization that induces self-hatred and self-abandonment. The less aware we are of ourselves and the socialization we've been exposed to, the more likely it is for us to think that our tastes, thoughts, feelings, desires and identity are our real self, and not the result of a lifetime of exposure to patriarchal culture and its institutions. Both the process of self-awareness and detaching from the family nucleus take time, require patience with oneself, a strong intuition, and an insatiable thirst for oneself, a thirst for dignity, a thirst for life: a biophilic impulse.

I was trapped in a cycle of heterosexual relationships with varying degrees of violence and exposure to pornography, including a marriage at 19 with a predator 24 years older than me. In that marriage, the breaking point was brutal. To my family, I only told the part about the infidelity; within myself remained the shock of having found that hard drive with pornography of the wives he had had throughout his life, myself included. It distorted my self-perception, but I lacked the capacity to understand the long-term repercussions of this traumatic wound. It wasn't until that relationship ended that I first heard the word 'patriarchy' and with it the possibility that there was something beyond my 'bad choices of men' that could explain a path of failed relationships and escalating violence. It was a turning point and an opportunity to create distance between my family and me, focusing on what I had left behind to get married: my photography studies, accompanied by basic notions of feminism.

I realized the discomfort I felt in university settings, as I was aware of the absence of women in all academic and artistic fields. I continued my path as a self-taught artist, and soon, I found myself immersed in the fascination for old chemical processes and with an undeniable reality: women seemed nowhere to be found. During that time, I had my first 'formal' romantic relationship with a woman. It was a chaotic bond that came to a painful end due to our inability to view relationships between women outside the framework of heterosexual dynamics and the pressure my family exerted on me, accompanied by psychological and economic violence.

Later, I found myself forced to engage in affective and sexual relationships with men due to the constant threat of instability in my immediate environment. During that time, I began to come into contact with discourses on sexual orientations, and their 'innate' character helped me dissociate myself from the systemic violence and self-abandonment that were behind heterosexual relationships.

My reconnection with photography was framed by the deep questions I was having about who I am, what life I wanted to build, and with whom I wanted to build it. Camera in hand, I began searching for a representation of what I thought eroticism was, through eyes beyond the male gaze (or so I thought). I focused my photography on the female nude, on building bridges between women. In this context, I began my last relationship with a man out of family pressure. It soon turned into an abusive relationship where I found myself emotionally and professionally exploited, which eventually lead me to choosing myself.

Centering my photography on looking at women, at our bodies, our stories, allowed me to interact intimately and non-sexually with women. Coexisting and looking at another woman naked, without wanting to consume her, is possible, necessary, and radically transformative. This confronted me with everything I had taken for granted about forming bonds with women. I felt in love, in ecstasy, but none of it was linked to the construction of sexual desire I had until that point; it was admiration and deep (self-)recognition.

The reflection had transformed, and so had I, and it didn't come from searching far away, but from turning to look at the women around me, and at the one standing in front of the mirror.

The photographs I created were the gateway to imagining other possibilities. Soon, I would turn the camera towards myself. Self-portraiture gave me a kind of internal-external image through which it was possible to recognize parts of myself that had been hidden in the images someone else created of me. My work started to be recognized in Mexico City and soon appeared in various digital and print publications around the world, opening many doors for projects and popularity.

Being focused on old chemical photographic processes and the 'absence' of female references, one of the premises of my artistic work was to 'fill historical gaps' in art history: 'gaps' of images that spoke of women's self-perception and not from what men imagine them to be. My first feminist intuitions made me notice the absence of women in their own representation and creation, but there was a problem with this premise: the gaps were not a product of no one having done it before. In reality, what I was doing was contributing to the systematic erasure of women in history. I wanted to build memory, but in reality, I deepened oblivion.

From leading a life marked by my family's rejection, I became recognized for my ties with women and the images resulting from those interactions, but at that moment, little did I understand about the active role that the hierarchy of popularity plays in the systematic erasure of women. Developing deep bonds with women is impossible in the margins of heterosexuality. I came to the understanding that the only coherent and liberating way to live my love for women and for myself was by becoming a lesbian.

But leaving behind heterosexual sex-affective relationships is only the first step in detaching from a whole relational model intrinsic to the socialization we are exposed to. When you start looking into lesbian herstory, you realize that there have been many lesbian feminists who have dedicated their work to revealing these seemingly invisible and unquestionable structures of the relationships between women. Prioritizing women does not inherently imply that you have managed to detach yourself from the patriarchal gaze; it is a meticulous process to trace the thought patterns with which we have built our reality and separate socialization from who one is.

During this time, I joined a *queer* collective. The discourses surrounding sexual orientations, and the lack of questioning of heterosexuality as an institution had a significant influence on my photographic work and its aesthetics. It depoliticized my feminist practice and artistic creation. This was a space where the way I began to expose and pornify myself on social media was not questioned, but applauded.

It was precisely at this point of growing popularity that, without realizing it, I separated from myself. It led me to seek transcendence in the world of patriarchal appearances and disconnected me from what had ironically led me to popular recognition. The Faustian desire to be a great 'whatever' kept me tied to their eyes. Aspiring to the intellectual recognition of the art world – run by men – implies silence and disloyalty to women, especially to oneself. I finally understood that being relevant means making consumable art, something that connects with the majority. It is easier to contribute to the misogynistic idea that you are reinventing the wheel than to confront the reality that we are silenced and erased in every chapter written in the history of art and 'humanity.'

By the time I had my first solo exhibition in Prague, I realized I was deviating from what I originally sought through my lens, and was not creating something honest. I was speaking the old language of patriarchy; I was creating images that made sense to the system. At that exhibition, a white man asked me if I was a lesbian. I replied yes, and he said it showed, because only men saw women that way. I got very angry, not only because of the misogynistic assertion that lesbians are men, because it also resonated with those intuitions that what I was creating had little to do with what I had set out to create: art with memory and feminist political consciousness. And it's an irrefutable reality that men make pornography out of everything, but there was a truth: I had become a broadcaster and participant in my own degradation and of other women. Such was that desire that I now found myself in Europe seeking that place. In that position, it could have been very comfortable to just follow the inertia of that popularity, of that intoxication that comes from being recognized by the hegemonic and dominant class, by patriarchal logics. The path was laid out; the only impediment was the voice of my dignity, which gradually grew until it was impossible to ignore.

Cutting ties with the patriarchal narratives meant the loss of that status and popularity, and it led me back to that place of rejection and ostracism in my environment. There is an abysmal difference between creating from our sense of Be-ing[1] and from performing femininity. The dazzling illusion of acceptance confuses you through the euphoria of applause that attempts to imitate the vertigo of creation. It is one thing to give free rein to creativity and another to feed the misogyny to which we are exposed and which will certainly be visible in the 'art world', by echoing that misogyny underlying everything we understand as culture, art, and tradition. Understanding that we live under an ideological regime gives us the clarity that desires and aspirations, as well as historical, artistic, and socially acceptable and unacceptable images, are not so by chance, naturalness, or divinity, but are part of a violent, artificial framework that sustains the patriarchal system.

---

1   Be-ing 1: "Ultimate/Intimate Reality, the constantly Unfolding Verb of Verbs which is intransitive, having no object that limits its dynamism 2: the Final Cause, the Good who is Self-communicating, who is the Verb from whom, in whom, and with whom all true movements move," as per Mary Daly's definition in the *Wickedary of the English Language*.

Spinsters can find our way back to reality by destroying the false perceptions of it that have been imposed by the language and myths of Babel.

—Daly, 2023, p. 54

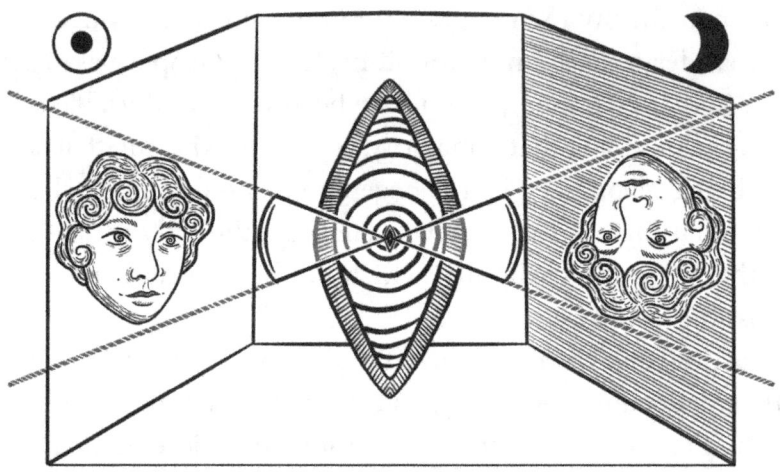

Our reality is constructed from mental images of what we see and feel, but these are not objects in themselves, but what our brain interprets from the light bouncing off them. In this sense, the construction of our imaginary is based on what we perceive through our eyes. The dazzling and misogynistic patriarchal conceptualizations distort the image we perceive through our eyes. Feminist analysis adjusts our gaze to the light to perceive reality without distortions. It can be intimidating to lose that sense of reality that connects you with society. Ostracism is a mechanism to keep women away from lesbianism and to ensure that those who still call themselves lesbians do so under misogynistic and pornographic terms that are acceptable.

I didn't fall into this place of recreating patriarchal images and calling them 'my true self' by chance; they are perfectly coherent with a life exposed to socialization, to systematic sexual violence, and to having found myself turned into pornography on more than one occasion. In narratives of sexual liberation, it is very common to seek to mitigate trauma by pretending that 'you desire it' (MacKinnon). Recreating trauma again and again, however 'safe and controlled' the environment (if such a thing exists), does not heal or 'empower'; it only deepens the wound and internal fragmentation. Performativity is not authenticity, and the fact that it is the norm in the context of patriarchal domination does not mean it is our only option for existence. It is necessary to create a distance between ourselves and the cultural expressions of patriarchy in order to flourish.

To live as a lesbian, to create from a lesbian political consciousness even when a system seeks to annul lesbians, is to **choose** to be a lesbian. When there is a social machinery to keep you and/or seek to return you to the heterosexual institution, prioritizing bonds with women and fostering the creation of a lesbian culture, in independent spaces both physical and emotional, is to choose life and its possibilities. Creating new worlds is possible, but it requires questioning the inherited construction of the vision of reality.

References

Daly, Mary. (2023). *Gin/Ecología: La Metaética del Feminismo Radical*. Sevilla, Spain: Labrys Editorial.

Daly, Mary. (1987). *Webster's First New Intergalactic Wickedary of the English Language*. Boston: Beacon Press.

MacKinnon, Catharine. (1987). *Feminism Unmodified*. Cambridge, Massachusetts: Harvard.

Pisano, Margarita. (2001). *El triunfo de la masculinidad*. Santiago de Chile: Surada Editorial.

Women, You Can Dodge the Dogma![1]

KatJ

The way I desperately wanted to fit in, but never did … the way my shirt was always wonky and my socks always fell down … the way I loved Abba at a time when they were well out of fashion … the way I fancied Agnetha and wanted to learn Swedish and never gave it a second thought … the way I felt I had to find a male singer to fancy … the way I was far too quirky for the prim-and-proper types … the way when someone told me I was "a lezzie" I was bemused and didn't care … the way I wondered why my friend was accused of being a lesbian and not me … the way I instantly thought it was a bad idea when a friend suggested going into town to find a boyfriend … the way I'd dream of girls and talk of boys … the way when I got close to girls I knew making any move was way too dangerous … the way I looked for a role model that I never found …[2]

Right from birth, pink is for girls, blue is for boys … stay in your place, girl, rigid and constricted by awkward and revealing clothes … it's boys who climb trees and play sport and take up the playground, you sit there quietly … look, all the men and boys are in charge, in charge isn't for you … look at all those couples around you, men paired with women, everywhere … freedom and power,

---

1   Extracts from *A Chaotic Journey to Radical Lesbian Feminism*, unpublished, 2025.
2   Format of this is borrowed from Alison Binney's poem 'The Way You Knew' in *Other Women's Kitchens*.

that's for men, not for you … you sit where you are … dress in a low-cut top and the tiniest skirts that reveal your legs … paint over your lips and your face … wear high heels that hurt your feet and stop you running away … one day a handsome prince might sweep you up … be like all those women you see in adverts, on videos, in films, on TV, not to mention on TikTok … you might be lucky and arouse a man's desire … marry him, serve him, take his name, delete your own, have his kids, be his inferior, suffer his abuses … do anything to keep that man … it's your duty, your destiny … you do want to fit in, don't you? … LESBIAN (shhh don't' say the word) is something you NEVER want to be …

A beautiful relationship blossomed suddenly, like gentle magic … and then just as suddenly crashed to an end, like concrete blocks shattering as a tower block crumbles to the ground … "I'm not like that," she says, angry but not so confident … she'd told her teasing, spiteful friends: it was only a phase, an experiment gone wrong, a mistake … I'm left too alone, only two lesbian friends both far away, everyone else straight, too many male friends, sexual harassment grinding me down … hetero-patriarchy whispers in my ear: "You'll be an outsider, you'll be lonely, you won't fit in to our world" … and you can only be a lesbian if you're BORN THAT WAY and you possess that magical gene … and maybe you're not and you don't … if our propaganda ever swayed you towards a man, if you ever doubted your lesbian self, if you ever dated a man, then you can't be a lesbian … go on, go on, get drunk, it helps, you need to hurtle fast into the hetero-patriarchal abyss …

I fell off the path, I'm ashamed to say, sisters … but I wasn't the first and I won't be the last … the golden lesbian path slipping further and further away … from early 20s all the way to late 30s trapped in hetero-patriarchy's lair … constricted and stifled, frustrated like a caged lioness longing to break free … on the outside pretending to be happy, on the inside sad as hell … But how did that happen, so many ask … if you were a lesbian that can't come to pass … It was oh so easy, I answer, don't you understand? … and they never do … I want to scream: but when did you realise you were straight? As you followed the path so carefully laid out for you … did anyone ask you if you chose heterosexuality? … did anyone ask if you wanted to be bound to men, to be second-class citizens?

There is a paradise out there somewhere … I found it once! Somewhere deep in a forest … thousands of women gather … the beat vibrates … courses the earth … up through our feet … we pump our fists, we pound the words … "Amazon women gonna rise again" … singing in riotous joy … unleashing our spirits … crushing out chains … a fire never to be extinguished … patriarchy burnt to a cinder … elation spreading…from sister to sister … you'd better believe us as we sing … "Amazon women gonna rise again" …

"Look!" she says, as she scans her eyes around her, "They're all women!!!"

Where had they been all of my life? … They were always here. The lesbian dream had never left me, the women were always waiting for me …

Bibliography

(by no means exhaustive) that has influenced the above:

Angelou, Maya. (2009). 'Still I Rise'. In *And Still I Rise*. London: Virago Press.
Binney, Alison. (2021). *Other Women's Kitchens*. Bridgend: Seren Books.
Dobkin, Alix. (1973). *View From Gay Head*. On: *Lavender Jane Loves Women* [LP]. New York: Women's Wax Works.
Faderman, Lillian. (1997). *Surpassing the Love of Men: Romantic Friendship and Love between Woman from The Renaissance to the Present*. London: The Women's Press Ltd.
Frye, Marilyn. (1982). 'A Lesbian Perspective on Women's Studies'. In Margaret Cruikshank (ed.) *Lesbian Studies: Present and Future*. New York: The Feminist Press, pp. 194–198.
Jeffreys, Sheila. (1993). *The Lesbian Heresy*. Melbourne: Spinifex Press.

Near, Holly. (2000). 'She'. In: *Simply Love* [song].

Rich, Adrienne. (1982). 'Compulsory Heterosexuality and Lesbian Existence'. Denver: Antelope Publications.

Watson, Jean. (2012). 'Lesbian Singalong' [song].

Wild, Angela C. (2019). *Lesbians at Ground Zero: How Trans Ideology Is Conquering the Lesbian Body*. Lampeter, Wales: Get The L Out UK. Available at: <https://www.gettheloutuk.com/attachments/lesbiansatgroundzero.pdf>.

Towards a Lesbian-centric Universe

Susan Hawthorne

I did not know the word 'lesbian' until my mid-teens. I was attending a girls' school and overheard one of my classmates use the term lesbifriends. I already had an inkling that boys had options as, not far from our school was the boys' school which was referred to as 'fairyland'. But they were just words. I had no real understanding of their meaning.

Words have come to be very important in my life, but the mid-1960s was not an easy time to use words like 'lesbian' or 'epilepsy'. The second I knew applied to me, but having come to understand its meaning, I simply did not speak it until I joined the Women's Liberation Movement in 1973 and became part of a consciousness-raising group. By then I did know the meaning of lesbian but was still in my heterosexual phase. It was a short-lived phase.

In my first year out of school when I was attending Melbourne Teachers College, I had a passionate friendship with a woman who was in the neighbouring room. I really fell for her, and I thought she had fallen for me too, though I would not have put that into words. We spent hours talking; we went ice-skating; I visited her in her hometown one weekend; we got drunk together.

One weekend when I was staying at my boyfriend's flat after getting drunk with him, I disappeared for a few hours. The police were not called, but my boyfriend called my girlfriend. I reappeared some hours later having climbed into the next-door neighbour's flat in error. When I walked in the door, I was greeted by a bevy of questions all asking where I'd been. "Just next door," I said.

After the weekend, I returned to the hostel and my girlfriend refused to speak to me. And not just on that day. The academic year was coming to an end, and she did not speak to me again. I was devastated. A quiet part of me said, maybe I'd loved her; maybe she'd loved me. It was a complicated question, but I was often dissatisfied with my relationship with my boyfriend and had attempted to end it a couple of times.

My girlfriend left the college to go teaching and I continued my teaching course for another two years. At the end of the teaching course, in 1973, I won a scholarship to extend my studies at university where I enrolled in an arts degree in Philosophy, History and Zoology. The first six months were lonely, but I was happy to be studying. I attended yoga classes and around halfway through the year, I stumbled across a bookstall run by the university's Women's Liberation Group. There, I picked up a copy of a pirate edition of Robin Morgan's collection of poetry, *Monster*.

I gave up yoga and attended my first meeting of the Women's Liberation Group and quickly became an activist. I joined a group spraying graffiti against a cigarette company; I painted posters for a protest; I wrote an essay on the 1929 Women's War by the Igbo women of Nigeria. In my African Studies class, I was asked to explain to the rest of the class what clitoridectomy was. In my classes in Philosophy, I began to make feminist arguments, some of which were not popular, but since philosophers like to argue, it gave students the chance to do so (often with me).

I met my first lesbian partner, Sue Ivanyi, in the university Women's Liberation Group in 1973. We became friends and just over a year later, lovers. Together we read books, we learnt about the misogyny of the witch burnings, we travelled to Crete, explored alternative health systems, we understood that women had fought for many rights previously and that lesbians were nothing new, just more obvious in our time. There was a lot of joy in our lives and for the first time intimacy was sensual, sexual and intellectual.

By late 1974, I finally left my male partner and threw myself fully into my lesbian life. The question about lesbian sexuality was no longer complicated and I could now see the sexism I had put up with. I was also tired of arguing with male and female flatmates who, by now, were accusing me of that familiar crime of 'going too far'. A year or so of feminism had completely shifted my view and made me impatient with the world of heterosexuality. When I read Germaine Greer's *The Female Eunuch*, my boyfriend suggested that it should be burnt. By now, I was able to see the systemic power structures which feminists were protesting.

I was volunteering at Melbourne's Rape Crisis Centre throughout 1974 and 1975. I attended Women's Dances, marched in protests and talked, talked, talked about all aspects of feminism. At the end of 1975, after some debate among the members of the Philosophy Department, I was accepted into my Honours year. I had not studied logic – a compulsory requisite – but in 1975 had studied the subject called Philosophical Logic which took me through the works of Bertram Russell, Ludwig Wittgenstein, Rudolf Carnap and Alfred Tarski. I wrote about Carnap and Tarski in my exam and when the question of logic came up, Jack Smart said, "But she's read Carnap and Tarski." Half the department would not have done so, and I was in.

I decided to write my thesis on the topic of separatism. It was a year of deep thinking for me with one major question: how could I make a philosophically strong case for separatism?[1] I came to it through an understanding of how power operates. With the first sections on power, oppression, domination and institutions dealt with, I simply had to apply a feminist framework and analysis. I then covered how these things operated to exacerbate women's oppression, to which I responded with heterosexuality (as an

---

1   *In Defence of Separatism* was finally published in 2019.

institution), rape and love. In my final section I wrote about strategies which included separatism and lesbian feminism. By year's end, I was very confident that my decision to be a lesbian was right.

While I had been allowed into honours, they were not going to make the same mistake twice and I was not invited into the postgrad stream. I made a number of attempts at being an academic, but on each occasion my lesbian and feminist world view was a stumbling block. After being kicked out of Classics in 1981, I decided that I had better be a novelist which would allow me to make up stories. And if they didn't like it, I could say, "It's a novel."

My lesbian life was – and is – rich. I occasionally wonder where I would be had I continued along the heterosexual trajectory, and it is not a happy thought. I had been exposed to pornography and to behaviours that today I would call 'male entitlement'. I decided to be a lesbian 52 years ago. It has taken me to wonderful places in the world and in the mind. At the end of 1976, after completing my honours year, I took off for Europe, spending the first month living in a London lesbian squat in Lambeth. I managed to buy a standing room ticket to a Joan Armatrading concert. I was introduced to ideas around matriarchal societies and when I travelled to Crete was able to *see* the remnants and to ponder how we got from there to here. In Europe, I went to lesbian dances, met lesbians in the Netherlands, France, Germany and Switzerland. Here was such richness and I felt I belonged in this international community.

In the 1980s, consciousness-raising went out of fashion, but three of us came together to talk about lesbian ideas in a group we called Cobweb. Kaye Moseley was an art teacher and deeply knowledgeable about archaeology, art history and practice. Throughout all the time I've known her, art has been at the centre of her life. Robyn Arianrhod was a mathematician who understood physics and the equations of cosmology. She was writing a PhD in Pure Maths. I was a budding novelist and poet. We met every three weeks for a meal, never pre-arranged who would bring what and always finished up with a feast. We met for about three years and after covering every subject under the sun, we then took up aikido for a year. Like the meals we shared, the balance was always right. Without those conversations, my novel, *The Falling Woman*, could not have been written.

My life as a writer – especially as a poet and novelist – has focused on the idea of the lesbian-centric universe. Since I started writing in the 1980s, I have drawn on concepts such as black holes, singularities, worm holes and other cosmological events which have helped me write my universe as if it were understandable. In most settings, I find that my world is regarded as a non-sense. Monique Wittig noticed this well before I did.[2]

In *The Falling Woman* (1992), I had my character, Stella, write the following:

> On a timeless day
> long ago or yesterday,
> in the immeasurable void of space,
> there occurred a remarkable event:
> a woman lay, with her self,
> a lover, a woman
> together she made love with her/self
> together she brought forth,
> created the universe
> created too the galaxies whirling through space
> the diamond planets
> the music of the spheres
> the rings of Saturn
> the cloudy veils of Venus
> and the moist fertile earth

---

2   Monique Wittig's books, *The Guérillères* and *The Lesbian Body* epitomise lesbian centrality.

> The big bang theory is really a story
> about one woman's orgasm (1992/2004, pp. 163–4)

Stella is faced with the power of gravity. The falling woman of the book's title is a reference to the epileptic seizures that knock Stella (Estella and Estelle) sideways from time to time. They are compared to galactic black holes in which gravity bends and absorbs all light.

In 1994, I joined two women's circuses and trained as an aerialist.[3] On the surface, aerials is about defying gravity and experiencing the exhilaration of flight. It is, in fact, about coming to terms with the power of gravity, harnessing it and with other women collectively creating performances that shock and delight audiences. I joined at age 42; some members were in their 60s and 70s. Each of us was encouraged to find the part she wanted to play. While not all members were lesbians, lesbian energy drove the stories we told and the ways in which we told them. It made me physically stronger, and I simply loved the creative possibilities of the trapeze and later the tissue (also called silks).

My book, *The Butterfly Effect*, includes poems that became scripts for performance, for example, 'Unstopped Mouths' in which I unpack the traces of lesbian culture that are more prevalent than are acknowledged. In 'Unstopped Mouths' I refer to, not the red shift, but the purple shift, "when a woman falls in love for the first time with another woman and the whole world turns purple" (2005, p.19).

I open the collection with the poem 'Strange Tractors'. This is a reference to strange attractors, a mathematical model of the earth's atmosphere which looks like a butterfly. Monique Wittig wrote, "The large labia spread out resembles a butterfly's wing" (1972,

---

3   I joined first, the Women's Circus, set up to work with survivors of sexual assault. A few months later I joined the Performing Older Women's Circus (POW) for which you had to be over 40. The focus here is my time in POW. I write about my experiences in this circus in my essay, 'The Aerial Lesbian Body: The politics of physical expression', published in my book *Lesbian: Politics, Culture, Existence* (2024) pp. 181–199.

p. 30). Reading Wittig in late 1974 was like entering a new world, an epiphany in which lesbians could make up the whole world. Every culture needs this sense of universal existence. The wings of Wittig and the shape of the strange attractor inspired me to write:

It's an ancient method of
ploughing— more ancient even than
boustrophedon— two cattle retracing
their steps in parallel lines

No, here there's not a
straight line to be seen anywhere— chaos
in the shape of two vulval wings—
the butterfly effect (2005, p. 3)

In my poetry collections *Cow* (2011)[4] and *Lupa and Lamb* (2014), I rewrite a lot of cosmology and prehistory. Queenie, the cow, for instance claims to have invented the universe and her proof is the galaxy: the word comes from Greek and means milk. Next time you look at the Milky Way, think of Queenie (that word comes from the Sanskrit word for 'cow'). She says of her travels that

she'd been to the moon
meandered with taureans
a herd of stars
as bison and boson (2011, pp. 13–14)

It was a lot of fun to write *Cow*, and a few years later I started my book *Lupa and Lamb*. The narrative follows the lives of two lesbian characters Diana/Lupa (wolf) and Agnese (lamb/lambda). The book is put together by Curatrix who has discovered a lot of 'Lost Texts' from 300,000 years to the present: from a wolf called La Donna Lupa Paleolitica to Sappho and Roman Sulpicia to a

---

4   In my first application for funding to travel to India, I mentioned lesbians; in my second, I mentioned women; in my third successful application, I stuck to cows and then turned all the cows into lesbians.

contemporary text (2011) about bones, probably written by a dog or her lesbian companion. Taking us into the realm of physics and cosmology again, in my research I came across (ΛCDM), the lambda-cold dark matter model.

the calculus of lambda (λ)

the variable x is a valid lambda term
what of xx
a valid identity?

lambda calculus solves my world
discovers the unknown
the dark energy driving the universe

or quintessence?

if t and s are lambda terms
then (ts) is a lambda term

calculus is about discovering the unknown
let us discover a universe in which lambda
is knowable

the observations click
purple shift
that emotional leap of faith into other realms
a transit out of time into timelessness

> *where*
> x = woman
> t = transit
> s = you work it out

In the poem, my reference to the lambda-cold dark matter model (ΛCDM model) is expanded by the artwork of my friend, Suzanne

Bellamy[5] whose sculpture, 'Observing and Documenting the Transit of Patriarchy' is forever in the back of my mind when thinking of lesbians and cosmology.

The ΛCDM model is the currently preferred and simplest model of the universe that best fits with observations; this model includes the Big Bang and the parameter lambda associated with dark energy.[6] And Suzanne's art is a hopeful comment on lesbian existence, the power of imagination, and our wish that patriarchy would transit away from us.

As with Curatrix, in this poem the narrator speaks of discovering the unknown, harking back to the purple shift which I referred to earlier.

I continue to write poetry, fiction and political non-fiction. My lens is always a lesbian lens. Since the early 2000s in non-fiction, my focus has been on war, globalisation, biodiversity, the torture of lesbians[7] and critiques of the trans ideology. The last has resulted in being kept out of the arts environment, but as Jenny Lindsay in her book, *Hounded*, says, "you cannot take an atmosphere to an employment tribunal" (2024, p. 92). Writing about lesbians, especially about the horrors of torture and the challenges for lesbian refugees, does not make friends.

Nearly 40 years ago, I met Renate Klein. Together we have forged worlds bound by love, silliness, lesbian friendship, and animal companionship. We have experienced the joys of travel whether to a remote campsite where only the birds, animals, trees, rivers, stars and the land itself surround us, or to places filled with lesbian energy of ideas, art practice, theatre, circus, music and politics. Living a lesbian existence has been the best decision of

---

5   There is more about Suzanne Bellamy in my essay, 'The Lesbian Art of Suzanne Bellamy: Creativity as political strategy' (2024, pp. 285–297) and in my 2022 obituary for Suzanne.

6   It was at the time of writing this book. Astrophysics keeps changing. I might be out of date.

7   The research on the experiences of lesbians who have been tortured resulted in essays (in *Lesbian*, 2024) and my novel, *Dark Matters* (2017).

my life. Lesbian existence is about having sex with women. But it is also an entire world – from the stars to the earth – of developing political analyses and initiating and participating in lesbian culture. Our dogs, River, Freya and Nala have helped me stay grounded and Renate has nourished my spirit and my life in many different ways.

References

Greer, Germaine. (1972). *The Female Eunuch*. London: Paladin.

Hawthorne, Susan. (1992/2004). *The Falling Woman*. Melbourne: Spinifex Press.

Hawthorne, Susan. (2005). *The Butterfly Effect*. Melbourne: Spinifex Press.

Hawthorne, Susan. (2005). 'Ancient Hatred and Its Contemporary Manifestation: The torture of lesbians', in *Lesbian: Politics, Culture, Existence* (2024), pp. 117–142.

Hawthorne, Susan. (2007). 'The Aerial Lesbian Body: The politics of physical expression', in *Lesbian: Politics, Culture, Existence* (2024), pp. 181–199.

Hawthorne, Susan. (2011). *Cow*. Melbourne: Spinifex Press.

Hawthorne, Susan. (2014). *Lupa and Lamb*. Melbourne: Spinifex Press.

Hawthorne, Susan. (2017). *Dark Matters*. Mission Beach: Spinifex Press.

Hawthorne, Susan. (2019). *In Defence of Separatism*. Mission Beach: Spinifex Press.

Hawthorne, Susan. (2022). 'Vale: Suzanne Bellamy'. <https://www.spinifexpress.com.au/blog/vale-suzanne-bellamy>.

Hawthorne, Susan. (2024). *Lesbian: Politics, Culture, Existence*. Mission Beach: Spinifex Press.

Lindsay, Jenny. (2024). *Hounded: Women, Harms and the Gender Wars*. London: Polity.

Wittig, Monique. (1971). *The Guérillères*. Translated by David Le Vay. London: Picador.

Wittig, Monique. (1975). *The Lesbian Body*. Translated by David Le Vay. London: Peter Owen.

Observing and Documenting the Transit of Patriarchy

Suzanne Bellamy[1]

The Lucid Darkness of the Lesbian

Kenia Namiliz Salas Pelaez

Translation: Tania Hernández Ortega

A woman in the shape of a Monster
a Monster in the shape of a woman
the skies are full of them

—Adrienne Rich, *Planetarium*

These places of possibility within ourselves are dark because
they are ancient and hidden; they have survived and grown
strong through that darkness. Within these deep places, each
one of us holds an incredible reserve of creativity and power,
of unexamined and unrecorded emotion and feeling.
The woman's place of power within each of us is neither
white nor surface; it is dark, it is ancient, and it is deep.

—Audre Lorde, *Poetry Is Not a Luxury*

From the depths of existence itself, from its bowels, the wild, the mystery, the lesbian is born. The lesbian originates in the woman. Her delivery is not superficial, it does not take place in the foreground.[1] The word 'foreground' references, evoking the greatness of Mary Daly, who set out to "return the treasures of

---

1 Translator's note: The Spanish version of Mary Daly's *Outercourse: The Be-Dazzling Voyage (2023)*, translates "foreground" as "superficial."

stolen words to the women in every time and place" (as cited in Franulic, 2023, p. 41), a "male centered and mono-dimensional arena where fabrication, objectification, and alienation take place; zone of fixed feelings, perceptions, behaviors; the elementary world: FLATLAND" (Daly, 1987, p. 76). The lesbian seems mysterious to this basic world, to the male order, which is certainly superficial. The lesbian inhabits the darkness and the mystery, outside of the FLATLAND.

This darkness is feared and loathed by men; prosecuted, punished and, in the most painful cases, mutilated. It's important to point out that I do not use the word 'mutilate' in a disrespectful manner; I invite you to think of it in its full scope. Furthermore, I invite you to reflect upon what this word implies: the male action of taking away our pleasure. The man performs a brutal cut, extracting "our innately ordained Self-direction toward happiness" (Daly, 1984, p. 2) which is, indubitably, a Self-direction toward women. The lesbian writer Adrienne Rich had brilliantly understood that this mutilation is performed both symbolically and materially, an action in dyad that men impose by denying women [their own] sexuality; by imposing it [male sexuality] upon them; forcing or exploiting their work in order to control its product; control or steal their children; physically confine them and impede their movement; use them as objects in transactions between men; limit their creativity; deprive them for large areas of knowledge of society and cultural discoveries (2003, pp. 18–19). This way, the mutilation of our Self-direction toward women takes place by the imposition of heterosexuality, and along all these aspects pointed out by Adrienne Rich, I would add the fear to our lucid darkness.

It is necessary to give substance to the concept of 'lucid darkness' that I propose to explore in this text. It's worth mentioning that this is a concept with body, that is, with substance; for which I quote the words of the Chilean radical lesbian of sexual difference Andrea

Franulic, who defines lucid darkness[2] as: "The journey proposed by some and which others refer to as an ancient knowledge, which is older and located deep within, in the roots of the body of words and history. And it comes from feminine rooting" (2023, p. 38).

So, the lucid darkness is constituted as the radical genealogical movement which directs us toward women, toward our pleasure, toward the lesbian orgasm,[3] and, hence, toward joy. Certainly, this is not a metaphor: all that joyous, powerful, sacred energy that flows within an orgasm is experienced and felt, just as its absence, its mutilation. Mary Daly (1984) states that *to be* is a verb, not a noun, one is-being. One is the pleasure of Self-direction toward women or its mutilation, this latter one, which directs women toward men, toward heterosexuality.

Thus, in this text I recover the word 'darkness' from the masculine misrepresentation, as Mary Daly and Andrea Franulic have done with different words, to account for the liberating meaning that I see in it, as well as distancing ourselves from incorrect meanings imposed by men, given that words possess a double dimension:

> [...] words wield/yield messages about the tragedy of women and all Wild be-ing confined withing imprisoning patriarchal parameters. Besides/beyond this, they radiate knowledge of an ancient age, and they let us know that they, the words themselves, are treasures trying to be freed, vibrations whose auras await awakening ears (Daly, 1984, p. 4).

It is important to point out that this is not an attempt to reduce social reality to discourse, as the neoliberal postmodern paradigm does. Rather, it is a genuine leap to flesh out our genealogy, which

---

2   Who in turn draws from the Brazilian writer Clarice Lispector.
3   I allude to what the historian María Milagros Rivera (2020) calls clitoral orgasms, which I also consider as lesbian orgasm.

Adrienne Rich named as lesbian continuum, an action in which women are not recovered in a compensatory way in order to integrate them into patriarchal history, but instead to account for a continuity of portentous existence that lives outside of the FLATLAND of men, in the darkness. To achieve this, it is necessary not only, although fundamental, to recover lesbian existence and the deep relationships between women from the past, but also, as Andrea Franulic so well states, to begin to name our perceptions:

> […] the action of silencing is not only achieved by erasing, but also through misrepresentation and fragmentation. To misrepresent is to construct a twisted version of our reality, using falsehoods about ourselves as mortar. And to fragment is to break our life into parts, in such a way that we constantly experience the feeling that we are disintegrated, torn apart, and that we feel hindered from making the connections that we need to live freely and without guilt (Franulic, 2023, p. 36).

Etymologically, the word 'darkness' means 'the quality to absorb light', hence the Italian philosopher Barbara Verzini says that no eye can exert its dominion there (2021, p. 13). Darkness escapes the order of sight. Sight, as a western supremacist sense, limits our openness to the mystery to feel-being, which is, to let ourselves be carried away by the underground marine currents that drift away from the superficial surface of men, from their rites, norms, laws, thoughts, dogmas … Darkness is fertile ground for creation, specifically for the birth of the lesbian.

Now, the word darkness has been distorted by patriarchal civilization to mean the opposite of light, which is completely linked to Judeo-Christian thought. For example, in the New Testament (the Catholic Bible), the word darkness is used to speak about four great themes:

The first, relative to hell; the second, relative to the power of gloom, its efficacy and its destructive power; the third … addresses the passion and death of Jesus; the fourth and last defines other aspects where gloom casts its darkness (Rodríguez, 2016, p. 30).

All these notions refer to the masculine necrophilia that is implemented as patriarchal sadospiritual indoctrination upon women, which places men, the male body, as creator and center of the energies of women. Mary Daly states that "sadospirituality demands the destruction of women's ancestral Memory, the blocking of our capacity to conceive, speak, and act upon our own Original Words" (1984, p. 36). In this manner, the mutilation of our radical genealogy needs to be legitimized by the masculine sadospirituality.

Likewise, the word darkness, from a patriarchal standpoint, is racist. The west has used skin color as a tool to create human typologies in which the dark has been defined as savage, primitive, evil, black; that which leans away from the Eurocentric patriarchal civilization. This way, the racialist theories of European colonization have used race to generate social hierarchies, still current, where the dark is associated with disease, criminality, the wild, the unclean and the evil (Silva, 2011). The dark is antagonist to the white, to purity and to capitalist development; that is why it is interpreted as monstruous, ugly, abject and perverse in the FLATLAND.

Hence, it is necessary to explore here how the imposition of orienting ourselves[4] toward men means mutilating our lucid darkness. As children we have been taught to fear darkness, and all which we cannot see, we are told, as a means of manipulation, that the most monstrous and perverse beings inhabit the darkness. For example, I remember when as a child I was not able to sleep

4 Which is why patriarchal neoliberalism speaks of sexual orientations, because it renders lesbian choice devoid of political content.

with the lights off in my room; I also remember spending sleepless nights for fear of experiencing the evil that supposedly defines the depth of night, fears derived from the stories I was told about fictional beings that inhabited the darkness. This generated great uncertainty in my childhood. Then, in my youth, begin the markers that limit our Self-direction toward women: the perverse, the angry woman, the brat, the ill-mannered, the lesbian, the spinster, the bad woman, among many others. It was a very frightening time; any of my movements could have disproportionate readings. Many of us young women live with paranoia, that is, with a great distrust of ourselves, given that all those labels generate confusion about what we are and what we are not.

The state of confusion is the beginning of patriarchal mutilation; the doubt, the suspicion and the paranoia reflect the misrepresentation that Andrea Franulic mentions: the way in which the distorted vision of reality is imposed. It is not surprising that many women, myself included, have placed men at the center, renouncing our creative possibilities, our freedom, and our pleasure. The fear is now not only in the horror stories, it was passed onto women, and it continues in the genre of fiction. The orientation, which is not Self-direction, becomes completely masculine: my first sexual experiences were with men, my first relationships were with men, but also my first great discoveries in literature, theory, photography and music, were through them, 'male geniuses and fathers', how they are called in the FLATLAND. Regarding this, Andrea Dworkin posed the question:

> I ask myself, what did I learn from all those books I read as I was growing up? Did I learn anything real or true about women? Did I learn anything real or true about centuries of women and what they lived? Did those books illuminate my life, or life itself, in any useful, or profound, or generous, or rich, or textured, or real way? I do not think so (1976, pp. 7–8).

Taking all the above into consideration, the lie is revealed: the monsters from the horror stories do not exist: what does exist is men. They indoctrinated us into distorting reality; thus, patriarchy has focused our fear into manipulative fantasies, diverting our attention from the real aggressors: men. The most miserable thing is that it also instils fear toward "our innately ordained Self-direction toward happiness" (Daly, 1984, p. 2) to women, it is important to repeat it.

Now I invite you to think about this 'evil' woman who you feared, the woman who lives in the shadows, unpleasant to the eyes, with a sharp tongue, with deep eyes, who wishes incessantly a life with other women; she who finds in the words of other women her creative impulse, who goes into the sea without fear of not finding the surface, who vanishes in total vulnerability at the touch of the woman she loves. That woman who has been labeled in a thousand ways, the one they don't want close to families, the one who fills herself with knowledge and searches other women from the past, the one who sprouts in the storm, the one who doesn't fear the night. I invite you to think about wild women, those who renounce western spirituality, who cast incantations, who invoke their ancestors, those who put their faith in life.

All of them live in the lucid darkness, which is why it's not just darkness and nothing more, but it is a timeless space for the power of women. It is lucid because it opens the possibility to center ourselves, because in the darkness the woman laughs, moans and dances, experiences the lesbian orgasm. It is lucid also because it moves away from the sadostate, the sadospirituality, and its heterosexual masochism. Lucidity is not sadomasochistic, which is no minor thing, it does not live simultaneously between agony and pleasure.

My final invitation to you is to believe in her.

References

Daly, Mary. (1984). *Pure Lust: Elemental Feminist Philosophy*. Boston, USA: Beacon Press.

Daly, Mary. (1987). *Websters' First New Intergalactic Wickedary of the English Language*. San Francisco, USA: HarperCollins.

Dworkin, Andrea. (1976*). Our Blood: Prophecies and Discourses on Sexual Politics*. New York, USA: Perigee Books.

Franulic, Andrea. (2023). *Confesiones de una amante de la lengua materna*. Madrid, Spain: Sabina Editorial.

Lorde, Audre. (1985). 'Poetry Is Not a Luxury'. In Audre Lorde, *Sister Outsider: Essays and Speeches*. New York, USA: The Crossing Press, pp. 36–39.

Milagros, María. (2020). *El placer femenino es clitorico*. Madrid, Spain: independent edition.

Rich, Adrienne. (2003). 'Compulsory Heterosexuality and Lesbian Existence'. *Journal of Women's History*, Vol. 15, No. 3 (Autumn), pp. 11–48.

Rich, Adrienne. (1973). 'Planetarium'. In Adrienne Rich, *Diving into the Wreck: Poems 1971–1972*. New York, USA: W. W. Norton & Company, pp. 27–28.

Rodríguez, José. (2016). 'La oscuridad en el Nuevo Testamento'. *Revista Scripta Fulgentina*, No. 51–52, Salamanca, Spain, pp. 29–59.

Silva, Christianne. (2011). 'Fotografías de amas de leche en Bahía. Evidencia visual de los aportes africanos a la familia esclavista en Brasil'. *Nómadas*, No. 35, pp. 118–137.

Verzini, Barbara. (2021). *La madre en la mar. El enigma de Tiamat*. Madrid (Spain) and Verona (Italy): independent edition, «A mano» collection.

Biographical notes

Lynn Alderson

Lucky enough to come of age in the UK Women's Liberation Movement of the 1970s, I have been a radical feminist, lesbian activist ever since. Founding member of Sisterwrite feminist bookshop, *Trouble and Strife* radical feminist magazine, and a member of the Onlywomen Publishing collective I have been in many other women's groups and projects over my lifetime. In more recent years I have worked to introduce new generations to the radical process of consciousness-raising, been active in fighting once again for women's rights in my political party and in 2025 I helped to organise lesbian sessions for Filia 2025. I live in the Southwest of England, walk dogs, feed birds and argue back with the radio. I have never stopped being shocked at the social acceptability of violent misogyny.

Alima

My name is Alima, I'm 30 years old. I'm a Russian expat living in Georgia. I am a lesbian feminist and political lesbian who previously identified as a 'born lesbian'. Currently, I run one of the largest Russian-speaking online communities for lesbian feminists as well as an online feminist reading group. In my activism, I aim to communicate a simple yet radical idea: no woman is destined to love her oppressor, and every woman can choose freedom and intimacy with other women.

Suzanne Bellamy

Suzanne Bellamy (22 September 1948 – 20 June 2022) was a giant intellect and artist, a lesbian writer, and an activist who had a powerful feminist vision. Like so many women before her she has been rarely noticed by the mainstream. But feminist and lesbian households across Australia and overseas have treasured examples of her work. She worked in mixed media, clay, printmaking, canvas and performance. She developed a form she called 'the visual essay' which combines ideas of text perception to explore the concept of visual thinking. She has written and created many works based on research about Virginia Woolf and Gertrude Stein.

Julie Bindel

Julie Bindel is a journalist, broadcaster and author. Her latest book is *Lesbians: Where Are We Now?* (Swift Press, 2025). She is the co-founder and co-director of the Lesbian Project, and a feminist campaigner against men's violence towards women and girls.

Ananda H. Castaño

Ananda Castaño, born in 1992, is a lesbian feminist and a woman with disabilities and chronic illnesses based in Spain. She's a self-taught poet, translator and writer and the director of the Spanish feminist press, Labrys Editorial. She has been involved in activism in health-related causes since 2014, with a special focus in advocacy for Myalgic Encephalomyelitis patients. In 2018, she started centering her efforts in divulging radical and lesbian feminism and organizing various groups, actions and events. She has translated into Spanish and published the works of lesbian feminist authors such as Mary Daly, Sheila Jeffreys and Marilyn Frye. Her articles and essays are available at <https://existencialesbica.wordpress.com> and Labrys Editorial's web <www.labryseditorial.es>.

Hazel Holloway

Hazel Holloway is a 50-something mother, nemophilist and ailurophile from the English midlands. An information scientist with lots of post-nominals to show for it, she is a long-time reader of radical feminist theory, attends marches and protests when she can, and has organised feminist conferences and socials alongside volunteering in the women's sector. Above all, she believes in supporting other women through the power of coffee and cake.

Anne Ehrlich

Anne Ehrlich is a feminist activist and organizer living in Berlin. She translated Dee Graham's ground-breaking work *Loving to Survive* into German.

Kelly Frost

Kelly is feminist artist specialising in puppet making. Her nostalgic, whimsical work includes intricate collage, amusing assemblage and carved puppets. She loves using vintage photographs and found objects gathered from junk markets and her mum's loft. Much of her work is in theatre where she makes puppets, props and costumes. She teaches art in primary schools and uses shadow puppetry to provide a healing space for female survivors of male violence. Kelly lives in south east London with her beloved cats. She organises a monthly lesbian night called Shabby She, a monthly Radfem social and other (women-only) events. She started these groups many years ago after deciding to purge men from her life and create a wider network of like-minded women.

Jesika Gonzalez

Jesika Gonzalez is a working woman, political lesbian, and activist in the struggle for women's liberation.

Susan Hawthorne

Susan Hawthorne joined the Women's Liberation Movement in 1973 and in 1974 came out as a lesbian. In 1976, she wrote *In Defence of Separatism* (2019). She is the author/co-editor of 30 books including fiction, poetry and non-fiction. Her work has been translated into Tamil, Spanish, German, Arabic, Czech, French, Polish, and Portuguese. Her recent books are *Dark Matters* (2017), *The Sacking of the Muses* (2019), *Vortex: The Crisis of Patriarchy* (2020) and *Lesbian: Politics, Culture, Existence* (2024). From 1994 to 2003 she was an aerialist in two women's circuses. She has won a number of prizes including with Renate Klein the Magdalen Berns Award in 2024.

Sheila Jeffreys

Sheila Jeffreys joined her first WLM group in 1973 in the UK and worked against men's violence against women and for lesbian feminism until 1991 when she moved to Melbourne to become a professor of feminist politics. She returned to the UK in 2015 and is a director of Women's Declaration International. Her thirteenth book *Uprooting Male Domination* was published in August 2025.

KatJ

KatJ is a London-based radical lesbian feminist who is passionate about the importance of building lesbian community and lesbian culture. She has organised weekends away and consciousness-raising groups, as well as attending many events organised by wonderful women. She writes the odd poem here and there, inspired by various women-only workshops and by the encouragement of other women.

Renate Klein

Renate Klein is a Swiss-Australian lesbian radical feminist who has degrees in Natural Sciences, Women's Studies and Sociology of Education. She has been a feminist health activist since the 1980s, particularly in the areas of reproductive and genetic technologies and is still heavily involved in bringing about the global abolition of all surrogacy. She was Associate Professor of Women's Studies at Deakin University until 2006 and in 1991 co-founded Spinifex Press with Susan Hawthorne.

Hyejung Kim

Hyejung Kim has been deeply involved in the anti-prostitution movement in South Korea for many years and has also participated in the lesbian rights movement. She wrote her master's thesis in Women's Studies on South Korea's 'Escape the Corset' movement. She currently lives in Canada with her partner and a dog.

Michelle Kerwin

Michelle is a lesbian feminist activist in her early 40s. She is based in Liverpool, England. Michelle is a feminist organiser (AKA herder of feminists!), helping to coordinate FiLiA, the largest feminist conference in Europe. She spends much of her time travelling around the UK, meeting lesbians and women from community groups, and making a small contribution to growing the Women's Liberation Movement. Michelle says, "The WLM and re-finding lesbianism saved my life. Creating the space for women to be together brings me much joy." Michelle is also a poet and is currently focused on helping women understand compulsory heterosexuality, the 4B movement, and building lesbian community. Anything that helps women leave heterosexuality!

Charlie May

Charlie is a lesbian, feminist, seafarer, writer, and scientist, with a long history of campaigning for human rights. She first stepped into radical feminism sharing her experiences living with a trans identity and extreme discomfort around her sex, with the intention to foster dialogue around the medicalisation of gender non conformity with her liberal peers. Despite ongoing threats and harassment, Charlie helped open dialogue around the unmet needs of women who were previously trans identified, and stepped aside as more voices came forward with more lived experience of the harm caused to gender non-conforming women and girls through surgical intervention. Though she still lives with discomfort around her sex, she continues to provide grass roots work to women and girls in her city.

Daniela Medina

I am a gender non-conforming lesbian of color born in Abya Yala – Indigenous Guna name for the territory currently known as America – during the first days of April in 2000. Everything is political for me, therefore I am an anti-speciesist philosopher and feminist who makes compost. In that same spirit, women and animals come first in my life. I am constantly learning about other women as well as myself. My work focuses on lesbian existence from an anticolonialist and lesbofeminist perspective, violence against animals, mystic philosophers and thinking about other possible worlds.

Ann E. Menasche

Ann E. Menasche is a radical lesbian feminist and revolutionary with roots in both the feminist movement and the socialist left. She is a founding member and co-coordinator of Feminists in Struggle (FIST) <www.feministstruggle.org>. She works as a civil rights attorney representing low-income tenants and unhoused people: <www.bulldogforjustice.com>. Ann is the author of *Leaving the Life*, and many poems and essays. Her essays have appeared on the FIST website and in the anthology, *Spinning and Weaving: Radical feminist for the 21st Century*, edited by Elizabeth Miller. She lives in San Diego with her partner, Rochelle Glickman, and a rambunctious puppy, Windy.

Kenia Namiliz Salas Pelaez

I am a lesbian, a radical feminist, raised in the southern waters of Mexico, Guerrero, within Abya Yala, the Indigenous name for the continent colonizers called America. My research focuses on the study of femicide through its cultural representations, misogynistic violence, and compulsory heterosexuality. I also write about the lesbian continuum, especially the bonds of friendship among women and lesbian existence throughout time. I was part of CETREG, a lesbian collective active from 2016 to 2024, which created spaces for lesbian women in Mexico City and across Abya Yala. From this work emerged the book *Illustrating the Lesbian Experience: Women Who Love Women in Abya Yala*, the result of our collective creative force.

Radfem Kollektiv Berlin

We are a small group within a larger network of women. The group was first established in 2018 and became more active from 2022. We organize meetings for women, protests, political events, parties and a yearly feminist camp. We support and encourage the growth of women's communities. We aim to strengthen a feminist understanding by developing and sharing knowledge with women. We challenge ourselves and others to think critically about our current environment(s) and to imagine a post-patriarchal world: <https://radfemkollektivberlin.net/>.

Margherita Rubin

I am a 21 years old programmer from Russia. During my activist path, I have been the manager or co-creator of several online communities and projects dedicated to feminist translations, art, and lesbian culture. I have translated two books (Walby's and Jeffreys') by myself, and I continue to help other activists with translating, proofreading, and typesetting. I developed a chat-bot for Emergency Contraception Fund that helps women in Russia to get free contraception. Currently I am working on a website with truths about pregnancy, childbirth, and motherhood in Russia. I also run a blog with a thousand followers to spread ideas of lesbian feminism.

Syldys

I am a 30-year-old programmer. In the past I was an organizer of offline feminist events (from five to 50 women), a facilitator of a consciousness raising group, an admin of several feminist online communities (from 500 to 2,000 followers). I have translated works about radical feminism, distributed leaflets, participated in pickets, marches and protest performances. Due to my political activity, I was forced to leave Russia. Now I am just an admin of lesbian feminist online community. I still translate some useful materials. I also run a twitter blog with 1,500 followers to spread the information about the lesbian and radical feminism.

Tabata Spinster

Tabata Spinster is a radical lesbian feminist, writer, and multi-disciplinary artist from Mexico, deeply committed to creation from political consciousness and lesbian rebellion. Early in her career, she explored the female body, eroticism, sisterhood, and self-awareness through photography and graphic art. Her work has been published and exhibited in cities like Mexico City, Prague, and Misiones (Argentina). She has collaborated with various feminist organizations focused on arts and independent cultural management. Curiosity drives her to question herself through her written work, swinging between personal diaries and essays. She is currently studying Sociology.

Yağmur Uygarkızı

Yağmur Uygarkızı is a 29-year-old political philosopher based in Paris, France. She writes on ethics and language, more specifically, on the interpretation of male violence against women and girls. She's developed a pastime in stalking pimp groups, and with that she's investigated clinical trials on victims of prostitution as well as Big Finance's collusion with pornography. When she feels like she's seen too much and is too mad, she'll dance. You can follow her work in English, Italian, French (hopefully more Turkish in the future!) on BorazanSesli.com.

Elizabeth Vigo

Elizabeth Vigo is a Peruvian freelance designer with a background in business administration. She works in graphic design, UX, and is a full-time learner. She participates in women's circles and feminist reading groups, and researches women-centered pleasure and sexual autonomy. She reads as a way of life and shares feminist ideas in Spanish, making them accessible and grounded in daily life and collective processes of unlearning.

WDI USA Lesbian Caucus

The WDI USA Lesbian Caucus is one of the working teams of Women's Declaration International USA, and its members collectively wrote 'Is Lesbian Political Potential Impacted by the Doctrine of Born-That-Way?' Other articles by the Lesbian Caucus can be found here: <https://womensdeclarationusa.com/?s=lesbian>. The following four members of the Lesbian Caucus are the authors of the article in this book.

Lauren Levey

Lauren Levey is a veteran of the Second Wave of the Women's Liberation Movement. She currently serves on WDI USA's board and also as coordinator of its Lesbian Caucus, which she created in 2021. A year later Lauren created Lesbian Bill of Rights International, an international network of radical feminist lesbian organizations. Some of Lauren's talks on lesbians and on radical feminism can be found on the YouTube channel of Women's Declaration International: <https://www.youtube.com/results?search_query=women%27s+declaration+international>.

KC Bianco

KC Bianco is a member of the WDI Lesbian Caucus, when she is not being an incorrigible nuisance to dinner party conversation everywhere. A writer and lifelong feminist, she found purpose in radical feminism's focus on systemic oppression and sex-based rights, along with being the last bastion of lesbian community. She can generally be found somewhere dangerous doing something peculiar hilariously badly, and having the most fun.

Mary Ellen Kelleher

Mary Ellen Kelleher has organized lesbian community-building events in upstate New York since 2012. In 2017, disturbed by the number of men infiltrating lesbian spaces, she sought information online and from radical feminist lesbians. She joined WDI USA's Lesbian Caucus in 2024.

Katherine Kinney

Katherine Kinney discovered radical feminism in 2018 and has been actively involved in the women's liberation movement since 2020. She joined WDI USA's Lesbian Caucus in 2021.

Cris Walker

Cris Walker is a Spanish 60-year-old woman who loves nature, books, food and white wine. She has got the time, but not the energy, due to a chronic illness. When she is half-well, she translates lesbian radical feminist texts and attends feminist events. She calls herself a Separatist, too.

Frances Woods

At a young age, Frances Woods became politically conscious in the late 1980s, shaped by the tail-end of the UK women's movement and feminist texts from the 1970s and 1980s. These influences helped her understand how heteropatriarchy oppresses all women and led her to love women and seek out lesbian feminist alternative communities. She became active again in the early 2000s, unable to watch the erosion of women's rights without responding. She has since withdrawn from social media activism, recognising the toll on her mental health for minimal political return, and instead seeks non-toxic connections with other lesbian feminists.

Yana

I'm a 27-year-old woman from CIS (Commonwealth of Independent States). I used to think that I was truly straight until I heard what Sheila Jeffreys has to say and after that I never looked back. Years ago, me and other women introduced political lesbianism to the broader feminist discourse in our part of the world. Nowadays I'm a political lesbian chat admin.

Sheila Jeffreys

The Lesbian Heresy: A Feminist Perspective on
the Lesbian Sexual Revolution

The backlash against feminism has been documented powerfully by Naomi Wolf and Susan Faludi: within the lesbian community too, there has been a parallel backlash. A lesbian sex industry is now making a profit from women's oppression, teaching lesbians to turn the pain of abuse and subordination into 'pleasure' and calling it liberation. Feminist theorist Sheila Jeffreys challenges the patriarchal and racist assumptions of the sex industry. In *The Lesbian Heresy* she advocates the continued creation of lesbian culture, community, friendship and ethics based on principles of equality and resistance. And for this call to freedom, lesbian feminists are deemed heretics.

ISBN 9781875559176   ebook available

Sheila Jeffreys
Trigger Warning: My Lesbian Feminist Life

I am in the very fortunate position of having been able to contribute to two waves of feminism: The Women's Liberation Movement and the new wave that is taking place now.

Trigger Warning: My Lesbian Feminist Life is both an engaging autobiography and a fascinating account of feminist history. From the heady days of the Women's Liberation Movement through to the backlash against radical feminism as neoliberal laissez-faire attitudes took hold. Fast forward to the current re-examination of feminism in light of the #MeToo movement and an emerging new wave of radical feminism.

Sheila Jeffreys' bold account makes it clear that the feminism and lesbianism she has championed for decades is needed more than ever. With honesty and frankness, she tells of victories and setbacks in her unrelenting commitment to women's freedom from men's violence, especially the violence inherent in pornography and prostitution. We also learn what her steadfastness has cost her in terms of personal and professional rewards.

Trigger Warning places radical feminism within a cultural, social and intellectual context while also taking us on a personal journey. Sheila Jeffreys has tirelessly crossed the globe to advance radical feminist theory and practice and we are invited to share in the intellectual and political crossroads she has encountered during her life.

Accessible yet detailed and rigorous, this landmark volume is essential reading for everyone who has ever wondered what radical feminism really is.

ISBN 9781925950205   ebook available

Renate Klein
Radical Reckonings: Survival in Patriarchy

What happens when an old radical lesbian feminist has an idea of publishing a collection of her papers? She looks at her writings and despairs. She has written too much. The idea gets shelved. Fifteen years later, she revisits the project. But it is worse now because she has written more … But being stared down by her publisher she gets a grip and (painfully) pares down her oeuvre to a manageable size.

This then is a skeleton journey through Renate's life and her survival in patriarchy. The book starts with her passion for autonomous Women's Studies as an intellectual necessity and radical feminist research methodology to give women a voice. And why men don't belong in Women's Studies classes. Next, she documents her immersion in a critique of reproductive technologies as a member of FINRRAGE. We hear about the exploitation of a desire in IVF followed with problems of egg 'donations', cloning, and of course the human rights violation of women and children in surrogacy. A critique of the illusion of 'choice' – endorsed by liberal feminists – has to be in the book and with it papers on long-acting contraceptives. Necessary warnings about the unethics of hormone replacement therapy and the French abortion pill RU 486 are included too.

As a feminist women's health activist, Renate Klein has always been concerned about the fact that women *are* our bodies and that reproductive technologies in tandem with postmodern and queer theories result in the fragmentation and dismemberment of women: from the one an egg, from the other a uterus … this erasure of women is helped by dissociation and a belief in delusions – such as the assault on women's existence by transgender ideologues.

ISBN 9781925950960   ebook available

Susan Hawthorne
Lesbian: Politics, Culture Existence

*A history of feminist and lesbian thinking
from the 1970s to the present*

Across almost 50 years of writing, Susan Hawthorne's essays on lesbian culture and politics take the reader on a journey through the concerns of radical feminists engaged in the Women's Liberation Movement. Not only does she trace the experiments of lesbians creating a vibrant woman-loving culture, but she also traces the backlash against lesbians and a history of violence perpetrated by the state, corporations and individual men.

She begins with a recollection of a rape in her pre-feminist days, followed by a critique of the institution of heterosexuality and the role of lesbian feminism as a strategy. She is soon asking questions about lesbian existence. The essays span reflections on lesbian literature and the development of lesbian culture, including the politics of physical expression in circus.

Susan Hawthorne writes about cultural appropriation, depoliticisation and the erasure of lesbian inventiveness. She researches violence against lesbians including rape, torture and murder and the way in which this violence is ignored and often distorted by the media.

Her investigations include lesbian refugees, lesbian economics, violation of lesbian human rights and the impact of the transgender industrial complex on the existence of lesbians as a political force.

ISBN 9781925950984   ebook available

Susan Hawthorne

Dark Matters: A Novel

A love letter from Kate to Mercedes. Mercedes is shot in a dawn raid on their home in Melbourne. Kate is arrested. In her despair of not knowing if Mercedes is alive or dead Kate writes to her, about her, about their lives. She invents stories and rearranges the rich mythic traditions of Greece.

This is a novel of resilience in the face of trauma and uncertainty.

Dark Matters is a transformative tour de force; lyrical as Sappho and revolutionary as Wittig in *Les Guérillères*.

—Roberta Arnold, *Sinister Wisdom*

With *Dark Matters*, Susan Hawthorne has written a remarkable novel that pulls lesbians out of the fissures of marginalization and obscurity to solid ground where lesbian visibility and meaning can emerge.

—Gariné Roubinian, *Rain and Thunder* (USA)

ISBN 9781925581089   ebook available

Suzanne Bellamy and Susan Hawthorne
Unsettling the Land

This chapbook, *Unsettling the Land*, is a celebration of a marvellous thirty-year friendship between Suzanne Bellamy and Susan Hawthorne. They have produced many combined performance works in Australia and overseas, combining image, music, circus and text. The Drought Project curated by Lella Cariddi, opened up a new way of joint production with Susan's poem taking visual form in Suzanne's art which in turn created additional poetic text.

Stunning. Like the birds and water on the Murrumbidgee, this collaboration too is dynamic and vital, a woven landscape of word and texture into a wrought gift.

—Robyn Rowland

ISBN 9781876756703   ebook available

Lara Fergus
My Sister Chaos

Winner: Edmund White Award for Debut Fiction (USA)
Shortlisted: Dobbie Literary Award
Finalist: Lambda Literary Award for Lesbian Debut Fiction (USA)

You will not elude me. I will measure your every dimension, I will trace your smallest lines. I will undo you from the inside. You will feel it like waves running across your floorboards, you will feel it like water rising through your walls, you will feel it like a sudden disorientation, you will wonder what happened to your foundations.

An obsessive-compulsive cartographer trapped in the mapping of her own house. A painter turned codebreaker trying to find the lover she lost in the war. Two sisters on a collision course.

In *My Sister Chaos* two sisters escape an unnamed war-torn country into separate lives of exile. The cartographer is obsessed with keeping the world in order, but finds it unraveling under her own demands. Her sister, an artist, arrives unexpectedly. Her very presence is a sign of chaos for the cartographer. But in spite of this, the sister has a firm grip on the real world, and a greater connection to the past. Chaos and order in tension provide the scaffolding for this compelling work of fiction. Presented within a world of obsession and trauma it asks whether any of us is immune to the forces of destruction.

ISBN 9781876756840   ebook available

*If you would like to know more about
Spinifex Press, write to us for a free catalogue, visit our
website or email us for further information
on how to subscribe to our monthly newsletter.*

Spinifex Press
PO Box 105
Mission Beach QLD 4852
Australia

www.spinifexpress.com.au
women@spinifexpress.com.au